THE SHROUD
A N D
THE GRAIL

Arcanum neque tu scrutaberis ullius unquam

HORACE

THE SHROUD
A N D
THE GRAIL

A MODERN QUEST FOR THE TRUE GRAIL

NOEL CURRER–BRIGGS

St. Martin's Press
New York

Library of Congress Cataloging-in-Publication Data

Currer-Briggs, Noel.
      The Shroud and the Grail : a modern quest for the true Grail / by
  Noel Currer-Briggs.
        p.   cm.
  "A Thomas Dunne book."
  ISBN 0-312-01510-0 : $19.95
  1. Holy Shroud. 2. Grail. I. Title.
BT587.S4C88   1988
232.9′66—dc19   87-27330
                                                        CIP

First published in Great Britain by George Weidenfeld & Nicolson Limited.

First U.S. Edition

10 9 8 7 6 5 4 3 2 1

CONTENTS

LIST OF GENEALOGICAL
TABLES

INTRODUCTION AND ACKNOWLEDGMENTS

Some mysteries defy solution for lack of evidence; others are solved by ingenious surmises. Near-solutions can be achieved by the assembly of circumstantial evidence. In this book I shall advance a new hypothesis which stems from something I read in Ian Wilson's well-known study of the history of the Shroud of Turin. Discussing the possible connection between the Shroud and so-called 'idol' or 'head' of the Templars, Wilson wrote: 'The crucial question is the head's identity. It is of considerable significance that it is precisely the most holy images of Christ that caused real fear at this time. Pope Alexander III in the twelfth century had ordered Gregory the Great's Acheropita image in the Sancta Sanctorum chapel to be veiled because it caused a trembling dangerous to life. In the Grail legend it was the image of Christ that similarly made the knight Galahad tremble. So what was the Templar head?'

At about the same time, I received a letter from Debrett inviting me to take part in a scheme to establish the historical existence of King Arthur. A lot of work had been done in France, I was told, and the English author of the proposed book needed a French-speaker to examine these sources and to act as a link between himself and French scholars. In the event, nothing came of this project, but my attention was drawn to another book on the Grail, which claimed that it was not a relic at all in the strict sense of the term, but a secret handed down from antiquity, and linked to the Cathars of Languedoc, concerning the descendants of Jesus and Mary Magdalene. The authors claimed that the Merovingian kings of France, who were approximately contemporary with King Arthur, were of this line, and as a genealogist I was naturally interested, though highly sceptical.

Catharism derives from a heresy known as Bogomilism, which

vii

arose in tenth-century Bulgaria, and which in turn derived from Manichaeism, an Eastern cult which began as a reaction against the deep fatalism of Persian Zoroastrianism. By the twelfth century it had put down firm roots in the Balkans and had spread to southern France. In spite of certain non-Christian elements, such as a belief in reincarnation, the Cathars regarded themselves as Christians. But like modern Unitarians, whom they resemble in other ways, they denied the divinity of Christ. They regarded the body and all material things as satanic: an attitude which coloured their view of relics. Since most relics are material objects such as the skin and bones of saints, the Cathars would have nothing to do with them. Consequently they would never have venerated material objects such as the Grail or even the Shroud of Christ itself.

A great deal of romantic nonsense has been written about the Templars, but the silliest is the accusation that they were Cathars and idolators. This arises from the fact that most of the evidence derives from hostile sources. The Inquisition, which was created to extirpate the Cathar heresy and to destroy the Templars, made sure that only its side of the case survives, so that all we have is slanted in its favour and against the Cathars and Templars.

I shall attempt to answer some of these questions by defining the true nature of the Holy Grail, and by showing how it was linked to the Shroud of Turin, and how the Templars were linked to both. I will show that the Fourth Crusade was, for some of those who took part in it, a quest for a historical Grail, and that the Grail romances were in some measure inspired by descriptions of Byzantine ceremonies of which the sacred burial linens of Christ were part, and that these secrets were known to a comparatively small number of men and women, all of whom were closely related to each other. I have sometimes to fall back on ingenious surmises, but I depend heavily on historical evidence, even though it may be circumstantial. I do not claim to have 'solved' the mystery of the Holy Grail any more than I can 'prove' its connection with the Shroud. I do, however, advance a new idea and bring forward historical facts to see if they fit what is already known. If my readers can produce conclusive evidence to show that I am wrong, they must offer evidence which is *more* conclusive and less circumstantial than mine to support an alternative hypothesis. I sincerely hope that they will, for there is not much point in finding the wrong answer to a mystery.

I owe a great debt of gratitude to David Batson, who read the typescript and gave me much help on matters theological, especially pointing out what was heretical and orthodox. Professor Peter Walsh of Glasgow University, who once served under me as a corporal, got his own back by translating a Latin epitaph and other Latin texts, which effectively put paid to one of my theories, and meant that I had to re-write a large section of Chapter Five, thus preventing me from committing a gross schoolboy howler. I am extremely grateful to him. Dr Willi Müller's kindness in guiding me through Franconia and drawing my attention to the evidence which supports the German episodes in this book went far beyond the limits of mere courtesy. David Reynolds, as often before, came to look after my bodily comfort for several weeks while I was typing the manuscript. Manfred Harnisch, likewise, went to great trouble to search out an obscure reference for me in Nuremberg. The list of those with whom I corresponded, and whose advice and comments have helped me greatly, is a long one, and includes G. Z. Graham of Dumfries Academy, Brian Inglis, Professor Robert Morris, Dr Detlev Schwennicke, Sir Steven Runciman, Dr Marc Heine, Dr Alexis Vlasto, Professor Bernard Hamilton, Father Kim Dreisbach, Ian Wilson, the Warburg Institute, Dr Eugen Csocsan de Varallja, the Salesians of Don Bosco, Editions 'Mage' and Rachel Brown, who read the script and offered her valuable comments.

FOREWORD
BY DAVID BATSON

———————●———————

Any attempt to assemble an early history of the Shroud has necessarily to face certain difficulties relating to the nature of the material available. It is, of course, to the Gospels that reference is primarily made. Both the Synoptists and the author of St John place a good deal of emphasis on the Passion narratives, since it is the death of Jesus, and the Apostles' subsequent experience of this event and what followed it, that determine the message (kerygma) that they proclaimed. The Christian Faith did not exist until there was a Christian kerygma proclaiming Jesus Christ the Crucified and Risen One to be God's eschatological act of salvation. It is important to remember that he was first so proclaimed in the kerygma of the earliest Church, not in the message of the historical Jesus. However, the fact remains that Jesus did proclaim an historic message which stands firmly in the context of Jewish expectations of the end of the world and God's new future.

The very first Christians were Jewish with all that that implies in cultural and religious terms. This is a fact of the most vital importance if we are to understand the Gospel material, for it means that the earliest traditions about Jesus were preserved by people utterly imbued with the traditions of the Old Testament. Jesus became the Christ as part of a three-act drama – three stages in one continuous operation by which the Kingdom of God was to be established, and since the first Christians were Jews, the drama was set against the background of Old Testament prophecy. The first Christians literally believed themselves to be living in the last days before the end of the world, at the most within a generation or so; consequently they had little leisure and less interest in antiquarian research into Jesus' earthly life. For them, act one of the drama was played out; act two was being experienced in the here and now; act three, the final establishment of God's reign on earth, was gloriously and terrifyingly imminent.

Against this background it is clear that the first Christians did not anticipate any posterity who might be expected to profit from the normal kinds of details of a person's life, such as we might reasonably expect to glean from a modern biography. Even when the oral tradition had reached the second or third generation of believers, and the need to commit something to writing arose in order to meet the needs, usually, of purely local churches and assemblies, the interests of the Evangelists lay still in quite different directions from those of personal histories.

If, therefore, the early generations of Christians had no regard for such details, it is a matter of considerable curiosity why they might be expected to preserve items of burial clothing which, in their deeply held Jewish belief and strict adherence to the religious practices of their forefathers, were ritually unclean objects. This brings us inevitably to a consideration of the story of the empty tomb.

The story of Jesus' burial was important in the early Church on two counts: first as establishing that he had really been dead (cf. Mark 5:35–43), and so, as far as the believers were concerned, had really risen from the dead; and secondly, from the point of view of the empty tomb, which had become a tradition as early as the post-Pauline period, it was important as establishing that the women who later found the tomb empty had not gone to the wrong tomb, but to the one in which they themselves had seen the body placed. However, it ought to be said that there has been a tendency for the possible influence of the Old Testament to be underestimated in connection with this account, although readily acknowledged by scholars elsewhere in the Gospels.

If one looks to the earliest of the synoptics, St Mark, and examines his account of the death and burial of Jesus, one finds difficulty in the chronology used. The assumption of 15:42 ('And now when the even was come, because it was the preparation, that is, the day before the sabbath') is that there was a hurry to get things done on the Preparation which could not be done on the Sabbath. But according to Mark's chronology of the Passion, the day of Preparation was that year the feast of the Passover, and the prohibitions with regard to Passover were as strict as those relating to the Sabbath. But the tradition says that Joseph of Arimathea bought the shroud that day, which if taken literally, would have meant a serious breach of the religious laws. Either Joseph did not buy the Shroud but already had it, or else, more likely, this section comes from a tradition which did not identify the

Crucifixion with the Passover. However, it is interesting to note that the tradition does not say anything either about the following day being Passover, although we do know that it was the Sabbath, so there was almost certainly a cycle of tradition that knew of no chronological tie-up between the Crucifixion and the Passover. What is important for our purposes is the fact, in all traditions, that Jesus' body had to be taken down and buried before nightfall, since if left on the cross, it would cause defilement. The Jews were scrupulous about this and charitable societies existed to bury those who died unattended. For an individual, therefore, to do this would be considered a work of merit. It would thus have been entirely natural for a pious Jew of means to arrange for the burial of Jesus, although the normal Roman custom (at least up to the time of Augustus) was to leave bodies on the cross until they had decayed. Subsequently it was possible for relatives and friends to request the body.

St Mark makes it quite clear that no anointing took place, no doubt because sunset was close at hand, and this point is emphasized in the opening verses of Chapter 16: 'And when the sabbath was past, Mary Magdalene, and Mary the mother of James, and Salome, had bought sweet spices, that they might come and anoint him.' Of course the question of this final chapter is highly problematic and has been called the 'greatest of all literary mysteries'. One fact is certainly true that what follows 16:8 (the account of the post-burial appearances of Jesus) is non-Marcan; consequently the earliest form of the Gospel ended with the account of the empty tomb.

From the point of view of establishing an early account of the burial clothes used in Jesus' case, the Gospel versions of the Resurrection and the empty tomb cannot be quoted as in any sense objective evidence. These are all highly subjective accounts based on the experience of those followers of Jesus whose inner-held conviction led them to proclaim him as the Crucified and Risen One. The two events, the Cross and the Resurrection, are really to be seen in the thought of the early Church as one single, indivisible salvation-occurrence. Consequently, it would seem that the two traditions of the empty tomb and the appearances are part of the mythology of the New Testament which arose from a belief of the first generations of followers of Jesus in the eschatological act of salvation.

Certainly there are elements of the narrative which may be termed 'historical', that is in the sense that they reflect generally held views in the early Church of what may have occurred.

Extreme caution needs to be exercised in deciding what may be 'historical' fact and what may not. Jesus' death on the Cross and subsequent burial in a rock tomb (according to normal Jewish practice) may well be all we can hold to with any degree of certainty. If the chronology is accepted (and there are very great difficulties in this) then it may well be that the body of Jesus was hastily wrapped in a cloth and conveyed to the tomb prior to the Sabbath observance beginning at sunset. However, there is evidence to suggest that proper burial of the dead in Jewish law was a permitted exception on the Sabbath.

It would seem most unlikely that the Shroud would be removed from the burial chamber in the days or weeks following. What is more likely is the possibility that, following the martyrdom of St James in AD 68 when the Christian community in Jerusalem removed to Pella in Decapolis at a time of persecution, and some two years before the destruction of the city by Titus in 70, relics of the saviour were sought for conveyance to safety and these included the Shroud, whose mysterious markings (always assuming that the Shroud of Turin is the authentic burial cloth of Jesus) would have ensured its preservation as an object of the greatest curiosity if nothing else.

But what of the ossuary containing the bodily remains of Jesus? Was this found then (for some reason unknown) to be missing, subsequently giving rise to the story of the empty tomb which probably does not appear until after AD 68?

The date limits for Mark's Gospel, which contains this tradition, and is the earliest of the four, are between AD 65 and 75, and there is some evidence to indicate a date at the top end of that scale. The final answer to this problem rests on the interpretation of Chapter 13 – the prophecy of the destruction of Jerusalem. I do not at all accept that this is a genuine prophecy before the event; it is the only place in the Gospel where we hear of Our Lord delivering a long, consecutive speech on a single topic, and my feeling is that it has been deliberately put in at this point to give significance to what follows, and to place the destruction of the city firmly in the context of Messianic prophecy. It is an integral part of Mark's structure.

Needless to say, much of this is conjectural.

CHAPTER 1

THE HOLY GRAIL
IDENTIFIED

———————●———————

The Holy Grail and the Loch Ness Monster have this in common: everyone has heard of them, but no one really knows what they are. Theories about both range from the scholarly to the absurd, and the most recent Grail theory, say the scholars, is the most absurd. But if you ask anyone what they think the Holy Grail was, most people will tell you that it was the Chalice of the Last Supper; that it had something to do with King Arthur and the Knights of the Round Table; that it lies buried on the top of Glastonbury Tor in Somerset; and that Joseph of Arimathea is said to have brought it to England. Probe a little deeper, and you will be told that the Grail stories have to do with Camelot, Lancelot and Guinevere, and if the person you are asking watches television, he may mention Monty Python too. If he is of a musical turn of mind, he may tell you that the Grail figures in Wagner's operas *Parsifal* and *Lohengrin*. If you are persistent, someone will mention Tennyson's *Idylls of the King*, and maybe Thomas Malory's *Morte d'Arthur*, but beyond that, you will be lucky indeed if you are told much more. So let me begin with the medieval Grail romances from which all our knowledge stems.

These stories tell us that the Grail was guarded by the Fisher King, a descendant of Joseph of Arimathea, whose successor is to prove his fitness for the office by asking a mysterious question. But the future Grail-winner is unaware of his destiny and knows nothing of the Grail, so he fails to put the question, and thus involves the world in mysterious enchantments which cease only when the question is put correctly. Coupled with the Grail is the Holy Lance the Roman soldier used to pierce Jesus' side on the Cross, which still reveals traces of his blood, and which in some versions is called the spear of vengeance.

The story was originally independent of the Arthurian legend, but

1

became incorporated with it during the twelfth century. At first the Grail quest was the task of a single predestined hero, but eventually became the crowning adventure of the Knights of the Round Table, all of whom took part in it. Some people say that the origin of the story is an ancient Christian tradition, some an oriental legend or a Celtic myth; others credit its invention to the medieval troubadours Chrétien de Troyes, Robert de Boron and Walter Map. The Grail has been likened to a wonder-working cauldron or horn of plenty, and the Lance to some kind of folk talisman, and we first meet them connected with the hero we know as Peredur, or Perceval. The Joseph of Arimathea element stems from the non-canonical gospel of Nicodemus. The claim that Chrétien de Troyes, Robert de Boron and Walter Map, or one of them, was the inventor of the story can be dismissed, but they were the first to write it down, and to give them their due, they only say that what they have to tell is based on what they have been told by others, or on books – now lost and otherwise not identified – that they have read. Whatever the truth of the matter, the Holy Grail became from about the middle of the twelfth century uniquely linked with the Passion of Jesus Christ and with the Arthurian cycle of legends. In a remarkably short time they became almost a cult of their own, in spite of being somewhat unorthodox from a strictly religious point of view.

Some Grail scholars suggest that the stories were deliberately written to mystify the uninitiated; that the authors set out to conceal something so sacred and secret that only a privileged and pious few would really understand them. As an example of this mystification, the Grail is described in one version as a vessel containing a single wafer; in another it is large enough to dispense food and drink to a large company of knights. Yet another account describes it as a receptacle for a severed head. In several versions it is a golden, jewel-encrusted dish or platter. Wolfram von Eschenbach, who wrote the earliest German version on which Wagner based his operas, calls it a magic stone in one section of his poem and a series of changing images of Christ in another.

Those who look for a pagan origin say that the Grail was an emerald or precious jewel from Lucifer's crown, which fell to earth when the Bringer of Light was thrust out of heaven during the war between the angels. Others believe that Seth, the son of Adam and Eve, went back to the Garden of Eden, where he was given the Grail by God as a sign that the Almighty had not forgotten mankind. A third theory, put forward by R. S. Loomis, makes the Grail into a food-and-drink-providing horn of plenty similar to the Celtic holy dish of Brân the

Blessed. But regardless of all this, the first time the Grail makes any appearance in history it is, as I have already said, in connection with the Crucifixion of Christ. By Thomas Malory's day – the late fifteenth century – it had assumed the distinct identity it still maintains as the Cup of the Last Supper. From the moment it appeared in the literature of France and Germany at the end of the twelfth century, it became a hallowed though utterly mysterious object, different from but more holy than all other relics.

The best-known version of the legend tells us that Joseph of Arimathea came to the West after the death and resurrection of Jesus with his son, Josephus, and a number of disciples. They were cast up on the shore hungry and thirsty, but there they met an old woman bringing twelve loaves from the bakery. These were not enough to satisfy them all, so Joseph ordered the loaves to be brought to him and told everyone to sit down on the ground. Just as Jesus had done in Galilee, Joseph then 'brake the bread and placed pieces here and there, and at the head of the table he put the Holy Grail' which he had brought with him from the Holy Land. 'As he set it in place the twelve loaves were multiplied in such a miraculous fashion that those present, who numbered four thousand, had every man his fill.' After further adventures the miracle-working Grail was brought by Joseph to Glastonbury, where he and his followers founded a church dedicated to the Mother of God, and where they enshrined the holy vessel.

This story was grafted on to the much older legend of King Arthur. Here it is envisaged as being kept in a castle variously called Munsalvaesche, Corbenic, Corbenoit, Corlenot and Carbonek, according to the various romancers. This castle is not wholly of this world, and is the goal to which the Knights of the Round Table, who have sworn to search for the Grail, must journey. To reach it they have to undergo many perils and trials, and it is from the accounts of this quest that we derive all we know about the Grail, its nature, form, function and purpose. In one version it appears to the knights in a ray of light to feed them with the food and drink of their choice; in another it is said to have various shapes – or changes of shape – which contain an inexplicable mystery. Although all the knights are searching for the Grail, some are doing so for worthy purposes, others for evil or dubious ones. It can only be found, however, by the truly pure and the truly holy.

The names of the knights vary from one version to another, but there are three principal ones: Galahad (or Gawain), Perceval (Parzival in German, Peredur in Welsh) and Bors. They alone of Arthur's men find their way to the Grail castle and the mysterious Fisher King who lives there and guards the holy vessel. He lies there wounded and ailing, and cannot be healed until a ritual question is asked and answered. This question differs from one version to another, but is either in the form 'Whom does the Grail serve?' or 'Who is it that serves the Grail?' When the question has been correctly answered, the king is healed, and the land over which he rules, until then a desert, begins to blossom. In Malory's version the three knights then take the Grail away by ship to Sarras, a holy city in the East, where the final celebration of the Grail mysteries takes place, and where Galahad, the purest of the three, dies a holy death after having been crowned King of Sarras. Perceval returns to the Grail castle to become its new king, and Bors journeys to Camelot to tell King Arthur and his Court about the miracles of the quest.

Let us now examine these early versions of the story a little more closely with particular attention to the descriptions of the sacred vessel. There are at least nine of them, and they can be summarized as follows:

1 The Grail is closely linked with Christ's Passion.
2 It is a vessel containing traces of his blood and sweat.
3 It is a series of changing scenes or images relating to Jesus.
4 It is a dish, or platter, on which is seen a bleeding head.
5 It is some kind of magical stone.
6 It is intimately linked with Joseph of Arimathea.
7 It is used for special celebrations of the Mass.
8 It is housed in a mystical castle variously called Corbenic (and variants) or Munsalvaesche.
9 It causes those who see it to tremble.

Let us start with the version known as *Perlesvaus*, written anonymously between 1206 and 1212, perhaps by a Templar. Here the first appearance of the Grail is described as follows:[1]

Two maidens come out of a chapel, one of them carries the Grail in her two hands, and the other the Holy Lance, which still carries traces of blood on it. They walk side by side and come into the room where Sir Gawain is eating. A sweet smell pervades the room. Sir Gawain looks upon the Grail and it seems to him there is a — within it.

At this point we are plunged into an area of debate. One version says that the Grail contained '*une chandoile*' (a candle or taper), while another says it contained '*un calice*' (a chalice). These discrepancies are due, of course, to the nature of the surviving manuscript texts, of which there are several versions which sometimes contradict each other. The point about this particular passage is this: Did Gawain seem to see a candle or a chalice within the Grail? Whatever he saw was *within* and not *on* the Grail.

Now, if the Grail was itself a chalice, as most people say, it makes nonsense to say that another chalice was placed within it. On the other hand, the word *chandoile*, if used symbolically, makes better sense, for it can be taken to indicate some kind of light or radiance. But the text is rather more explicit, for it goes on to say '*donc il n'est gaires a icel tens*', which can be translated as 'albeit there was none at that time', so the whole sentence should read: 'Sir Gawain looks upon the Grail and it seems to him that there is a light [or radiance] within it albeit there was none at that time.'

Now it seems to me that the author is suggesting that Gawain did not see a literal candle within the Grail but that he had the impression of some kind of light or radiance emanating from it. The association of light and radiance with things holy – and for that matter with saints and members of the Holy Family – in the form of haloes and auras is nothing unusual, and occurs in other religions besides Christianity. I would therefore suggest to you that the idea of light within the Grail in this context makes a good deal more sense than the idea of another chalice within it. And the passage which follows seems to bear this out, for Gawain 'seems' to behold two angels carrying a golden candelabra with lighted candles after he has seen the Holy Lance from which blood seems to be flowing. The French text is careful to use the words '*senble*' ('*semble*' in modern French) and '*voit*' very deliberately to distinguish between what Gawain actually sees and what he seems to use. Thus the author is making the point that he is describing something symbolic, or conveying the idea that Gawain is experiencing some kind of dream or vision.

A little later the two maidens come out of a second chapel. This time Gawain 'seems' to behold three angels, where before he had beheld only two. He also 'seems' to behold the form or image of a child *within the midst* of the Grail. Here again, the concept of a child within a chalice makes nonsense. Clearly the anonymous author has something much larger than a chalice or Communion cup in mind.

Gawain's third vision resembles the other two insofar as the author makes a distinction between what he sees and what he seems to see. Once again the two maidens appear and come to a table, but Gawain seems to see three figures. He looks up and there appears before him a man nailed to a cross with a spear in his side – obviously the crucified Christ immediately before he was taken down from the Cross. The maidens return to the chapel taking the Grail and the Lance with them.

The other knights who have been present with Gawain now retire, leaving him to contemplate what he has just seen.

The vision-like character of this episode is emphasized by the recurring motif of three drops of blood which Gawain sees after the image of the child. He cannot take his eyes off them 'and would fain pick them up but they elude him . . . wherefore he is very doleful, for he cannot put his hand out to them or to anything within his reach'.

Finally I should draw your attention to one other aspect of the Grail which appears in the *Perlesvaus*, and which I would like you to remember in connection with what I shall tell you later: the hermits who guard the Grail are also knights, who wear red crosses on their robes and surcoats like the Knights of the Order of Templars.

The *Perlesvaus* is but one of many versions of the Grail story. There are, in fact, five main groups of legends, comprising a much larger number of anecdotes and stories. The earliest is called the *Conte del Graal* by Chrétien de Troyes, a troubadour from Champagne in eastern France. The Counts of Champagne, although nominally subject to the King of France, were in reality almost independent princes at this period. Their lands occupied an area rather larger than Wales to the east and south-east of Paris as far as the borders of the Holy Roman Empire, which in those days ran well to the west of the Rhine. For these scattered lands the Counts of Champagne owed allegiance not only to the King of France but also to the Emperor, the Duke of Burgundy, the Archbishops of Reims and Sens, the Bishops of Autun, Auxerre and Langres and the Abbot of St Denis. They were, in any case, kinsmen of many of these potentates, being closely linked by blood and marriage to the Capetian Kings of France and Dukes of Burgundy, and to the Norman and Plantagenet rulers of England. Champagne, together with the neighbouring and interlocking duchy of Burgundy, was the intellectual and religious heartland of western Europe from the middle of the eleventh century to the end of the thirteenth, occupying together an area as extensive as England, and much larger than that of their titular overlord, the King of France.

Chrétien wrote his *Conte del Graal* at the behest of Philip of Alsace, Count of Flanders. The count paid his first visit to the Holy Land ostensibly on a pilgrimage, but with the secret intention of marrying off his two cousins, the Princesses Sibylla and Isabella, the daughters of the late King Amalric I of Jerusalem, to the two young sons of his favourite vassal, Robert of Béthune. He failed, and at the end of October 1177 he left Jerusalem for Tripoli and Antioch, but returned to Jerusalem for Easter 1178, after which he sailed for France by way of

Constantinople. Ten years later he joined the Third Crusade, and died in the Holy Land in 1191.

Chrétien tells us that he 'will not have wasted his effort, who strives and toils to turn into rhyme, at the command of the Count [Philip of Flanders], the best tale that may be told in a royal court: it is the story of the Grail, of which the Count has given him the book'.

What, precisely, did this book contain? The answers to this question tend to be influenced by theories concerning the origin of the Grail legend. Some have surmised that it was written in Latin and described a ritual about a certain Christian relic: others that it was a book of Celtic adventure stories. I am inclined, for reasons which will become apparent, to believe that it was the former.

The second group of Grail legends likewise originated in Champagne and Burgundy and consists of Robert de Boron's metrical *Joseph of Arimathea*, the *Lesser Holy Grail*, the *History of Merlin* and what has become known as the Didot-Modena *Perceval*. The third group is known as the *Great Vulgate Cycle*, a version consisting of four works entitled the *Quest of the Holy Grail*, *Merlin*, *Launcelot* and the *Death of King Arthur*. Its authorship is hotly debated in spite of the fact that there are quite specific statements in both the *Quest* and the *Death* on the subject. The fourth group is known to scholars as the *Pseudo-Robert de Boron Cycle* and is generally seen as an alternative version of the *Great Vulgate Cycle*, and as such need not concern us here. Finally there is the German cycle which we shall consider in due course.

We will look at the *Great Vulgate Cycle* next, so let me quote from Dr Pauline Matarasso's translation.[2] This is what the author of the *Quest* has to say in conclusion:

When they had dined King Arthur summoned his clerks who were keeping a record of all the adventures undergone by the knights of his household. When Bors had related to them the adventure of the Holy Grail as witnessed by himself, they were written down and the record kept in the library at Salisbury, whence Master Walter Map extracted them in order to make his book of the Holy Grail for the love of his Lord King Henry, who had the story translated into French from Latin. And with that the tale falls silent, and has no more to say about the Adventures of the Holy Grail.

The first paragraph of the *Death of King Arthur* in James Cable's translation[3] reads:

After Master Walter Map had put down in writing as much as he thought sufficient about the Adventures of the Holy Grail, his Lord King Henry II felt that what he had done would not be satisfactory unless he told about the rest of the lives of those whose prowess he had related in his book. So he began this last part; and when he put it together he called it the Death of

King Arthur because the end of it relates how King Arthur was wounded at the battle of Salisbury and left Girflet who had long been his companion, and how no one ever again saw him alive. So Master Walter begins this last part accordingly.

The last paragraph of this book reads:

At this point Master Walter Map will end the story of Lancelot, because he has brought everything to a proper conclusion according to the way it happened; and he finishes his book here so completely that no one can afterwards add anything to the story that is not complete falsehood.

I want to examine the question of the authorship of the *Great Vulgate Cycle* because there is so much controversy about it among Arthurian scholars. Many, including both the translators from whose work I have just quoted, refuse to take these three statements at their face value. Their chief reason for not doing so is because Walter Map is known to have died in about 1209, and modern scholarship is of the opinion that the cycle was written between 1215 and 1235. One translator backs his opinion with the observation that the author, whoever he might be if not Walter Map, reveals a very sketchy knowledge of England and English geography, for he believes that Salisbury Plain is near the sea. If he had been Walter Map, he argues, or any other Englishman, he would certainly have been aware that the monks of Glastonbury had discovered in 1191 what they claimed to be King Arthur's tomb in the chancel of their abbey, and that he would not have placed it in the Black Chapel by the sea.

This is all very well, but no one can explain why the author, if he were *not* Walter Map, should have pretended that he was. At the same time, they all admit that there are no internal means of dating the *Death of King Arthur* precisely. The general consensus seems to be that various scraps of internal evidence *tend* to suggest that the cycle as a whole was written around 1230 to 1235 in France, possibly in Champagne. I hope to show that while I agree with the location, I disagree with the date, and why. One translator makes the point that the author was not a layman – nor was Walter Map – but confines herself to general speculation. The text from which these translations have been made is to be found in the British Museum, but there is nothing to indicate whether the MS was written by Walter Map himself, by the unknown author, or by a clerk at his dictation, or later copied from an earlier version. Notwithstanding, the opinion of these scholars is not unanimous, for the author of the article on Walter Map in the *Dictionary of National Biography* states, albeit with some reservation: 'probably the author of *Lancelot* and the *Quest of the Holy Grail*, written in French'.

What, then, of Master Walter Map? Who was he? When did he live? Should we attach great importance to the statements I have just quoted, or should we agree with the Arthurian scholars who think he had nothing to do with the *Great Vulgate Cycle*?

Well, quite a good deal is known about Walter Map. He was born in Herefordshire about 1140. His parents are known to have been in the service of Henry II both before and after he became king. In 1154 young Walter went as a student to Paris, probably to read law, where he remained for at least six years. He returned to England in 1161 or early in 1162 when he seems to have gained the king's favour early in his career. From Herefordshire Walter Map joined the king at Limoges in 1173, and six years later, Henry II sent him to the Lateran Council called by Pope Alexander III. This is of great significance to our present investigation, for it was there that he met the historian, William of Tyre.

In 1168 William, then Archdeacon of Tyre, was sent by King Amalric I of Jerusalem as his ambassador to the Emperor Manuel I Comnenus of Constantinople to discuss his proposal for the conquest of Egypt, where he was received warmly. Two years later, King Amalric invited Stephen of Champagne, Count of Sancerre, to Palestine to marry the Princess Sybilla, his daughter. Stephen was the youngest son of Theobald (Thibault) Count of Blois, Chartres and Troyes, and a brother of Henry I, Count of Champagne, the patron of Chrétien de Troyes. Stephen was born about 1130, and made a runaway marriage in 1151, though by 1170 he was a widower.[4] Amalric had invited Stephen to be his son-in-law as a consequence of the tragic discovery that his nine-year-old son, Baldwin, was suffering from leprosy. Baldwin was being educated by William of Tyre, who attributed this misfortune to the judgement of God for the 'incestuous' marriage of Baldwin's parents, Amalric and Agnes de Courtenay. It boded ill for the kingdom of Jerusalem, he said, for even if Baldwin survived, he would never be able to father children. For safety's sake, therefore, Amalric considered it wise to marry his eldest child, the ten-year-old Princess Sybilla, to a rich, experienced Western prince, who could act as regent or king. Stephen accepted the invitation, and arrived in Palestine in the summer of 1171, a few days before Amalric himself, who had been on a visit to Constantinople in connection with his own marriage to the emperor's daughter. Stephen took one look at the Holy Land, disliked what he saw, broke off the marriage negotiations and left for France, intending to call in at Constantinople on the way. He had much to tell his brother when he got back.

In 1175, William was raised from Archdeacon to Archbishop of

Tyre. On his way to the Lateran Council in 1179, he paid a seven-month visit to Constantinople, and was present when Manuel's daughter married Rainier of Montferrat (one of four brothers of whom I shall have much more to say in the course of this book). He also assisted at the wedding of Manuel's son, the future Emperor Alexius II, then ten years old, to the nine-year-old Princess Agnes of France.

William of Tyre was well informed of life at the Byzantine Court, as well as with current events in the Holy Land and the Eastern empire. Furthermore, there can be little doubt that Walter Map would have come to know him well during the course of the Lateran Council, where the pope had deputed Map to argue the case for orthodoxy against the Waldensian heretics. Both on his way to Rome in 1179 and on his return to the Court of King Henry II, Walter Map was hospitably received by Count Henry of Champagne, so there was plenty of opportunity to make himself conversant with the work of Chrétien de Troyes, and to learn from him about the Grail.

Walter Map must have learnt about the Holy Grail between 1179 and 1183, but for the moment I want to conclude this brief account of his life. In 1176 he had been appointed a Prebendary of St Paul's Cathedral in London, and was already a Canon and Precentor of Lincoln. He was with King Henry II in Anjou in 1183, and at Saumur when the king's eldest son, Henry Courtmantel, known as The Young King, died there in June. He returned to England around 1184, and was appointed Chancellor of Lincoln before 1186. His connection with the Court lasted until Henry II's death in July 1189, after which he seems to have returned permanently to his native country. In 1197 he was appointed Archdeacon of Oxford, and resigned the Precentorship of Lincoln. He was alive in March 1208 but dead before 1210.

It is important to realize that Walter Map was a cosmopolitan cleric of considerable standing in Europe as well as in his own country. He had a large circle of acquaintance not only at the English Court, but also at the Courts of Champagne (at Troyes) and at Rome. Throughout his life he was engaged in public affairs, and for more than thirty years – between 1154 and 1185 – he lived outside England. He is best known for his *De Nugis Curialium* (*A Courtier's Triflings*), which is a gossipy account of life at three of the most sophisticated Courts of Europe. Map wrote in Latin, but spoke French well, possibly as his first language in spite of his West Country origins. He incorporated in *De Nugis* a great deal of historical information, and like William of Tyre is a major source for modern medievalists. It grew out of a request by a friend named Geoffrey to write a poem about his experiences at Court and abroad. Elsewhere he implies that he wrote it at the request of Henry II. There is general agreement that he wrote it between 1182 and 1192, but there is nothing in it about his authorship of the Arthurian stories, although a near contemporary, Hélie de Borron, says that Walter Map wrote '*le propre livre de M. Lancelot du Lac*'.

Before leaving Walter Map, let us consider the three quotations attributed to him which are on pages 7–8. If these are to be believed – and I can see no reason for not believing them – Walter Map must have set down his account of the Grail between 1162 and 1189, during the lifetime of his lord and master, Henry II. I would go farther, and say that if he wrote them at all, it must have been after 1179, when he first met William of Tyre, and after he had met Chrétien de Troyes, for I am firmly of the opinion that it was from one or both of these men that he first heard about the Grail. He would not have had time to compose such a long work during the course of the Lateran Council, when all his energies must have been taken up with the business of refuting the Waldensian heresies. So it is highly unlikely that he would have started until after his return to Court in 1183. The *Quest*, being the first book of the cycle, must have been completed before the death of Henry II in 1189, but it does not necessarily follow that the rest of the cycle was. The king, having read the *Quest*, expressed the opinion that it needed a sequel, and Walter may have begun this before the king died. If *De Nugis* was still in course of compilation up to 1192, the remaining parts of the cycle would probably have had to wait until after that date, and they could have occupied his old age.

But how should the critics who say that Walter Map could not have been the author of these stories be regarded? I think it is important to remember that Henry II and his sons, especially his three eldest sons, Henry, Geoffrey and Richard Coeur de Lion, spent the greater part of their lives outside England. They saw themselves first and foremost as French princes who happened to own a valuable piece of real estate called England on the northern shore of La Manche. They ruled vast areas of France, and their capital was as much Rouen as it was London. A great deal of their time, like that of later Kings of France, was spent in the delightful valley of the Loire. Consequently a courtier like Walter Map, who first went to France as a boy of fourteen, and who remained abroad for the better part of the next thirty years, can be forgiven for thinking that Salisbury Plain is near the sea. From the point of view of someone living in the heart of France it *is*. So, for that matter, is Glastonbury; the former is no more than twenty-five miles as the crow flies, and the latter no more than twelve. To say that

Walter Map, an Englishman, could not have written the stories because of his apparently inaccurate geography, doesn't hold water. Walter Map's benefices in Lincoln, London and Hereford probably claimed little of his personal attention, for many ecclesiastical positions were held *in absentia*. So until his return to England in 1189 or 1190 there are good reasons for thinking that he knew very little about his native country. By the time he returned he was an old man by the standards of his day.

Let us now look at the Welsh version, *Peredur*, which forms part of a collection of more ancient stories known as the *Mabinogion*, written down between 1050 and 1250.

The hero, Peredur, as I have already said, is the counterpart of Perceval or Parzifal in the other versions. His first encounter with the Grail is very similar to the one I have quoted from the *Perlesvaus*. Peredur

> saw two lads entering the hall and then leaving for another chamber. They carried a spear of incalculable size with three streams of blood running from the socket to the floor. . . . After a short silence two girls entered bearing a large platter with a man's head covered with blood on it, and everyone set up a crying and a lamentation. . . .

It is hard to say whether this is a gloss on the *Perlesvaus* or vice versa, but that is of minor consequence for our purpose. We are only concerned with the size and shape of the object known as the Grail, and here it is clearly seen as something bigger than a chalice, for two maidens are required to carry it. Moreover, it is described unequivocally as a platter. This indicates something flattish and big enough to carry a man's head. In more prosaic terms, the author is envisaging something measuring not less than one foot by eighteen inches, since the average human head measures roughly fourteen inches by eight. This imagery is also found in the *Perlesvaus* where, in addition to the changing forms I have described, the Grail is likened to a severed head which Sir Gawain saw 'in the midst' of it 'all in flesh'.

In his study of the *Perlesvaus*, Thomas E. Kelley refers to a comment concerning the Grail by Hélinand, Abbot of Froidmont, a Cistercian abbey founded during the first half of the twelfth century not far from Beauvais, north of Paris. Hélinand writes of '*li estoires du saintisme vessel que on apele Graal o quel li precieus sans du Sauveur fu receuz au jor qu'il fu crucifiez por le peuple racheter d'enfer. . . .*' (The stories of the most holy vessel called the Grail into which the precious blood of the Saviour was received on the day he was crucified to save mankind from hell. . . .)

Abbot Hélinand wrote this in May 1204, and it is perhaps the earliest reference we have to the Grail, apart from the stories themselves. Up to now the passage has been taken to refer to the cup into which Joseph of Arimathea is said to have received drops of Jesus' blood and sweat. In the Latin version of the passage, Hélinand uses the word *Gradalis* for Grail, which in medieval Latin means a shallow dish. In another passage, Hélinand refers to the Grail as *scutella lata*, which can likewise be translated as a saucer, dish, or flat, broad bowl. That is not all: Hélinand states that the vessel called the Grail was one into which Christ's blood was *received* on the day he was crucified. I stress the word 'received' and that this happened on the day Jesus died. The use of the word 'received' in connection with the drawing off of blood into a cup is strange. Clearly Hélinand was thinking of no such thing. The medieval French word *vessel* is a neutral term, and can stand for any hollow object capable of holding liquids or solids, and can be of almost any shape. Two modern French words derive from it. One is *vaisseau* meaning a receptacle, and by extension a ship, or the nave of a church. The other is *vaiselle* meaning a table service, plates and dishes (the modern French term for a dish-washer is *lave-vaiselle*). Quite emphatically the term does not mean a cup or chalice.

So what Hélinand had in mind was something flat or dish-shaped, corresponding to the platter-like object described in the *Peredur* and the *Perlesvaus*. It is the same with Walter Map; he represents the Grail as a vessel from which Jesus and the disciples ate the paschal lamb at the Last Supper, which appears to 'feed the Companions of the Round Table'. He continues:

> The Holy Grail (covered with a cloth of white samite) entered through the great door, and at once the palace was filled with fragrance as though all the spices of the earth had been spilled abroad. It circled the Hall along the great tables, and each place was furnished in its wake with the food the occupants desired. When all were served, the Holy Grail vanished they knew not where nor whither; and those who had been mute regained their speech, and many gave thanks to our Lord *for the honour he had done them* [my italics] in filling them with the Grace of the holy vessel.

Hélinand is not alone in describing the Grail as a dish or platter. Walter Map obviously thinks of it in this way, but he implies something more. By recounting how the knights gave thanks to our Lord, he goes on to make the point that our Lord had done them an honour of some particular kind. He seems to be implying that Christ himself was there in person. In other words the knights and the king were in the Real Presence of Christ when the Grail was among them.

Elsewhere, Walter Map likens the Grail to a shield. Here is a brief summary of what he says:

Forty-two years after the Crucifixion, Joseph of Arimathea left Jerusalem and came to the (mythical) city of Sarras, ruled over by King Evalach (a fictional character), who was then an infidel. Evalach was at war with his neighbour, Tholomer (another fictional character) who is defeated by a shield bearing the emblem of a bleeding figure of Christ crucified. Evalach, having overcome Tholomer, returns to Sarras and proclaims the truth that Joseph has revealed to him, and bears witness to Jesus Christ. He and his family are baptized, and Evalach takes the new name of Mordrain.

Then there is the story of Lancelot, who comes during his quest to a ruined chapel, in which he sees a richly decked altar. He is unable to enter, so he lies down outside and falls asleep. In his dreams he seems to see a sick knight approaching in a litter slung between two horses. The holy vessel (once again not specifically identified) appears, and the sick man prays earnestly to it to be healed of his afflictions, so that he, too, may undertake the quest 'wherein all good men are entered'. The Grail then appears on a silver table, and when the sick knight sees it, he falls on his knees, crying, 'Gracious God, who through this Holy Vessel that I now see before me, hath performed so many miracles in this and other lands, Father, look upon me in thy mercy, and grant that I may presently be healed of my infirmities. . . .' He drags himself towards the silver altar and kisses it, pressing his lips and eyes against it, and immediately finds relief from his suffering.

In another passage, Percival meets his aunt, a holy recluse, who tells him how Joseph of Arimathea, his son and disciples, went to Britain, and about the miracle of the loaves I described earlier. There can be no doubt that Walter Map is here reflecting the story of Jesus' miracles of the loaves and fishes as told in Matthew 13, Mark 6 and 8, Luke 9 and John 5. This seems to be yet another instance of his wish to imply that in the presence of the holy vessel we are in the Real Presence of Christ. The Grail's function in all these passages is the same. Walter Map seems to be telling us that the miracles Jesus performed here on earth can still be performed by the Grail and what it contains.

It is now time to look at the German version of the legend. Wolfram von Eschenbach tells us that his *Parzival* was based on Chrétien de Troyes', but that Chrétien was not in possession of all the facts, and more specifically, that the Grail is not an object of fantasy, but a means of hiding something of great significance and consequence. In a passage where Parzifal meets his hermit uncle, Trevrizent, the latter describes the Grail in the following manner:

14

It is well known to me that many formidable fighting men dwell at Munsalvaesche with the Gral. They are continually riding out on sorties in quest of adventure. Whether these same Templeisen [Wolfram uses the term derived from *Tempelritter*, whose generic meaning indicates a member of any military order of monks, and not exclusively the Templars] reap trouble or renown, they bear it for their sins. A warlike company lives there. I will tell you how they are fed: they live from a stone whose essence is pure. . . . It is called *Lapis Exilis*. By virtue of this stone the Phoenix is burned to ashes, in which she is reborn. Thus does the Phoenix moult her feathers, after which she shines dazzling and bright, and as lovely as before. . . . The stone confers such powers on mortal men, so that their flesh and bones are made young again. This stone is called the Gral, and it is unknown, save to those who are singled out by name to join the company of Munsalvaesche.

At first sight this seems to be an entirely new and different description of the Grail. The only point in common with the others is the reference to the Phoenix as an analogy of the resurrection. Wolfram seems to be pointing more to the Grail's religious significance and power than to its actual shape or form. But that is not all. He says somewhere that he derived his account of the story of Parsifal and the Grail from one Kyot, whom he qualifies as '*ein Provenzal*'. Oceans of ink have been spilt on attempts to identify Kyot. The epithet *Provenzal* looks at first sight as if it indicated someone from Provence, but no troubadour or minnesinger[5] of that name is known to the history of literature. On the other hand, Wolfram, whose knowledge of French was, on his own admission, very sketchy, may have been speaking of one Guyot de Provins, a troubadour from Champagne who flourished in the first part of the thirteenth century.

Wolfram's ignorance of languages other than his native German may account for some of the obscurities of his text if, as he tells us, he derived his information from the Frenchmen, Chrétien de Troyes and Guyot de Provins. But nowhere is he more obscure than when dealing with the Grail. His Latin name for it has caused scholars immense trouble and confusion. To begin with, the surviving MSS disagree with one another. The St Gall MS calls it '*Lapsit exillis*', where all the others have variants. *Lapsit* varies with *lapis* and *iaspis* (meaning stone and jasper respectively); and *exillis* varies with *exilis*, *ereillis*, *erilis*, *exilix* and *exillix*. Only *exilis* and *erilis* are proper Latin words. The former means thin, lean or slender; the latter means heir, or more properly 'of the master' or 'of the mistress' – there is no exact English equivalent, for the word really means something that has been inherited, or has belonged to one's father or mother, which you now own yourself.

15

In another passage referring to the Grail, Wolfram writes: 'Always on Good Friday [the dove] brings a white wafer to the stone [*lapis*]. . . .'

There seems to be ground for thinking that Wolfram had more than one object in mind to which he applied the word 'Gral'. His limited knowledge of French might have led him to misunderstand what Chrétien meant by the term, although he reproaches Chrétien for inaccuracy. R. S. Loomis[6] thinks that Wolfram assumed that the stone and the Grail were one and the same. But did he truly misunderstand the Grail's nature? He tells us that in its presence each man obtained whatever he sought. In the *Quest of the Holy Grail* it is written that as the Grail passed before the tables, the knights were instantly filled with such food as they desired. These and similar passages must refer to spiritual rather than material nourishment, although some commentators have taken them literally. But whichever way you look at it, these descriptions of the vessel fit a dish or platter better than a cup or chalice.

Professor Hatto, the translator of Wolfram's *Parzival*,[7] puts forward good reasons for believing that the work was written between 1205 and 1208. Wolfram was one of the many poets, or minnesingers, who were welcome at the Wartburg, the Court of the Landgrave Hermann of Thuringia. He was born and buried at Eschenbach in Franconia, about twenty-five miles south-west of Nuremberg. From Book III to the middle of Book XIII Wolfram's *Parzival* agrees closely with the *Perceval* of Chrétien de Troyes; but it possesses an introduction and concluding portion to which no parallel has hitherto been found. The swan-knight, Lohengrin, is Parzival's son; the Grail-bearer becomes the mother of Prester John, and the whole poem bristles with oriental allusions. Lohengrin is also Duke of Brabant by marriage. Now the historical Duke of Brabant at that time was called Henry. In 1198 his daughter Marie was betrothed to Otto, Count of Poitou, and in 1204 was named Henry's heiress, as it seemed unlikely that he would have any sons of his own. But a son was born to him in 1207. Thus until 1207 the inheritance of Brabant was through the female line, which brings Professor Hatto to the conclusion that Lohengrin's inclusion as Duke of Brabant by marriage must date from the period before the real Duke Henry's son was born. Hence he dates the composition as a whole to between 1205 and 1207. This gave me an important clue for my search for the true nature of the Grail.

Before I leave Wolfram, I want to have another look at Kyot. In 1934 the Nazi activist, spy and author Otto Rahn published a book entitled *Kreuzzug gegen den Graal* (*Crusade against the Grail*), in which he makes out that Wolfram had had Montségur and the Cathars in mind when he wrote his poem. I do not propose to enter into this controversy here, for the identification of the Grail with the Cathar Treasure has been dealt with at great length by Messrs Lincoln, Baigent and Leigh. Nevertheless, parts of Rahn's theory are less dotty than others, and worthy of at least some respect. He advances the view that Guyot de Provins wrote a version of the Parsifal story which was lost during the Albigensian Crusade (launched against the Cathars in 1209 and lasting till 1244). From Wolfram's Book IX, Rahn claims that the poem is based on Guyot. He bases his thesis to a large extent on the similarity of names found in the countryside around Montségur with those in the poem. For example, he suggests that Wolfram chose the name of the Grail castle – Munsalvaesche – with Montségur in mind. It cannot be denied that the notions of safety, security and salvation have something in common. The name Munsalvaesche derives from two Latin words – *mons* – mountain, and *salus/salvare* – safe/to save. Montségur's name likewise derives from Mons and *securitas* – security, safety. Alternatively, it can be argued that 'salvaesche' derives from *silvaticus*, which means wooded or savage. The sheer strength of Montségur is certainly impressive; perhaps the name Munsalvaesche was chosen to convey the idea of the spiritual nature of the Grail which the castle was supposed to house, yet at the same time to hint at a secure fortress which may have really existed.

Although a native of Champagne, Guyot had as patron the King of Aragon, in whose territory Montségur had at one time been situated. (By the time that Wolfram wrote, it belonged to the Count of Toulouse.) Wolfram says that Kyot derived his information about the Grail from Spain. It is known that Guyot did travel extensively in southern France and Spain, and to reach the Court of the King of Aragon, he would almost certainly have gone up the valley of the Ariège near Montségur. On the other hand, it is possible that Wolfram met the French poets Guyot and Chrétien at Mainz in 1184 or at Beaucaire in 1198, during the great festivities there in connection with the wedding of Richard Coeur de Lion's sister to the Count of Toulouse. Or they might have met at the Wartburg, the Landgrave of Thuringia's Court, in 1203, where a great festival of troubadours and minnesingers was held. But however Wolfram acquired his knowledge of the legends, there was ample scope for confusion and misunderstanding.

Whether or not Guyot ever wrote a Grail romance is something we are unlikely to discover now. The fact remains that during the Albigensian crusades which took place in the first half of the thirteenth century in southern France, a vast amount of Occitan literature was burnt as heretical by the Inquisition. It is also true that some troubadours were Cathars, but there is nothing to support Rahn's theory that Guyot was one, or that he came from Provence. If we identify Kyot with Guyot then his birthplace was Provins, not far from Troyes in Champagne. But in fairness to Rahn, it has to be said that Catharism was not unknown in that province and in neighbouring Burgundy. It comes to this: there is some evidence to support the view that Wolfram's Kyot was Guyot de Provins; there are less solid grounds for believing that either Guyot or Wolfram had Cathars in mind. Such oriental influences as can be detected in Wolfram's poem – and there are many – can be attributed insofar as they correspond to any extent with Catharism to contacts his informants may have had with the Bogomils of the Balkans, whose heresy was the basis of Catharism.

Versions of the story after Chrétien's and Wolfram's include the sequel to Chrétien's *Conte del Graal*. In this, the Grail is portrayed somewhat differently, as the following synopsis shows:

Gawain enters a great hall and sees a bier on which a corpse is lying with half a sword-blade on top of it. A priest enters bearing a cross, and wearing over his alb a tunic of 'precious cloth of Constantinople'. He and his acolytes celebrate the Mass of the Dead. The priest then leaves the hall, and the king and his courtiers enter and sit down to eat. They are served by the Grail, which is not described, though the inference is made that it is the vessel from which the Host is offered to the courtiers, rather in the way a ciborium would be used at Mass. Each communicant receives the Host as though directly from the hand of Jesus himself. Gawain's vision of the Requiem and the 'Feast' that follows it is, of course, symbolic, for the company suddenly vanishes, leaving him alone with the bier and the bleeding lance, which we have met before in other versions of the story. This lance is subsequently identified with the one which pierced Jesus' side on the Cross. The Grail, however, is differentiated from the bier, and this is a significant point to which I shall return. The episode can be summarized by saying that it was a special Mass at which Christ himself is present, a concept we encounter in the religious art of this period, and about which I shall also have more to say in the final chapter of this book.

A. E. Waite has made an exhaustive study of the Grail legends and their symbolism.[8] He points out that the legend depends upon certain values attaching to various sacred objects. The most holy is the Grail itself, followed by the lance and the sword. The fourth is the dish which he finds the most difficult to define, since he assumes that the Grail itself is the Chalice of the Last Supper. Of these sacred objects, the lance and the sword present no problem, for they are known to have been among the many relics of the Passion kept in the Church of the Virgin Mother of God of the Pharos in the Bucoleon Palace at Constantinople. Other relics of the Passion kept there included the crown of thorns, the nails, the sponge, the sandals of Christ, the burial linens and a phial of his blood.

Having considered the Grail as a dish or platter, I want now to consider it as a chalice. There are several versions of the chalice legend. Following Jesus' ascension into heaven, his earthly body was removed from the world. All that remained was the vessel into which his blood and sweat had been received by Joseph of Arimathea. Endowed with the virtue of the risen Christ and the power of the Holy Ghost, it sustained him spiritually for forty years of imprisonment. After his release the holy vessel became the sign of saving grace to a certain number of initiates whom Joseph selected to accompany him to the West. When they arrived in Britain, these sacred objects were added to the Chalice and all of them were kept in a secret place.

Because of the central part he plays in the Grail legends, we must now examine the evidence that has been handed down to us about Joseph of Arimathea. It comes, of course, from the four canonical Gospels, but there is a great deal more about him in the non-canonical gospel of Nicodemus, which is an early tradition of the last days of Jesus' life and of the events that took place immediately after the Crucifixion. Although not included in the New Testament, the gospel of Nicodemus is none the less a valuable historical document. But let us begin with St Matthew, Chapter 28:

> 57. When the even was come, there came a rich man of Arimathea, named Joseph, who also himself was Jesus' disciple:
>
> 58. He went to Pilate, and begged the body of Jesus. Then Pilate commanded the body to be delivered.
>
> 59. And when Joseph had taken the body, he wrapped it in a clean linen cloth,
>
> 60. And laid it in his own new tomb.

This is St Mark's account (Chapter 15):

> 42. And now when the even was come, because it was the Preparation, that is, the day before the sabbath,
>
> 43. Joseph of Arimathea, an honourable counsellor, which also waited for the Kingdom of God, came, and went in boldly unto Pilate, and craved the body of Jesus.
>
> 44. And Pilate marvelled if he were already dead: and calling unto him the centurion, he asked him whether he had been any while dead.
>
> 45. And when he knew it of the centurion, he gave the body to Joseph.

46. And he bought fine linen, and took him down, and wrapped him in linen, and laid him in a sepulchre.

Let us now see what St Luke has to say (Chapter 24):

50. And behold, there was a man named Joseph .... he was of Arimathea, a city of the Jews: who also himself waited for the Kingdom of God.
52. This man went unto Pilate, and begged the body of Jesus.
53. And he took it down, and wrapped it in linen, and laid it in a sepulchre. . . .
54. And that day was the preparation and the sabbath drew on.

Finally, so far as the canonical Gospels are concerned, we have St John's account (Chapter 29):

25. Now there stood by the cross of Jesus his mother, and his mother's sister, Mary, the wife of Cleophas, and Mary Magdalene. . . .
31. The Jews therefore, because it was the preparation, that the bodies should not remain upon the cross on the sabbath day, (for that sabbath day was a high day,) besought Pilate that their legs might be broken, and that they might be taken away.
32. Then came the soldiers, and brake the legs of the first, and of the other which was crucified with him.
33. But when they came to Jesus, and saw that he was dead already, they brake not his legs:
34. But one of the soldiers with a spear pierced his side, and forthwith came thereout blood and water. . . .
38. And after this Joseph of Arimathea, being a disciple of Jesus, but secretly for fear of the Jews, besought Pilate that he might take away the body of Jesus: and Pilate gave him leave. He came, therefore, and took the body of Jesus.
39. And there came also Nicodemus which at the first came to Jesus by night, and brought a mixture of myrrh and aloes, about an hundred pound weight.
40. Then took they the body of Jesus, and wound it in linen clothes with the spices, as the manner of the Jews is to bury.
41. Now in the place where he was crucified there was a garden; and in the garden a new sepulchre, wherein was never man laid.
42. There laid they Jesus therefore because of the Jews' preparation day; for the sepulchre was nigh at hand.

The gospel of Nicodemus is divided into two parts – the Acts of Pilate and Christ's Descent into Hell. Let us see how this account differs and augments the ones we all know so much better (Chapter 11):

3. But a certain man named Joseph, a member of the council, from the town of Arimathea, who also was waiting for the kingdom of God, this man went to Pilate and asked for the body of Jesus. And he took it down, and wrapped it in a clean linen cloth, and placed it in a rock-hewn tomb, in which no one had ever yet been laid.

Chapter 12:
When the Jews heard that Joseph had asked for the body, they sought for him and the twelve men who said that Jesus was not born of fornication, [Note: the twelve apostles] and for Nicodemus and for many others who had come forward before Pilate and made known his good works. But they all hid themselves, and only Nicodemus was seen by them, because he was a ruler of the Jews. . . . Likewise also Joseph came forth [from his concealment?] and said to them: 'Why are you angry with me, because I asked for the body of Jesus? See, I have placed it in my new tomb, having wrapped it in clean linen, and I rolled a stone before the door of the cave. And you have not done well with the righteous one, for you did not repent of having crucified him, but also pierced him with a spear.

Then the Jews seized Joseph and commanded him to be secured until the first day of the week. They said to him: 'Know that the hour forbids us to do anything against you, because the sabbath dawns. But know also that you will not even be counted worthy of burial, but we shall give your flesh to the birds of the heaven' . . . and they laid hold on Joseph and seized him and shut him in a building without a window, and guards remained at the door of the place where Joseph was shut up.

2. And on the sabbath the rulers of the synagogue and the priests and the Levites ordered that all should present themselves in the synagogue on the first day of the week. And the whole multitude rose up early and took counsel in the synagogue by what death they should kill him. And when the council was in session they commanded him to be brought with great dishonour. And when they opened the door they did not find him. And all the people were astonished and filled with consternation because they found the seals undamaged, and Caiaphas had the key. And they dared no longer to lay hands on those who had spoken before Pilate on behalf of Jesus.

Chapter 13:
And while they still sat in the synagogue and marvelled because of Joseph, there came some of the guard which the Jews had asked from Pilate to guard the tomb of Jesus, lest the disciples should come and steal him. And they told the rulers of the synagogue and the priests and the Levites what had happened: how there was a great earthquake. 'And we saw an angel descend from heaven, and he rolled away the stone from the mouth of the cave, and sat upon it, and he shone like snow and like lightning. And we were in great fear, and lay like dead men. And we heard the voice of the angel speaking to the women who waited at the tomb: Do not be afraid. I

21

know that you seek Jesus who was crucified. He is not here. He has risen, as he said. Come and see the place where the Lord lay. And go quickly and tell his disciples that he has risen from the dead and is in Galilee.'

2. The Jews asked: 'To what women did he speak?' The members of the guard answered: 'We do not know who they were.' The Jews said: 'At what hour was it?' The members of the guard answered: 'At midnight.' The Jews said: 'And why did you not seize the women?' The members of the guard said: 'We were like dead men through fear, and gave up hope of seeing the light of day; how could we then have seized them?' The Jews said: 'As the Lord lives we do not believe you.' The members of the guard said to the Jews: 'So many signs you saw in that man and you did not believe; and how can you believe us? You rightly swore: As the Lord lives. For he *does* live.' Again the members of the guard said: 'We have heard that you shut up him who asked for the body of Jesus, and sealed the door, and that when you opened it you did not find him. Therefore give us Joseph and we will give you Jesus.' The Jews said: 'Joseph has gone to his own city.' And the members of the guard said to the Jews: 'And Jesus has risen, as we heard from the angel, and is in Galilee.'

I have quoted these passages in full because, taken as historical evidence, they have a profound bearing on the identity of the Holy Grail.

What are the salient points we should consider? First the people who were watching the Crucifixion. Imagine to yourself the scene: three criminals are being brought to execution in public by the paramount power represented by the Roman soldiery. They have the uprights of the gallows already set up, and now the crosspieces have to be attached and the victims nailed to the completed crosses. While this is being done, the friends of the victims must be kept at a distance lest they attempt to rescue them. Matthew, Mark, Luke and Nicodemus are all agreed that the women and other acquaintances of Jesus were not allowed to come too near. Only John seems to suggest that they were close enough to the Cross for Jesus to be able to address them so that they could hear what he said. Thus there is some doubt about this, though there can be no doubt that the soldiers would have endeavoured to keep the crowd at a distance, simply in order to keep control of the situation, which might so easily have got out of hand. In order to fill a cup with Jesus' blood and sweat while he was still on the Cross, therefore, it would have been necessary for Joseph of Arimathea to be right beneath it and close enough to reach Jesus' feet, the lowest part of his anatomy from which blood was flowing. It would have been a physical impossibility to get it from any higher point of his body. Moreover, in such a situation, sweat would have been flowing more profusely from his head and body than from his feet. But apart from these practical difficulties, the very idea is quite disgusting. Put yourself in the position of Joseph and the disciples. You have just seen the man you revere most on earth arrested on a trumped-up charge, insulted, beaten to within an inch of his life; forced to walk something like half a mile with a heavy wooden beam on shoulders already lacerated by the vicious beating he has just undergone; nailed to a cross and now dying a slow and agonizing death. Would you add to his agony by approaching him to get a drop of his blood as a souvenir? Of course you wouldn't. The very idea is utterly revolting. And I submit that Joseph of Arimathea did no such thing either.

So we can dismiss the notion that Joseph gathered drops of Jesus' blood and sweat during the Crucifixion. But we have to reconcile this with the repeated allegation that the Grail was the vessel containing traces of Jesus' blood and sweat, and the tradition that Joseph of Arimathea was closely concerned with it. Once more let us turn to the accounts of what happened on Good Friday and the following Sabbath day. Let's start with the chalice itself. The Last Supper took place on Thursday evening – let us say about seven o'clock. It would have lasted at least an hour, if not longer. Afterwards, say about ten or eleven o'clock, Jesus and the disciples went to Gethsemane. They were sleepy, so it was probably later. They are most unlikely to have taken any cups or plates with them, and must surely have left them in the upper room where the meal had been held. How, then, did Joseph of Arimathea get hold of the cup Jesus had used? He wasn't among those who took part in the meal. Indeed, he only appears on the scene after Jesus had been put on the Cross, about twelve hours later. Jesus was arrested before dawn – say about five o'clock in the morning. The trial took place before midday, for that was the time of the Crucifixion. The eclipse lasted till about three (the ninth hour) and Matthew, Mark and John all agree that Joseph did not appear on the scene until 'even had come', say about five o'clock.

The biblical evidence is quite clear: Joseph of Arimathea is only mentioned in connection with the burial of Christ. He provided the cloths in which the body was wrapped before it was placed in the tomb and Nicodemus provided the myrrh and aloes to prevent putrefaction. Everything was done in a hurry because Jesus died in the late afternoon of the eve of the Sabbath, and nothing could be done after nightfall or on the Sabbath itself. As soon as Jesus was dead, Joseph of Arimathea went to Pilate to ask for the body. Pilate could not believe that Jesus was already dead, so he sent a centurion to make sure. All this took time. Pilate's office in the Antonia is about half a mile from Golgotha, so it would have taken Joseph nearly two hours to go to Pilate, to gain admission to him, for Pilate to summon the centurion, for the centurion to go to Golgotha and back to make his report. Only then was permission given for the removal of the body. It was not until then that Joseph went out to buy the cloths and Nicodemus the myrrh and aloes, both of which would have taken yet more time. After that Joseph and Nicodemus had to return to Golgotha and persuade the guard to release the body of Jesus to them. Having done this, the body had to be taken down and laid on the cloth. The herbs and spices had then to be packed round it and the whole bound together with bandages before it could be placed in the tomb. Everything points to the intention to give the body a proper burial on the following Sunday. The result of this was that the linen became stained with Jesus' blood and sweat. They buried the body in the tomb because it was 'nigh at hand' and because it was growing late, not because it was the intended tomb of Jesus. Joseph of Arimathea was the only person responsible for all this. As soon as they completed their task, according to the non-canonical version Joseph and Nicodemus were arrested by the Jews and thrown into prison until Sunday morning. When, pray, could Joseph have obtained the Cup of the Last Supper? And even if he had, what happened to it when he was arrested? Surely the Jews would have taken it from him, for they would not have been likely to allow him to keep it in prison. No! The evidence is utterly against the idea of the Grail being the Cup of the Last Supper. So where does this leave us? The only acceptable conclusion the evidence points to is the burial linen in which Joseph wrapped Jesus' body. But that is all very well, you may say, how are we to reconcile the notion of a flattish, dish-like vessel with the grave cloths? The answer must surely be that the Grail was the vessel, casket, reliquary, call it what you will, in which the linen was kept in later years. But that is not the end of the matter, for we still have to explain why this vessel was called a Grail, and we have yet to discover which of the six or seven linen cloths associated with Jesus' burial was the one concerned.

St John tells us that Jesus was buried in the 'manner of the Jews' (19:40). At the time of Jesus' death it was the custom of the Jews to wash the body, then dress it in clean linen clothes, generally garments worn at festivals, to bind a cloth or bandage under the chin and tie it at the crown of the head to prevent the jaw sagging. A cloth was sometimes placed over the face, but invariably the feet and the wrists were also bound (as we learn from St John in Chapter 11, where he describes the raising of Lazarus: Jesus tells those who were caring for him to 'unbind him and let him go free'). When all this was done, the body was laid on the long linen shroud, which ran the full length of the body and then back over the head to the feet again. Before the shroud was bound to the body, it was packed with spices and herbs, and coins were placed over the eyes. Months later, when the body had sufficiently decomposed, the bones were placed in an ossuary, a small stone or wooden chest, and placed alongside others in the family tomb. Jews did not swathe their dead in bandages like Egyptian mummies, and the Romans cremated their dead. Consequently there were at least six, and possibly seven pieces of cloth involved in a Jewish burial. Any one of these – apart, perhaps, from the outer bandages – could have been stained with sweat and blood.

When they came on the Sunday the body had disappeared. Let me remind you what the Gospels have to say about the cloths that remained behind. There is much controversy surrounding the whole matter of the burial and the burial cloths, and it is impossible to be absolutely certain of what took place. Matthew, Mark and Luke speak only of the *sindon* that Joseph of Arimathea bought for the burial, and this word is often translated as 'shroud', though it is not solely confined to this meaning. St Mark, for example, uses it to indicate an article of clothing, while St John, on the other hand, does not use the word at all. He says that the body was wrapped in *othonia*. Furthermore, he is the only Evangelist to describe how the cloths were found after the disappearance of the body. He tells us that the *othonia* were lying with the 'napkin that was about his head, not lying with the linen clothes but wrapped together in a place by itself'. The word translated as 'napkin' is *soudarion*, which literally means a sweat-rag.

The distinction between *othonia* (the plural form of *othonion*) and *sindon* is a matter of debate. The most balanced opinion holds that *othonia* is the generic term for all the cloths I have mentioned, and *sindon* refers to the largest of them only, namely the Shroud. The *soudarion* seems to indicate something smaller, probably the cloth which was sometimes laid over the face, rather than the band of cloth tied under the chin and over the top of the head.

Thus we have at least two cloths which might show traces of Jesus' sweat and blood – the *soudarion* and the *sindon*. Assuming that one or both of these survived, together with other relics of the Passion, they would certainly have been kept during the Middle Ages, if not earlier, in some kind of casket or reliquary. Since it held cloths such a casket must have been more like a flattish dish or a shallow box than a cup. But of all the relics of the Passion, these alone are connected with Joseph of Arimathea, so let us have another look at the Grail legends to see how this theory fits.

To begin with, Wolfram's magic stone does not at first sight appear to have anything to do with this concept of the Grail, but what about Chrétien's description of it? Those who follow him waver in their understanding of the Grail between the notion of a paschal dish and a cup, but when we come to Robert de Boron, we find something different. He says:

> *Cist vaisseau ou men sanc meis*
> *quant de men cors le reuiellis*
> *calices apelez sera. . . .*

(The vessel in which the blood from my body shall rest shall henceforth be called a chalice.)

A. E. Waite says:

> It is difficult to read the later verses in which the Eucharistic Chalice is compared with the Sepulchre of Christ, the Mass Corporal with the grave-clothes, and the Paten with the stone at the mouth of the tomb, without concluding that by the Grail there was intended the first Eucharistic vessel. . . . If it be objected that this idea of a Chalice does not correspond to a vessel, whose content is sacramental, it should be remembered that a reliquary which by this hypothesis contained the precious Blood was obviously in correspondence with Eucharistic wine. . . . It seems certain that when Robert de Boron speaks of the Grail as a vessel *in* which Christ made his sacrament, this ought to be understood as referring to the Paschal Dish.

Substitute in your mind's eye a casket or shallow box containing the blood- and sweat-stained *sindon* and *soudarion*. Does this not make better sense than a chalice containing drops of blood and sweat? A casket such as this, containing a cloth upon which Christ's features were imprinted, would seem to those who saw it at Mass as if Christ himself were there in person. Robert de Boron speaks of 'The great secret uttered at the great sacrament performed *over* the Grail – that is over the chalice.'

This does not seem to me to make sense, for the sacrament is not celebrated *over*, but *with* a chalice. It is, of course, celebrated at an altar on which, or within which, a relic has been placed, and such a relic could be the *sindon* or *soudarion*. The *Greater Holy Grail*, even when it reproduces Robert de Boron, calls the sacred vessel the dish in which Jesus partook of the Last Supper. At first sight this seems preposterous, since no dish could at the same time be a reliquary. On the other hand, it might have been the outward witness of what it contained. The first unveiled vision of it is on a chapel altar, on one side of which were the Nails used at the Crucifixion and the Holy Lance, and on the other a 'dish' in whose centre was an exceedingly 'rich vessel of gold in the semblance of a goblet'.

But can we be quite sure that the word translated here as 'goblet' is correct? There are good reasons for believing that by the time this was written the memory of the Grail's precise form and identity had been forgotten. For example, this so-called 'goblet' is said to have had a lid 'after the manner of a ciborium'.

Now a ciborium is a receptacle for the reservation of the Host, i.e. the Body of Christ, and it performs quite a different function at Mass from the chalice which contains the wine, which signifies his blood.

In the *Roman de Saint Graal*, a late, though still medieval version of the legend, Christ's blood is said to have been 'drawn into the vessel after Joseph and Nicodemus had taken the body of Our Lord down from the cross'. This seems to support our theory that the blood and sweat were obtained *after*, not *during* the Crucifixion, and so upholds the view that they were to be found on the burial linens.

Before we finish with this subject, I want to consider the role played by women in Grail ceremonies. I have already quoted passages where the Grail is carried by two maidens. In Chrétien's version the sacred object is likened to a deepish platter large enough to hold a lamprey or salmon, though it only contains a single wafer. Now lampreys and salmon grow to a length of three feet and more, which gives us a good idea of what Chrétien had in mind. But some commentators have found this association of women with the Grail and the Eucharist not only unorthodox but inexplicable. If, indeed, the Grail had really been the Chalice of the Last Supper, then it is easy to agree with them. On the other hand, if it were the casket containing the burial clothes, then nothing could be more logical, for women play a big part in the story of Jesus' burial, whereas there were only men at the Last Supper.

So where do we now stand? The earliest poets did not think of the Grail as a chalice, but rather as a shallow, dish-like reliquary containing the blood- and sweat-stained cloths used at Christ's burial. Later writers, unaware of the existence and nature of these cloths, began to think of the vessel as a chalice, because a cup seemed to be the obvious type of vessel to contain liquids such as blood and sweat. The Grail first appeared in Western literature around 1180, but within a century and a half its nature and form as described by later writers had undergone a subtle change, suggesting that its authentic character had been forgotten. Why? Until the end of the twelfth century, there is no record in the West of the Grail in any form, yet since that time it has become intimately associated with the Passion. Why is there this odd gap in its history? If the Grail was associated with the burial cloths of Christ, why had no one in the West heard of it before the twelfth century? Suddenly, and apparently spontaneously, the Grail and its sacred contents dominate Western literature for nearly fifty years. It is suddenly introduced by writers in France, Germany and England into much older stories surrounding the quasi-mythical figures of King Arthur and his knights: why? These writers didn't invent the Grail any more than they invented the stories into which they introduced it. But supposing for a moment that they had: why? Almost as suddenly as it had appeared in literature, its precise nature became clouded, and later writers began to think of the Grail as a cup – the Chalice of the Last Supper: why? But most puzzling of all; why was the reliquary containing the burial cloth of Christ called the 'Grail' in the first place? What does the word mean? Who coined it, why did they coin it, and when? Why was the original identity of the Grail forgotten? If it had *not* been forgotten, there would not have been so much speculation about it today.

I said earlier that some students of the Grail romances believe that the stories were written with the deliberate intention of mystifying people; that their real purpose was to conceal something so sacred and secret that only the initiated would understand. There may be something in this, but I am not inclined to take this view. I do not think that the earliest writers were out to mystify their readers; I think that most of their readers knew perfectly well what the Grail was – so much so, that there was no reason to be more specific about it than they were.

I am by no means the first to ask what the word 'Grail' really means. Until we can answer that we can make no progress. I sought my answer in the religious and political history of the twelfth and thirteenth centuries and in the pages of dictionaries, glossaries and lexicons. I was looking for an historical object which could reconcile all the different descriptions I have quoted; which became known in the West during the twelfth century; which disappeared again about a century later; and which has remained hidden ever since.

If you look up the word 'Grail' in any dictionary or encyclopedia, you will find that its origin is said to be uncertain. You will next discover that it is said to derive from a Low Latin word *gradalis* or *gradalus*, and that this word means a shallow vessel. On the other hand, you may light on one of those dictionaries which says that it derives from a 'lost' Latin word *cratale*, and that this derives from the classical Latin *cratus* or *crater*, and ultimately from the Greek κρατηρ, from which our modern word crater, as in volcanoes, is derived. *Cratus* and κρατηρ mean, of course, chalice or cup, so we seem to have come full circle, for the lexicographer is chasing his tail and has produced an origin to fit the meaning he has already decided upon. But in any case, how can a word get lost? If a word is used at all, it gets written down, and once it is written down, it can't be lost. It's true that words go out of fashion – who, today, says that anything pleasant is 'ripping'? – and their meaning can be forgotten or modified. 'Prevent us, O Lord, we beseech Thee . . .' now means almost the exact opposite of what it meant when that collect was written. In primitive, unwritten languages words can, of course, be lost, and medieval words may lose their meaning, but they cannot, strictly speaking, be lost. No! The lexicographer who derived 'Grail' from '*cratale*' was guessing.

If you look in a dictionary of the Langue d'Oc, that variant of French spoken in the south-western part of the country, you will find *grazal* meaning a large, clay vessel: in Provençal of south-eastern France *grasal* means a bowl or platter; in Anglo-Norman *Graal* means a dish made of some costly material for the purpose of great feasts (another guess, I guess). If, however, you get as far as Larousse's *Dictionary of Ancient and Medieval French* and look up the word *greil* or *greille* you will find it translated into English as grid, grill, trellis or lattice, deriving from the low Latin *craticula* or *gradella*, which both in turn derive from the classical Latin *cratis*. Virgil uses the word *cratis* to mean 'a shield', and the reason for this is that the Roman shield was made of a lattice framework over which tough leather was stretched. But the more usual Latin word for shield is *scutum* (its diminutive is *scutella*) and it in turn derives from the Sanskrit *skauti*, meaning to cover.

Now you will recall that Abbot Hélinand referred to the Grail as '*Gradalis*' and '*scutella lata*'. This must mean that the object he had in mind was a shallow, platter-like or shield-like casket in some way associated with the idea of lattice or trelliswork. Hélinand was writing in May 1204, during the time before the Grail came to be thought of as a cup.

So here we have it: two words extremely similar to one another – *gradalis* and *gradella* – each deriving from Latin words which differ by one letter only – *cratis* and *cratus* (sometimes *crater*). By the twelfth century these words in medieval French have become *greil* (or *greille*) and *calice*, and by today they have become, in English, grill and chalice.

You may ask, So what? What possible connection can a dish or platter-like Holy Grail have with a word meaning grid, grill, trellis or lattice? This is what I now hope to explain in the rest of this book.

CHAPTER 2

THE SHROUD OF
TURIN:
1353–1985

———●———

In November 1973 Cardinal Pellegrino, Archbishop of Turin, agreed that the *Santa Sindone*, or Shroud of Turin, should be shown for the first time on television. It was seen throughout Europe and in parts of South America; the pope spoke about it in the course of the programme, and it was shown to an international group of journalists the day before the television broadcast. On Thursday 22 November the cardinal addressed the gathering, explaining why he had chosen this modern method of showing the Shroud in preference to the more traditional expositions of the past. Television would enable millions more people to see the Shroud in detail with little or no risk to the fabric itself.

One who was present at the press conference has written:

> One sensed in him [the Cardinal] a great reluctance that the Shroud should at last be submitted to public spectacle and scrutiny. Yet one sensed also that in agreeing to the exposition he tacitly acknowledged a real twentieth-century need – the need to find an antidote to doubt, the need for some tangible evidence of Christ in an age that demands proof of everything.[1]

That the Shroud might be the twentieth-century equivalent of the proof demanded by doubting Thomas when he asked to see the holes that the nails had made in Jesus' hands, and to put his own hand into the hole in his side before he consented to believe in the Resurrection, was voiced by one of the TV commentators present, who insisted that it needed to be approached from the point of view of the doubter.

This is an attitude that I shared when, like many others, I heard of the Shroud for the first time twelve years ago. I still share it, for until the Shroud can be scientifically dated, and its age more precisely determined than is possible at present, either through the application of archaeology or other techniques, doubt must remain that this is the

actual cloth in which Christ's body was wrapped by Joseph of Arimathea and Nicodemus nineteen hundred and fifty years ago.

Since that press conference in 1973 the Shroud has been examined
by experts from many disciplines and many countries. The list is
impressive, and includes textile specialists, haematologists, historians
and genealogists, theologians, forensic scientists, physicists, photo-
graphers, criminologists, space scientists, numismatists, art historians
– all of whom have contributed new information from their individual
fields, but none of whom has yet been able to prove conclusively – and
I stress the word 'conclusively' – that the relic is a medieval forgery.
This has been essentially a quiet investigation, as Ian Wilson says,
which has been largely ignored in academic circles. Yet the mystery
surrounding the Shroud, far from being cleared up by all this effort,
has, if anything, grown as deep and as fast as the case for its authenticity. For now the onus is on those who doubt its authenticity to
explain how, when and why it was made; for whom it was made;
who was this otherwise unknown genius who painted or created it.
His knowledge of human anatomy rivals that of Leonardo da
Vinci and Michelangelo, yet he must have lived and worked in
total obscurity in fourteenth-century Burgundy. Why have we
never heard of him – or, I suppose, since we live in an egalitarian
age – her?

Having said this, it is not part of my case to claim that the Shroud *is*
authentic. That must wait for more evidence. I do, however, claim
that it has existed for at least a thousand years, and that it is the same
sacred object with which the Holy Grail was so intimately linked in
the twelfth and thirteenth centuries. On that basis we will now look at
its history to see how valid my claim is, and whether it can be
substantiated. To quote Ian Wilson again, those of us who have
studied the Shroud include men and women and all Christian sects,
believers and non-believers, atheists and Jews. It is not my intention to
make religious converts, and my own study of the Shroud and the
Grail has made no difference to my personal religious and philo-
sophical convictions, but in the spirit of a doubting age, I seek to make
a case for linking two of the greatest mysteries of our era. I do not
write so much for those who already believe in Christ as for those, like
myself, who consider themselves agnostics. There is much about the
Shroud and the Grail that is still baffling; more that will be unfamiliar,
as the evidence I shall produce will demonstrate. That there should
still survive a cloth which *may* have been used at Christ's burial does
not seem to me to be any more, or any less, miraculous than that
the Dead Sea Scrolls or the treasure of Tutankhamen should have

survived. My mind is likewise open regarding the possible survival of the Grail.

Indeed, the survival of relics of famous men is an interesting subject in its own right. Keeping relics is a natural, human impulse. In the immediate aftermath of the Crucifixion when the cloth with its strange markings, which even modern science has so far failed to explain, was found, it would have been extremely odd if it had *not* been carefully preserved. Indeed, the very fact that the burial cloths bore these inexplicable markings could well have cancelled out their ritual uncleanliness. This is not to say that many relics do not possess very dubious credentials, or that unscrupulous ecclesiastics and lay-men have not from time to time manufactured spurious relics for financial gain and to fool the superstitious. In the case of the Shroud and this present study, only scientific dating can 'prove' how old it is. All the textile experts and numismatists, all the botanists and forensic scientists in the world can only draw our attention to certain of its features and provide us with a little more circumstantial evidence in support of its authenticity. They have shown (to my satisfaction, at least) that the cloth we see today was certainly in existence at the time the Grail legends first appeared in Western literature, and that it had been in existence for at least three hundred years before that. Beyond that it is not necessary to go. Those who created the poems and romances about the Grail, and their readers, lived in an age of faith (the cynics call it an age of superstition, and, if it was, it doesn't matter) and they accepted the authenticity of the Shroud and of the other relics of the Passion without question. That is enough for my purpose.

The exposition of the Shroud in November 1973 took place in the Hall of the Swiss in the former royal palace of the Dukes of Savoy and Kings of Italy in Turin. It was suspended in a plain, wooden frame fastened at the top by a batten. Its full length hung down, in contrast to previous expositions which had always displayed it horizontally. The linen, although sear with age, looked surprisingly clean and where it had not been damaged by fire and water, and where it had not been patched, the herringbone weave of the cloth was in remarkably good condition, resembling a coarse twill bed sheet. It measures 14 feet 3 inches in length and 3 feet 7 inches wide. It is made in a single piece, apart from a strip about 3½ inches wide running the length of the left-hand side and joined by a single seam. What makes this linen cloth so extraordinary is the frontal and dorsal image of a man just under six feet tall with a powerful and well-proportioned physique, the limbs well formed and without any obvious signs of a life given to undue physical labour. The only exception to this is that the right shoulder appears a little lower than the left, a feature more pronounced in the dorsal image than in the frontal. Perhaps one arm was dislocated during the process of crucifixion? The face is bearded and the man wears his hair long. The hands are folded over the lower abdomen or pelvic region, as in death, the left over the right. The figure appears like a shadow on the cloth, and is of a colour not unlike that made by a domestic iron which has scorched the cloth of the ironing board. To those who have never seen a photograph of it, the two figures (front and dorsal) appear head to head, suggesting that the body was laid on one end of the cloth while the remainder was drawn over the head and down to the feet. The face on the frontal image has a mask-like quality and in some degree seems to be detached from the rest of the body: the crossed arms are likewise particularly well defined, and so are the thighs and upper part of the shins. The rest of the body is somewhat blurred. There is absolutely no trace of any paint or colouring matter, a fact which has baffled sceptics even more than believers. Another curious feature of the image is a total lack of outline: the legs on the frontal image and the greater part of the dorsal image are indefinite and fade away in a blur, quite unlike any painting one has ever seen. This same blurred effect applies also to the apparent blood and sweat stains. On the upper forehead there are flows from wounds just below the hairline, and on the dorsal image at the back of the head. There are more blood flows from the wrists and feet. The side has been wounded and a massive quantity of blood has flowed from it. More traces of blood can be seen on the dorsal image across the small of the back, possibly from this same wound. These stains in ordinary light appear very much the same colour as the body stains, but under bright television lights they appeared a quite different colour, almost a clear, pale carmine, with a hint of mauve.

Even when looked at through a magnifying glass, the wounds carry no trace of matter such as might be expected if the cloth had been in touch with a major injury. In other words, these are not the remains of blood clots. Equally strange, they appear to bear no visible trace of pigments either. Nevertheless, a chemical analysis of fibres taken from these parts of the cloth does reveal the existence of iron oxide, present always in blood.

Numerous paintings of the Shroud exist, some of them dating from as early as the fourteenth century, but none of them adequately reproduces the original: they appear, without exception, crude and sharply defined. These copies are useful for the record they provide of various incidents in the Shroud's history. All copies painted since about 1540 show the figure framed by the ugly, arrow-shaped patches, which were added after the Shroud had narrowly escaped destruction in a fire which destroyed the chapel in Chambéry, where it was then kept, in December 1532.

This fire was not the only one in which the Shroud suffered damage. There was another, unquestionably earlier, but exactly when is not certain. Its occurrence is apparent from four sets of triple holes in the linen, which can be identified in a painting made in 1516 and kept at Lierre in Belgium. The charring at the edges of the holes is blacker than what one can see of the 1532 damage. They seem to have been made by something like a red-hot poker. If the Shroud is folded once lengthwise and once widthwise the holes match up exactly and appear to be in the exact centre of this folding arrangement, which leaves one with the impression that the burning was done deliberately. Ian Wilson suggests that at some time the Shroud may have been subjected to an 'ordeal by fire'. When this may have been is uncertain, but Dr W. K. Müller thinks that it took place in the Holy Land in about 1225 or thereabouts. Whenever it occurred, it was certainly before the sixteenth century.

So much for the physical appearance of the Shroud of Turin: what of its history? There is no dispute about this as far back as 1453, for in that year it came into the possession of Duke Louis of Savoy and his wife, Anne of Lusignan, after somewhat obscure negotiations with its former owner, an elderly French noblewoman called Marguerite de Charny, Comtesse de Villersexel. There is a good deal of evidence of its history during the previous one hundred years from 1353, when it was the property of Marguerite's father and grandfather. Before that there is a gap of a century and a half, during which time its history can be traced circumstantially, but with no absolute certainty. Before 1204, in which year it vanished from Constantinople in circumstances which will be described in due course, its history can be traced once more to 944, though there is an alternative history which takes it back to the fifth century. Both these will be examined later, as well as the hitherto 'missing' years between 1204 and 1353. While it was in Constantinople it was kept under the close guardianship of the emperor, though there are reasons for believing that he may not have been its legal owner. There is no dispute over whom it belonged to from the middle of the fourteenth century, and there are good reasons for believing that, unlike other relics of the Passion, the Shroud has been the private heirloom of one, or several, families descended from or linked with Fulk of Anjou.[2] It was never the property of the Church or of any state, and remained the private property of the descendants of

Table 1   DESCENT OF MARGUERITE DE CHARNY FROM JEAN DE JOINVILLE & JEAN DE VERGY

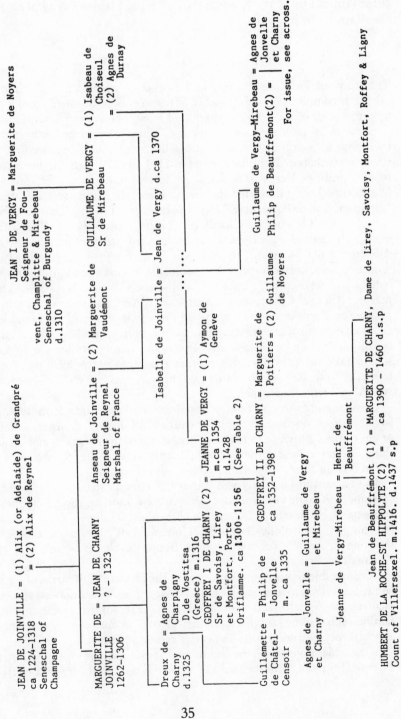

35

these families until 1984, when the late King Umberto of Italy left it to the Vatican in his will.

GENEALOGICAL NOTE

The study of French genealogy and especially medieval, aristocratic genealogy, is complicated by the absence of registers of birth, marriage and death, by the absence of wills, by the absence of fixed, hereditary surnames, and by the custom of noble men and women of calling themselves by the names of their estates. No one, unaware of these difficulties, would realize that of the seven Seneschals of Burgundy between 1191 and 1310, all but one belonged to the family of Vergy. The six were, in chronological order, Etienne de Mont-Saint-Jean, Guillaume de Vergy, Henri de Mirebeau, Guillaume de Mirebeau, Jean de Fouvent and Henri de Fouvent. The only one who was not a Vergy was Gaucher de Châtillon. The titles used by the Vergy family during the period in which we are interested were as follows: Seigneur d'Autrey, Châtel-Censoir, Belvoir, Mirebeau, Fouvent, Champlitte (shared with another family who were also Seigneurs de Champlitte, but of the other half of the seigneurie), Fontaines, Port-sur-Saône, de la Fauche, Dampmartin, Rigney, Champuant, Mantoche, d'Arc, Montferrant, Fontaines-Françaises, Bourbonne and Charny. In the course of one lifetime a nobleman could change his name three or four times, as happened on more than one occasion in the de Joinville family. It was also quite common for a younger son to take his title from his mother's estates, as for example, Jean de Joinville, Sr de Reynel (the name by which he was known), whose mother was Alix, Dame de Reynel.

Consequently the genealogist must depend on references to individuals in such historical documents as public treaties and decrees, transfers of land or grants to the Church or to religious orders, marriage contracts and heraldry, though it has to be said that individual arms were frequently carried, which differed from the family coat, properly so called.

The custom in Germany was rather less complicated, for the hereditary surname was carried on from one generation to another, though hyphenated to the name of the estate. Thus in the Hohenlohe family we find Hohenlohe-Hohenlohe, Hohenlohe-Brauneck, Hohenlohe-Weikersheim, Hohenlohe-Roettingen, which subdivides into Brauneck-Neuhaus and Brauneck-Brauneck and so on.

Considerable significance is attached to the identity of the arms of Charny/Mont-Saint-Jean in Burgundy and Weinsberg in Franconia – Gules, three escutcheons argent – and while there is good reason for equating the two families, it has to be said that similarity of arms in one country with those in another does not necessarily indicate a common ancestry.

In the tables given here, the commonest family surname – e.g. Courtenay, Brienne, Joinville, Montbéliard and so on – is used in the interest of clarity.

Marguerite de Charny, Dame de Lirey, Montfort, Savoisy, Roffey et Ligny, was born about 1390, the only daughter and sole heiress of Geoffrey de Charny II, and his wife, Marguerite de Poitiers (see Tables 1 and 2). She was twice married and twice widowed, but it is her second husband, Humbert de la Roche-Saint Hippolyte, Comte de Villersexel (died 1437), who played the more important part in the Shroud's history. Marguerite's father, Geoffrey de Charny, died in 1398 when she was still a child, leaving her extensive properties in Burgundy and Champagne, and at Thory, near Beauvais in northern France. Her mother married as her second husband Guillaume de Noyers, a member of a Burgundian family with whom the de Charnys had intermarried on several previous occasions (see Table 4). Geoffrey, in his turn, had inherited the Shroud from his father and namesake, who died at the Battle of Poitiers in 1356. Geoffrey the Elder had obtained permission to build a collegiate church on one of his estates, Lirey, some twelve miles west of Troyes, in 1353. There he installed the Shroud, where it was exposed for public veneration from time to time, not without controversy. In 1389, Pierre d'Arcis, Bishop of Troyes, sent a long memorandum to the pope, Clement VII, in which he drew the pontiff's attention to what he described as a grave scandal in his diocese on the estate of the de Charny family at Lirey. The canons of the church were, he said, exposing for veneration a cloth which the bishop described as 'a likeness or representation' of the 'Sudarium Christi'.

Because of its subsequent history, there can be no doubt that the cloth exposed at Lirey was identical to the Shroud of Turin. But, as I have been at pains to point out, the *Soudarion* (or *Sudarium*, to give it its Latin name) was *not* the *Sindon*, which is the name by which the Turin Shroud is known today, namely, *La Santa Sindone*. This confusion of terms has been the cause of much debate, and a number of pertinent questions arise from it. Can we, for example, assume that the Bishop of Troyes did not know the difference between the *Soudarion* and the *Sindon*? Had he seen the cloth at Lirey to which he gave the name 'Sudarium Christi'? If he had seen it, why did he call it the *Sudarium*, when quite obviously it was a much bigger cloth than that name implied? Can we really believe that a medieval bishop – and one who was well known for his scholarship and probity – would have been ignorant of the size, number and nature of the burial cloths described by the Evangelists? It seems most unlikely. If Lirey had been in a remote part of his diocese, one might assume that he had never visited the parish, but Lirey is not remote; it is no more than twelve miles from Troyes, so it seems very odd indeed if he had not seen the cloth

Table 2   VERGY, SEIGNEURS DE FOUVENT, MIREBEAU, AUTREY, CHAMPLITTE. SENESCHALS OF BURGUNDY

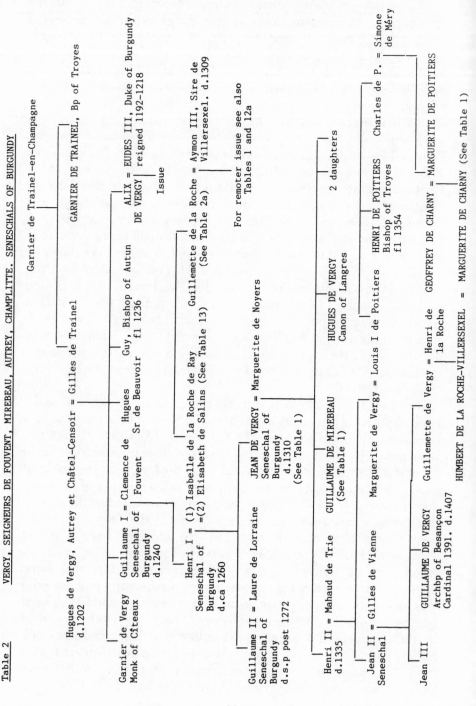

Table 2a

DE LA ROCHE/VERGY

Pons de la Roche-sur-l'Ognon, Sire de Ray
1140-1193

OTTO DE LA ROCHE = Isabelle de Ray
fl 1180-1234

Pons, Seigneur de Flagey
1179-1197

Guy I, Duke of Athens 1208-1263

Dukes of Athens

Otto, Sire de Ray = Marguerite de
fl 1210-1233   Tilchâtel
                      m.ca 1238

Guillemette = Aymon III, Ct of Villersexel

Isabelle = Henri I de
           Vergy

For issue see Table 2

Number of generations uncertain

HUMBERT DE LA ROCHE-SAINT HIPPOLYTE
Count of Villersexel
(See Tables 1 and 12a.)

that was being exhibited there. And yet the evidence strongly suggests that Pierre d'Arcis did *not* know the precise nature of Geoffrey de Charny's cloth, which is even odder, because the bishop was Geoffrey's cousin (see Tables 12 and 12a). We can be sure of one thing: Bishop d'Arcis was annoyed and suspicious about what Geoffrey de Charny was doing at Lirey, mainly because his nose had been put out of joint. Geoffrey had not approached his cousin before exposing the cloth for veneration, but had gone instead directly to the papal legate for permission. On enquiry, and to make matters worse, the bishop discovered that the de Charnys had exhibited the cloth thirty-four years earlier, when the canons of Lirey had claimed quite openly that their relic was the true Shroud of Christ. Bishop d'Arcis' predecessor, Henri de Poitiers, was also closely related to the de Charny family, for he was an uncle of the older Geoffrey's wife (see Table 2). He had investigated the matter, and had announced that this could not be the real Shroud of Christ because the Gospels made no mention of there being an imprint on it. If it had been genuine, he asserted, it was unthinkable that the Evangelists should have made no mention of the fact. But is it? Assuming that Joseph of Arimathea took it after the tomb was found empty – after all it belonged to him, since he had bought it in the first place – it is not inconceivable that the markings were known only to him and a few very close intimates, among whom the Evangelists were not included. But Bishop Poitiers had a good point. Maybe the explanation is that the disappearance of the body, and the belief that Christ had risen from the dead, were so much more extraordinary that there was no point in saying that the burial linens had been left behind bore the imprint of his body. Indeed, it is only John who mentions their survival at all.

But to return to Bishop d'Arcis: he included a sentence in his memorandum which has justified sceptics believing that the Shroud is far from authentic. It reads as follows in the translation of the Rev. Herbert Thurston:

'Eventually, after diligent inquiry and examination, he [Bishop Henri de Poitiers] discovered the fraud and how the said cloth had been cunningly painted, the truth being attested by the artist who had painted it, to wit, that it was a work of human skill and not miraculously wrought or bestowed.'[3]

Since so much depends upon our interpretation of this memorandum, I propose to quote further passages from it.

Some time since in this diocese of Troyes the Dean of . . . Lirey, falsely and deceitfully, being consumed with the passion of avarice, and not from any motive of devotion but only of gain, procured for his church a certain cloth

40

cunningly painted, upon which by a clever sleight of hand was depicted the twofold image of one man, that is to say, the back and the front, he falsely declaring and pretending that this was the actual shroud in which our Saviour Jesus Christ was enfolded in the tomb, and upon which the whole likeness of the Saviour remained thus impressed together with the wounds which He bore. This story was put about . . . so that from all parts people came together to view it. . . . The Lord Henry of Poitiers, of pious memory, then Bishop of Troyes . . . set himself earnestly to work to fathom the truth of this matter. For many theologians and other wise persons declared that this could not be the real shroud of our Lord having the Saviour's likeness thus imprinted upon it, since the holy Gospel made no mention of any such imprint, while, if it had been true, it was quite unlikely that the holy Evangelists would have omitted to record it, or that the fact should have remained hidden until the present time. Eventually, after diligent inquiry and examination, he discovered the fraud and how the said cloth had been cunningly painted, the truth being attested by the artist who had painted it, to wit, that it was a work of human skill and not miraculously wrought or bestowed. Accordingly . . . he began to institute formal proceedings against the said Dean and his accomplices in order to root out this false persuasion. They, seeing their wickedness discovered, hid away the said cloth so that the Ordinary could not find it, and they kept it hidden afterwards for thirty-four years or thereabouts down to the present year.

And now again the present Dean . . . suggested . . . to the Lord Geoffrey de Charny, Knight, and the temporal lord of the place, to have the said cloth replaced in the said church, that by a renewal of the pilgrimage the church might be enriched with the offerings made by the faithful.

Acting upon the Dean's suggestion . . . the knight went to the Cardinal de Thury, your Holiness' Nuncio and Legate in French territory, and suppressing the facts that the said cloth . . . was asserted to be the shroud of our Saviour, and that it bore the Saviour's likeness imprinted upon it, and that the Ordinary had taken action against the canons in order to stamp out the error which had arisen . . . he represented to the Cardinal that the said cloth was a picture or figure of the shroud . . . which had previously been much venerated . . . but on account of the war and other causes . . . had been placed for a long time in safer keeping, petitioning that . . . it might there be shown to the people and venerated by the faithful.

Then the said Lord Cardinal . . . granted to the petitioner the Apostolic authority that . . . he might set up this picture or figure of the shroud of Our Lord in the said church or in any decent place. And under cover of this written authority the cloth was openly exhibited on great holidays . . . to wit by two priests vested in albs with stoles and maniples and using the greatest possible reverence, with lighted torches and upon a lofty platform constructed for this special purpose; and although it is not publicly stated to be the true shroud of Christ, nevertheless it is given out and noised abroad in private, and so it is believed of many, the more so because . . . it was on the previous occasion declared to be the true shroud of Christ, and by a

41

certain ingenious manner of speech it is now in the said church styled not the *Sudarium* but the *Sanctuarium* [the French term for the Shroud is *Sainte Suaire*] which to the ears of common folk ... sounds much the same thing....

The memorandum concludes with a request to the pope to oppose these expositions and to

bestow your attention upon the foregoing statement and to take measures that such scandal and delusion and abominable superstition may be put an end to both in fact and seeming, in such wise that this cloth is held neither for Sudarium nor Sanctuarium, nor for an image or figure of our Lord's Sudarium, since our Lord's Sudarium was nothing of the kind, nor, in fine, under any ingenious pretext be exhibited to the people or exposed for veneration, but that to express horror of such superstition it be publicly condemned....

Ian Wilson argues that the passage about the artist who had painted the offending cloth is not quite what it at first sight appears in this translation, and I agree with him. Latin has no definite article, so it would be perfectly legitimate to replace 'the artist' by 'an artist'. Similarly, although '*depingere*' certainly means 'to paint', it also means 'to depict, portray, draw, describe, represent and copy', so the phrase could be translated 'the truth being attested by an artist who had copied or depicted it'. This puts a very different complexion on the matter.

There is, however, a perfectly reasonable explanation for Geoffrey's behaviour and for the bishop's suspicions, which is, perhaps, better left to a later point in this narrative. Bishop d'Arcis makes it quite plain that Geoffrey de Charny the Younger openly involved himself in the attempt to establish the Shroud as an object of veneration. He describes how Geoffrey held it in his own hands to show to pilgrims on important feast days, and how he supported the canons of Lirey throughout. We should therefore know something about his career and character.

In 1362 he became a soldier, taking up arms against the English under the Count of Tancarville, a Norman nobleman, and later under his overlord, the Duke of Burgundy, of whom his mother, Jeanne de Vergy, was a cousin. Under Kings John the Good and Charles V of France he carried out diplomatic missions, for which he was rewarded in 1375 by the appointment to the post of Bailli of Caux, that region of France to the north of the lower reaches of the Seine bounded by Rouen, Le Havre and Dieppe. This was a most important position, for baillis like seneschals were the chief executive officers of a province directly responsible to the king.

In terms of wealth and status Geoffrey de Charny had nothing to complain of, and by 1389 he was a prominent and successful man, unlikely to wish to involve himself in any kind of religious controversy. In spite of the bishop's reaction, it is clear that the Shroud expositions were the result of careful thought and preparation, almost certainly at the prompting of his mother, Jeanne de Vergy, now about sixty years old. A year earlier she had lost her second husband, Aymon de Geneve,[4] an uncle of the reigning pope, Clement VII. Geoffrey may have felt that while the family link with the papacy lasted, he could be sure of the Holy Father's protection and approval. We can be certain that the pope knew most if not all the true facts about the Shroud's history and how it had come into the possession of the de Charny family, and that he would have been sympathetic to Geoffrey's cause. This explains why Geoffrey, a layman, by-passed his cousin, Bishop d'Arcis, and applied direct to the pope through his nuncio. Nevertheless, it seems strange that the cardinal made no attempt to consult or inform the bishop about such an important matter within his diocese. From our point of view, however, the most important feature of the affair was the careful formula for describing the cloth agreed between the pope and Geoffrey de Charny. It is described as an image or likeness only, but as Bishop d'Arcis was quick to point out: '. . . although it is not publicly stated to be the true Shroud of Christ, nevertheless, this is given out privately, and so it is believed by many, the more so because as stated above, it was on the previous occasion [1356] declared to be the true Shroud of Christ. . . .'

It is as a result of this statement that the Shroud of Turin has come to be regarded (up to 1973, at any rate) as a fourteenth-century forgery, and why its owner, the late King Umberto of Italy, and its guardian, the Cardinal Archbishop of Turin, are to be commended for allowing it to be subjected to so many scientific tests.

One can sympathize with Bishop d'Arcis and understand the course he took. He did not know that the pope already knew about the Shroud, its history and how it came into the possession of his nephew, Geoffrey de Charny; and why these facts must remain a secret. But the fact that the pope *did* know what the bishop did not explains what lay behind the pontiff's otherwise eccentric action. Presented with such a serious and well-argued complaint from a respected bishop, you might have thought that the pope would have ordered an immediate investigation. On the contrary, he did nothing of the kind. His immediate reaction was to attempt to stifle all further discussion and to sentence Bishop d'Arcis to perpetual silence. It was this totally unexpected action that spurred the bishop to compose his memorandum.

Notwithstanding, the pope persisted in his refusal to hold an enquiry. By way of a sop to the bishop all the pope asked for was a modification of the number of candles used and the vestments worn, and he reaffirmed that the Shroud should be termed only 'a likeness or representation' – a splendidly ambiguous and vague definition. He refused to order the expositions to be stopped, and reiterated his demand that the bishop keep silent on the matter.

Practically everything Bishop d'Arcis had to say was correct, but the issue hinged not only on how this was interpreted, but on the fact that some vital pieces of information, which I shall reveal in due course, were, for excellent reasons, withheld from him. D'Arcis wrongly saw, in the furtive manner in which the Shroud had been brought before the public, evidence for thinking it was a fraud. The lack of evidence about its provenance only served to strengthen his view of the matter. He did not realize that by protesting so vigorously he was preventing a pious attempt to bring the relic before the people so that they might venerate it.

Geoffrey de Charny died in May 1398 soon after his return from a visit to Hungary, and was buried in the Cistercian Abbey of Froid-mont, near Beauvais, whose abbot, Hélinand, I mentioned in the last chapter. On his death the Shroud fell to his daughter, Marguerite, who was little more than a child when her father died. Her first husband, Jean de Beauffremont, was killed at Agincourt; her second, to whom she was married in 1416, was Humbert de la Roche-St Hippolyte, Comte de Villersexel. Following the French defeat at Agincourt, Lirey was thought to be unsafe for the Shroud, so Marguerite and her husband removed it for safekeeping to her castle at Montfort, near Montbard in Burgundy, about twenty miles north of her ancestral castles of Charny and Mont-Saint-Jean. There on 6 July 1418 Count Humbert issued this receipt:

> During this period of war, and mindful of ill-disposed persons, we have received from our kind chaplains, the dean and chapter of Our Lady of Lirey, the jewels and relics of the aforesaid church, namely the things which follow: first a cloth, on which is the figure or representation of the Shroud of our Lord Jesus Christ, which is in a casket emblazoned with the de Charny coat of arms. . . . The aforesaid jewels and relics we have taken and received into our care from the said dean and chapter to be well and securely guarded in our castle of Montfort.

It is likely that Marguerite and Humbert had every intention of returning the Shroud to Lirey when the times were more propitious, but they changed their minds and took it to the church of St Hippolyte-sur-Doubs, a parish belonging to the family of de la Roche in what is now Franche-Comté, but was then the County of Burgundy within the Empire. Here in the heart of Count Humbert's domains it remained for thirty-four years. Expositions were held once a year in a meadow, still called the Pré du Seigneur, on the banks of the Doubs. Ian Wilson points, correctly, to the establishment of a Shroud cult here, and claims that painted copies of the relic were made. There were certainly a number of paintings in which the Shroud figures, but whether the Besançon Shroud, which was installed in the cathedral there, and which was destroyed at the French Revolution, was one is debatable, as I hope to show. Sculptures and paintings of the entombment of Christ became popular about this time, perhaps under the Shroud's influence, but these are to be found outside the borders of Burgundy and eastern France.

Marguerite was a sadly troubled woman, for she was barren. Herself an only child and the last of her line, she longed for an heir to whom the sacred heirloom might be handed on. When Count Humbert died in 1438, this became a more pressing problem for her. She was determined that it should not return to Lirey, where it would fall under the protection either of the sceptical Bishop of Troyes, or of those who became the owners of the Charny estates after her death, and where the church built by her grandfather was already falling into disrepair. In May 1443 she agreed to hand over to her husband's heirs all the jewels and reliquaries Count Humbert had taken into safekeeping in 1418, except the Shroud, which she arranged to retain for another three years in return for the payment of certain sums of money for the repair and upkeep of the church at Lirey. This arrangement was extended twice more for a total of five years in return for yet further payments. During this period Marguerite, for reasons that are not altogether apparent, decided to take the Shroud to Belgium in 1449, where she exhibited it at Chimay in Hainault in the diocese of Liège. This might have been in connection with the institution of the Feast of Corpus Christi, which Pope Urban IV in 1264, at the instigation of the Blessed Juliana of Liège, had included in the calendar of Church festivals. The Blessed Juliana had seen a vision thirty or so years before while Pope Urban, then Jacques Pantaléon, had been Archdeacon of Liège. The feast commemorates the doctrine of transubstantiation and is observed on the Thursday after Trinity Sunday.

Jacques Pantaléon was the son of a cobbler of Troyes, and apart from his association with Corpus Christi, he is remembered for the gift of an icon, now known as the Sainte Face de Laon, which he sent to his sister, the abbess of a Cistercian nunnery at Montreuil-en-Thiérache exactly two hundred years before, in 1249. This icon, I was later to discover, plays a crucial role in the identification of the Holy Grail, and will be described at some length in the appropriate place.

But like the Bishops of Troyes, the Belgian clergy were suspicious of the cloth's credentials, and the Bishop of Liège asked Marguerite to produce some documentation to certify its authenticity. All she could offer were the bulls Pope Clement VII had given to her father describing the cloth as a 'figure or representation' of the Shroud of Christ. Another exposition was held three years later at the castle of Germolles near Macon. A year later, in March 1453, Marguerite was in Geneva where a curious transaction took place between her and Duke Louis of Savoy and his wife, Anne de Lusignan. In return for what were euphemistically described as 'valuable services' Louis ceded to Marguerite the castle of Varambon and lands at Miribel between Pont d'Ain and Bourg-en-Bresse.

This is not unlike an earlier transaction in which the Shroud had changed hands, which I shall describe later. In both cases it was unthinkable to sell such a sacred object outright. Marguerite, the duke and the duchess all believed that the Shroud was the authentic burial cloth of Christ, and as such it was the nearest anyone could get to his real body. To have sold the body of Christ would have amounted to gross blasphemy, and could not have been contemplated for an instant. But the duke and duchess wanted to express their gratitude in a tangible way, so the transfer of these estates to Marguerite took care of that. But in any case, there was never any question of a commercial transaction in the strict sense, for both the duke and the duchess were Marguerite's kin, albeit distant.

Both Marguerite's marriages had had dynastic purposes. Indeed, there was nothing unusual in that, for nearly all aristocratic marriages were dynastic, and many are even today. Her first husband, Jean de Beauffremont, was the son of Henri de Beauffremont and of Jeanne de Vergy, who was the niece of Marguerite's grandmother (see Table 1). Count Humbert de Villersexel was a direct descendant of Pons de la Roche (see Table 2a), and a member of a family which I was later to find playing a leading part in the Shroud's history in the thirteenth century. Duke Louis and Marguerite were both descended from Count Humbert II of Savoy and Maurienne, and Duke Louis was a direct descendant of St Louis, who had not only acquired the reputed Crown of Thorns, for which he built the still-standing Sainte Chapelle in Paris, but had been endowed by the Latin Emperor Baldwin II with the right to all other surviving relics of the Passion in Constantinople. Duchess Anne, for her part, was not only one of the most beautiful as well as one of the most pious women of her day, but the heiress of the former kingdoms of Cyprus and Jerusalem. In the twelfth century Amalric de Lusignan, King of Cyprus, succeeded to the throne of Jerusalem as King Amalric II, and from the date of Duke Louis' marriage to his descendant, Anne de Lusignan, the House of Savoy assumed the somewhat empty but none the less venerable titles of King of Cyprus and King of Jerusalem.

On coming into the possession of its new owners the Shroud took on an apparently new, but in reality ancient, role. It became the palladium of the House of Savoy – the divine protective device to be invoked in times of trouble. In the years immediately after they obtained it from Marguerite de Charny, they carried it about with them like a holy charm to preserve them against every kind of danger and mishap. A seventeenth-century engraving shows the Shroud as a standard fluttering above Duke Victor Amadeus and his wife, inscribed with the words '*In hoc Signo, Vinces*' (In this sign you will conquer), the injunction that inspired the Emperor Constantine at the Battle of the Milvian Bridge, when he won the Roman Empire and converted it to Christianity.

On 7 October 1460 Marguerite de Charny, Comtesse de Villersexel, de la Roche-St Hippolyte, Dame de Lirey, Montfort, Savoisy, Roffey, Varambon, Miribel et Ligny was gathered to her forefathers, the last of her line, but not the last of the hereditary owners of the Shroud. She died, one hopes and believes, content that she had done her duty in handing on the cloth to other decendants of those who had been its owners two and a half centuries before. From her death to the present day, the story of the Shroud does not concern us, but it has been necessary to trace its history from its appearance in Lirey in the mid-fourteenth century because those who declare it to be a forgery claim that it was manufactured by or for Geoffrey de Charny about 1350. In order to counter this charge on historical grounds it is necessary to go back a little over a century to the time of Marguerite's grandfather, to look at such evidence as there is to show how it came into his possession; when this might have been; and how the Shroud became associated with the Holy Grail.

The first recorded owner of the Shroud in the West was Geoffrey I de Charny, Porte Oriflamme de France (see Table 1). He begins to appear in French records in about 1337, and continues to be mentioned until his death in battle in 1356. He was one of France's most outstanding generals during the reigns of Philip VI and John II (see Table of Ruling Monarchs, pages 74–5). His military career took him throughout Europe, and in 1346 to Smyrna.

During the thirteenth century Christendom had its last chance to deal effectively with the Turkish invaders of Anatolia. The Byzantine emperors, living in exile in Nicaea, were aware of this chance, but their European preoccupations and their longing to recover Constantinople from the Latins hampered their efforts. By the end of the century it was too late. The Latins, however, were not unaware of the importance of Anatolia, both as a base against Moslem aggression as well as for the control of the eastern Mediterranean. The Knights Hospitallers had occupied the island of Rhodes, partly by chance, but also for these strategic reasons, and the Italian republics had long been interested in the Aegean islands. It was only natural that the whole Latin world should concern itself with the adjacent mainland. When the Emir of Smyrna built a fleet in order to indulge his fondness for piracy, the Venetians and Hospitallers at Rhodes took action in 1344. A squadron under the command of the Latin Patriarch of Constantinople defeated the emir and captured Smyrna on 24 October. Encouraged by this easy victory, the Latins decided to try to invade the interior, but they were heavily defeated a few miles from the city, though the Turks failed to retake it. In 1350 a treaty was signed, by which the Hospitallers were entrusted with the city of Smyrna, although its citadel remained in Turkish hands. The knights held it until 1402.

While the fate of Smyrna was still in the balance, a French nobleman, Humbert II, Dauphin of Vienne, announced his wish to go on a crusade. He was a weak though pious man, who succeeded in persuading the pope to give his crusade his blessing. After some indecision on the part of the pope, it was decided to send Humbert and his army to supplement the Christian effort at Smyrna. He set out from Marseilles with a company of knights and priests, which included Geoffrey de Charny the Elder, in May 1345 and reached Smyrna the following year. His army defeated the Turks in a battle outside the walls, but by 1347 the expedition had returned to France. The whole thing had been a singularly pointless exercise, but its importance lies in the theory advanced by some students of the Shroud's history, that Geoffrey de Charny obtained it in the course of the campaign. It must be said that there is singularly little evidence to support this theory, but as it has been recently repeated in a reputable article on the Shroud, I should mention it.

Geoffrey de Charny was back in action against the English following their victory over the French at Crécy, in 1349, when he made a gallant attempt to recapture Calais – an attempt which was foiled by treachery, and in which he was captured. He spent the next eighteen months a prisoner in England, where it is thought that he formulated his plan to build a church for the Shroud. Soon after his release and return to France, he obtained funds from the king in 1353 to begin work on it. Most commentators assume that Geoffrey owned the Shroud by this time, and that his intention to keep it in the church was already obvious. The first premise is almost certainly correct, but the second does not seem to be quite so certain. The documents concerning the foundation of the church in 1353 and its consecration three years later on 28 May 1356 have survived, but they contain no reference to the Shroud. Moreover, the bishop who consecrated it, Henri de Poitiers, was the very one who later condemned the Shroud as a forgery. On 19 September 1356 Geoffrey de Charny, Porte-Oriflamme de France, had fallen on the battlefield of Poitiers facing the English army of Edward, the Black Prince. The chronicler, Froissart, records how valiantly Geoffrey fought against hopeless odds, when, seeing an English knight bearing down with his lance on the king, he thrust his body in front of his sovereign and fell mortally wounded. Fourteen years later this gallantry was publicly recognized when his remains were given a state funeral and reburial in the Eglise des Céléstins in Paris.

Writing in 1934, Monsignor Arthur Stapylton Barnes, Domestic Prelate to Pope Pius XI, advances a theory about the way in which the Shroud came into Geoffrey de Charny's possession which differs from Ian Wilson's, written forty-four years later. Since neither of these theories is totally satisfactory, I propose to look at both of them before advancing any theories of my own.

Both Wilson and Barnes agree that the Shroud vanished from Constantinople in 1204 when the city was sacked by French, Flemish, Burgundian, Italian and German soldiers of the Fourth Crusade. What happened to it in the intervening century and a half will occupy a large part of the rest of this book. At this stage, however, all I want to do is present such evidence as we have – and it is meagre enough – but which I hope you will find useful when we come to discuss what probably happened.

In 1204 the forces of the Fourth Crusade under the supreme command of Boniface, Marquis of Montferrat, turned aside from their avowed purpose of fighting the infidel in the Holy Land to attack their fellow Christians at Constantinople. The relics of the Passion were kept with other treasures in the Bucoleon Palace, which was captured but never plundered.

There were others in the church of St Mary, the Mother of God, in the Blachernae Palace, and orders were given to surrender these to Garnier de Trainel, Bishop of Troyes, one of the crusaders' spiritual leaders, who made an inventory of them. But as Robert de Clari, who was an eye witness, tells us rather naïvely: 'Some brought them in well, others badly.' Certainly the Shroud does not figure in Bishop Garnier's inventory, nor anything like it, and it is clear that it never passed through his hands. According to Monsignor Barnes, the Shroud came into the possession of Otto de la Roche, one of the Burgundian leaders, who was later created Duke of Athens, and that he sent it, when the opportunity offered, to his father Pons de la Roche at his home in Franche-Comté. Pons gave it to Amadeus de Tramelay, Archbishop of Besançon, who put it in his cathedral, where it remained for a century and a half, the focus of pilgrimages and honoured by a special liturgical ceremony every Easter, when public expositions were held.

In 1349 the cathedral of Besançon was struck by lightning and burnt to the ground. After the fire no trace of the Shroud could be found. It seemed to have disappeared with the reliquary in which it was kept, and everyone concluded that it had perished in the flames. What had really happened, Monsignor Barnes tells us, was that it had once more been looted in the general confusion by a member of the Vergy family, who took it to Calais and presented it to King Philip VI. This, he says, was done for political reasons, because the de Vergy family were members of a faction that wished to see the County of Burgundy, of which Besançon was the capital, transferred from the Holy Roman Empire to the Crown of France. But of this, even the good monsignor admits, there is no proof, and it is otherwise impossible to imagine what motive the Vergy family could have had for doing such an odd thing. But to continue Monsignor Barnes's version of events: Philip VI, having received the Shroud from this unnamed member of the de Vergy family, entrusted it to Geoffrey de Charny at a ceremony at Amiens.

The main objection to this theory lies in the total lack of any evidence implicating the de Vergys in a theft of the Shroud from Besançon in 1349. Admittedly this was at the height of the Black Death, when such a theft might have been easier than at other times, but between 1347, when he returned from Smyrna, until 1350, when he was taken prisoner by the English, Geoffrey de Charny was campaigning with the king. He did not return to France until 1352. Monsignor Barnes postulates that Philip VI gave the Shroud to Geoffrey de Charny in trust to restore it to its rightful owners, the Dean and Chapter of Besançon, from whom it had been stolen by the politically-minded member of his wife's family,[5] and that Geoffrey decided to keep the authentic Shroud and to fob the Besançon Chapter off with a copy painted on linen of the frontal image only. The two Bishops of Troyes were sceptical of the relic at Lirey because they presumed that the authentic Shroud had been returned to Besançon, and that the copy was at Lirey, but this seems an unlikely explanation.

Indeed, the monsignor's theory supposes that the Dean and Chapter of Besançon could not distinguish between the authentic Shroud we know today, which they were said to have owned for more than a century and a half, and a painted copy of the frontal image only, and since there is no record of their ever having made any complaint, that they were quite content with it. This really seems to stretch one's credulity too far. There was no investigation of the matter, so Pope Clement VII gave his decision without one, and nothing was settled one way or the other. The Lirey canons ceased to hold public expositions; Bishop d'Arcis, still angry over the whole affair, held his peace; the Canons of Besançon continued to believe that they had the true relic and, the times again becoming exceedingly difficult through the renewed war with England, the Shroud from Lirey once more (in 1421) passed into the keeping of the de Charny family in the person of Marguerite. The Shroud of Besançon remained unquestioned, though very seldom shown. It was not until the period of the French Revolution that any examination was made. Then it was found to be a painted copy and it was destroyed with the consent of the clergy themselves.

I believe that the monsignor's theory cannot be sustained, for there are much more plausible explanations than his for what happened.

In 1449 peace was restored with England and the Canons of Lirey pressed Marguerite de Charny for the return to the Shroud, but she refused to give it up. From this point Monsignor Barnes' narrative corresponds to the one I have already given. There is, however, another account of the Besançon Shroud, which comes from a paper published by the Académie des Sciences, Belles-Lettres et Arts de Besançon in 1883 by one Jules Gauthier. He tells us that the Besançon Shroud was made up of two cloths

> delicately sewn together. Those who have seen and touched it tell us that it was made of ordinary soft linen such as that made in Egypt. It was eight feet long and four feet wide and the body of Jesus Christ was painted on it in pale yellow, equally impressed on both sides without any noticeable difference, having the two hands crossed, one over the other in such a way that the wounds of each hand could be clearly seen, as well as that in the side. The head of Christ has a beard and long hair, and the size of the body from the heels to the top of the head was five feet nine inches.

The person giving this account, named Durrod, seems to have been an eye witness, but if he gave his account directly to M. Gauthier he must have been a very old man speaking of something he had seen in his youth. This information is valuable because it confirms that the Besançon shroud was painted, and that it was a little over half the length of the Shroud of Turin. Durrod also says that the casket in which the Besançon shroud was kept was a red chest decorated with precious stones. The shroud within was wrapped in crimson satin. This small box or chest was placed in a wooden casket decorated with rich cloth and secured by five different locks, whose keys were kept by five of the canons. The shroud itself, although extremely fine and folded several times, was perfectly preserved and showed no signs of ever having been torn.

The Besançon shroud was not the only burial cloth to be venerated in France and elsewhere in Europe during the Middle Ages. The best known was kept at Cadouin, a Cistercian abbey in Périgord, founded in 1115 by monks from Cîteaux, the Order's mother house in Burgundy. Two years after its foundation, the monks of Cadouin were given a linen cloth by a crusader, who told them he had obtained it in Antioch, and which purported to be the napkin which was laid over Jesus' face and head at burial. It soon became the object of a fervent cult, and pilgrims came from all over Europe to venerate it. Cadouin became rich and famous, and was visited by Richard Coeur de Lion, Saint Louis and King Charles V of France. During the Hundred Years War the cloth was removed to Toulouse for safety, but when the war was over, the cloth was returned to Cadouin, though not without costly lawsuits between the monks of Cadouin and their brethren of Toulouse who, realizing its value as a source of revenue for their abbey, wanted to hang on to it. It was so highly prized throughout the Middle Ages and right up to the eighteenth century that the monks and citizens of Cadouin combined at the Revolution to hide it from the iconoclasts, and it was only during the reign of Napoleon that it was brought out of hiding and displayed once more in the abbey. However, increasing doubts about the authenticity were expressed by the church authorities in Périgueux and among the higher ranks of the French clergy. In 1933 it was decided to submit the cloth to scientific examination, when it was found to be of tenth-century Egyptian provenance, and that the inscriptions on it were quotations from the Koran. It was consequently removed and eventually destroyed, though the medieval casket, which resembles a glass dog-kennel with brass adornments, can still be seen in the former chapter house. Neither the Cadouin nor the Besançon caskets could in any way be equated with a reliquary whose chief characteristic gave it the name of the Grill or Grail.

There were less well-known shrouds elsewhere in France, one of which was supposedly given to Charlemagne in 797. In 877 his grandson, Charles the Bold, gave it to the church of St Cornelius at Compiègne. Like many other relics, it was destroyed during the French Revolution. Another much venerated cloth was the *Sudarium Christi* of Andechs in Bavaria. Andechs, now belonging to the Benedictine Abbey of St Boniface in Munich, was originally a castle of the powerful Counts of Wolfratshausen, who became Counts of Andechs about 1130, and later Dukes of Meran (or Merania). They owned extensive estates in Bavaria, Main-Franconia, the Tyrol, Istria and Burgundy, and the family's piety showed itself in the number of saints and bishops it produced before it became extinct.

The counts were great relic collectors, and throughout the crusades they sent a steady stream from the Holy Land and Italy, which were kept in the chapel of Andechs Castle, where they were looked after by the Benedictines. After the family died out in 1248 the castle was destroyed. The relics passed into the care of the Bishop of Augsburg, but none were exhibited again until 1388. In 1846 Andechs, having been extensively rebuilt in the eighteenth century, was given to its present Benedictine owners.

There was another cloth at Oviedo in Spain. Monsignor Ricci and Dr Alan Whanger of Duke University who have made a study of this cloth are convinced that it touched the same face as the man of the Shroud, but they differ as to its position: Ricci believes it was in direct contact with the face, whereas Whanger thinks that it was on the outside of the Shroud and absorbed blood which had completely penetrated the cloth of the shroud proper. Alternatively, the Oviedo cloth might have been in direct contact with the face, but removed before the whole body was enveloped in the Shroud.

Finally, there is the 'Veronica' tradition of cloths impressed with the features of Christ. This, quite simply, is a minefield, for there is so little solid ground to tread on. Briefly the Veronica story is as follows: Veronica (or Berenice, to give her her Latin name) was in her house when she heard a commotion outside. Opening the door to see what was going on, she found that it was Christ being led to crucifixion. She was so deeply moved by the sight of him struggling beneath the weight of the cross beam that she took her veil and, oblivious of attempts to stop her, pushed her way through the soldiers who were escorting him. Seeing Jesus' face pouring with sweat and blood, she wiped it clean with her veil, and when she retreated once more into her house, she discovered that he had left the imprint of his features upon it.

So widespread did this story become in Christian mythology that it was incorporated as the sixth of the fourteen Stations of the Cross, and tourist guides to this day point out the place on the Via Dolorosa where the incident is supposed to have happened. So firmly did it become part of Christian tradition that many people are surprised to learn that it is not mentioned in any of the Gospels.

In attempting to investigate the tradition, the discovery one makes is that the original veil which was once venerated by medieval pilgrims no longer exists. It is said to have been stolen by troops of the Emperor Charles V when they sacked Rome in 1527, and when last seen was being auctioned by drunken soldiers in a Roman pub. The square, medieval silver reliquary in which it was once kept is still preserved in St Peter's in Rome, and carries the faint outline of the face it originally framed. In 1907 it was examined by art experts, but revealed nothing of the cloth so frequently portrayed by medieval artists and sculptors, and which was exposed for veneration in the papal jubilee years of 1300 and 1350.

Contemporary descriptions, and the work of many painters who recorded it, present no consistent picture of the relic's appearance. Fifteenth- and sixteenth-century artists like Albrecht Dürer, William of Cologne and the unknown artist of the Bronnbach altarpiece all depict Christ as a disembodied head crowned with thorns. Earlier artists, such as Robert Campin, illustrators of the French and English manuscripts of the fourteenth century, the anonymous sculptor who carved the tympanum of the south door at Heilsbronn in the twelfth or thirteenth century, and the Master of Hallein, whose 'Man of Sorrow' and Veronica head are part of a diptych painted about 1450,[6] likewise show a disembodied head, but without the crown of thorns. These earlier versions show a striking resemblance to the face on the Shroud. Still earlier versions, such as the thirteenth-century *Chronica Majora* of Matthew Paris and the Westminster Psalter show the Veronica likeness with the neck and the upper part of the body. Quite independently Gervase of Tilbury, who flourished in the early thirteenth century and who was a contemporary of Walter Map, describes the Veronica as portraying Jesus from the waist upwards. All these variations are hard to equate with the 'miraculous' impression of Christ's features on Berenice's veil.[7]

Notwithstanding these inconsistencies, the history of the cloth can be determined without too much difficulty. In 1207, Pope Innocent III instituted a procession of the Veronica from St Peter's to the Hospital of the Holy Ghost in Rome. In 1191 Pope Celestine III showed it to the King of France, Philip Augustus; in 1143 a canon of St Peter's casually remarked how the pope 'made his way to the Sudarium Christi, which is called Veronica, and censed it'. In 1011 Pope Sergius IV consecrated an altar to the Sudarium in St Peter's, which was probably the occasion of the cloth's first arrival in Rome.

How does all this fit our theory that the Holy Grail was the casket in which the Shroud (or a shroud) of Christ was kept? There were six cloths associated with Christ's burial – seven if the loin-cloth he was wearing on the Cross is counted as well. The burial cloths consisted of the Sindon, or Shroud; the Soudarion or napkin which was placed over his face; three bandages for tying the chin, wrists and ankles; and the Othonia, or bandages used to secure the Shroud to the body. We can eliminate the Othonia and the wrist, ankle and chin bandages, since they could not conceivably have borne any image of the face or the body as a whole. This leaves the Soudarion and the Sindon only.

The manner in which the imprint of the body comes to be on the Shroud of Turin has not yet been explained scientifically, and I do not propose to enter the controversy for or against those who claim that it 'proves' the Resurrection. Suffice it to say that so far no naturalistic explanation has been found to explain the phenomenon. Whether the Shroud is the authentic burial cloth of Christ or not, the fact remains that it bears these unexplained imprints of a man who appears to have suffered the same fate as Jesus, and they have every appearance of having been made by contact with the body immediately after death. How they were made does not, I repeat, matter very much: it is the fact of their existence which is important. The cloth which survives today was imprinted by some emanation from the body itself, so it follows that any other cloth which might have been in close contact with the body at the same time as these marks were made must likewise have been imprinted with the same markings (see Appendix A). Insofar as the Soudarion was in closer contact with the face and head, seeing that it was between the flesh and the Shroud, which was imprinted, then it is not unreasonable to believe that the process which marked the upper cloth must also have marked the lower one. Consequently it follows that the Shroud of Turin cannot have been the *only* cloth with markings of this kind upon it, if we accept the existence of a separate, smaller cloth which was placed over the head and face. If, eventually, the Shroud is proved to be a forgery, or the image to have been made by a clever artist; then that artist, knowing that the Soudarion had been between the face and the Shroud, would have been perfectly capable of producing a second, bodyless image. The assumption that there were originally two burial cloths – one bearing the image of Christ's face alone and the other of his entire body, back and front – and that both these cloths were kept as relics, goes a long way to explain some of the confusion which has arisen since the Shroud of Turin has been the subject of intensive historical and scientific investigation. There are, in fact, two quite distinct accounts of how the burial cloths came to Constantinople: Robert de Clari speaks about 'sindons' in the plural; and there are other references to the Soudarion and Sindon as two separate and distinct relics.

Let us, therefore, assume that there were, in fact, two cloths bearing an image of Jesus not-made-by-human-hand. The smaller bore the imprint of his face alone, the larger a frontal and dorsal image of the whole body. The smaller has vanished; the larger survives in Turin to this day.

Ian Wilson makes out a convincing case for thinking that the Veronica saga is a distorted version of the Gospel story of the Hemorrhissa, the woman with the issue of blood who was cured by touching the hem of Jesus' garment (Matt. 9:20–22; Mark 5:25–34; Luke 8:43–8). Those who wrote down these traditions were not charlatans who invented the stories out of nothing; nor was the likeness on the Veronica cloth the brain-child of a medieval artist any more than the Shroud of Turin is. Sir Steven Runciman[8] is not alone in being sceptical about the Shroud's authenticity, but he recognizes a common source in a deeply-rooted tradition in the East, and in particular in the story of another famous cloth portrait of Christ, the image not-made-by-human-hand (or Akheiropoietos, to give it its Greek name) of Edessa, which was known in Constantinople as the Mandylion. This word literally means a kerchief, and cannot possibly refer to anything as large as a shroud. It corresponds in size, therefore, to the napkin or Soudarion, and can only refer to the Veronica image. The Mandylion has an early historical existence, and is the parent not only of the Veronica cloth itself – indeed it must have been that very cloth if my hypothesis is correct – but of several post-sixth-century elements of the Veronica story, and even of some Grail legends.

Part of this history is semi-legendary, but from its sixth-century rediscovery in Edessa to 944 when it was transferred to Constantinople, and then to 1204 when it disappeared without trace, it is well documented.

I should explain at this point that Ian Wilson equates the Shroud of Turin with the Mandylion, but this is where I now part company from him. Before I explain why, I should summarize his thesis in order to compare it with my own. One of the problems concerning the Mandylion stems from the secrecy surrounding it before 944 when it was in Edessa, during which time there is not a single record of a viewing of the cloth, let alone an exposition. After its transfer to Constantinople only a privileged few ever saw it. As Wilson says:

> The most crucial aspect of study is therefore to determine what one can of the overall physical characteristics of the Mandylion vis-à-vis the Shroud. There is a reasonable amount of artistic and documentary information available, but what rapidly becomes clear is the importance, as in an archaeological dig, of placing each item in its chronological sequence. Only by this method do certain details make sense.

Wilson notes a significant difference between copies of the image before the cloth's disappearance in 1204 and after that date. Professor Grabar, one of the leading experts on icons, shows that copies made after about 1260 were of what he calls the 'suspended' type, that is to say the head of Christ is shown on a cloth hanging free. This style first appears about 1265 on a mural painting at Sopočani in western Serbia, which, he says, is an isolated case among orthodox Mandylion representations of the time. None like it appear in the East until the end of the fifteenth century or later, whereas in the West, there were innumerable Veronica images of the suspended-cloth type as early as the fourteenth century. This, he suggests, was a result of Western and, more particularly, Italian influences. Copies made before this time are not only rarer, and date from the eleventh to the thirteenth centuries, but show the cloth apparently stretched taut, with a fringe, and frequently with a curious trellis pattern as background. The Sainte Face de Laon belongs to this earlier type of portraiture. The fringe and trellis design as on the Laon icon dates from the late twelfth and early thirteenth centuries, and is typical of the period of the Comnenus Emperors of Constantinople, namely from about 1150 to 1200. Examples of this kind can be seen in frescoes at the monastery of Spaso-Mirozski at Pskov (1156), at Spas-Nereditsa near Novgorod (1199) in Russia, and in the church of Dzurdzevi Stupovi near Novi-Pazar in Serbia (twelfth century).

A common feature of these early representations is the background colour of the cloth, which is consistently ivory white, the natural colour of linen, just as on the Shroud of Turin; the face is frontal and disembodied, a feature shared by the shroud when it is folded in such a way as to conceal the body image.

Then there is the colour of the face itself. This ranges from a pale sepia to a rust-brown, sometimes slightly darker in shade than the colouring of the face on the Shroud, but otherwise virtually identical. In the case of the Sainte Face de Laon, a later artist has added small traces of colour in certain areas, but Professor Grabar makes it clear that these were absent when the icon was originally painted. This facial colouring was mentioned by Jacques Pantaléon in the letter he wrote in July 1249 which accompanied his gift of the Sainte Face to his sister, Abbess Sibylle:

> Do not be surprised if you find his [Christ's] face blackened and sunburnt, for those who dwell in temperate and cold climates and who live all the time in pleasant places, have fair, delicate skin, whereas those who are always in the fields have burnt, darkened skin. This is the case with the Sainte Face, bronzed by the heat of the sun, as the Song of Songs has it, Our Lord has worked in the field of this world for our redemption.

Although the majority of depictions are without a neck, those in the Codex Rossianus and the Alexandria Menologion, two early examples, do show a truncated neck. All versions of the portrait show a bearded face, but the style of the beard and hair differs slightly, which can be explained by the blurred nature of the face on the Shroud, and, presumably, also on the Soudarion face which we have lost. There is yet another way in which these images can be related to the Shroud. Artists have copied certain characteristic details, technically known as Vignon markings, after the scientist who analysed fifteen of them, such as a transverse streak across the forehead of the Shroud image, a V-shape at the bridge of the nose, two curling strands of hair in the middle of the forehead, a hairless area between the lower lip and the beard, and so forth. In some of the earliest copies – those painted before 1260 – as many as thirteen of the fifteen details are discernible, which strongly indicates that these earliest artists were working from the Shroud. Indeed the Sainte Face de Laon has an inscription in Slavonic, contemporary with the icon itself, which reads OBRAZ GSPDN NAUBRUSJE (Obraz Gospodin na Ubruzje) which means 'The Lord's picture on the Cloth'.

Wilson concludes from all this that the earliest artists were working from the image as seen on the Shroud; and the corollary he advances, which Runciman rejects, is that the Mandylion and the Shroud were one and the same. But can Wilson's identification of the Shroud really be sustained? Only, I believe, if there was one cloth upon which the mysterious image of Christ's features were impressed. If, however, there were two such cloths, we have a very different set of circumstances. The unknown author who was commissioned by the Emperor Constantine Porphyrogenitus in 945 to write the official history of the Mandylion had no doubt at all about its size and nature. It was, he tells us, either a cloth with which Christ had dried his face, or it was an image formed during Jesus' agony in the garden of Gethsemane when, according to St Luke, sweat poured from his brow like drops of blood. 'Then, they say, he took this piece of cloth, which we see now, from one of the disciples and wiped off drops of sweat on it. At once the still visible impression of that divine face was produced.' This account is clearly the parent of the identical tradition relating to the Veronica that became popular in the West two hundred years later. But the cloth itself is smaller than a shroud.

As in the case of the word 'grail', we should examine the precise meaning of the word 'mandylion'; names are given for deliberate reasons, in order to describe the object to which they are attached. Sir Steven Runciman rejects the equation Mandylion = Shroud because he says that the word means 'kerchief' or a small cloth. It comes from the same root as the Spanish word mantilla, which means a cloth that covers the head. Today we might translate it 'head scarf'. It would be logical to give this name to a cloth known to have been laid over Christ's head at burial, but not to the shroud in which his whole body was wrapped. In modern parlance we would not describe a shroud or winding sheet as a scarf or kerchief: the two are of completely distinct and different sizes. If, for the sake of this argument, we assume that the Shroud of Turin *is* the authentic winding sheet of Christ, which has survived to our day, then it is inconceivable that those who kept it after the tomb was found empty would not have taken the other burial cloths with them as well, more particularly if the two largest – the Sindon and the Soudarion – were impregnated with the mysterious image of his body and features. I repeat: there can be no logical objection to the belief that if, in some as yet unexplained manner, the imprint of Christ's body was transferred to the Shroud in the way we see it today, it could not have been imprinted on the Soudarion. After 944, therefore, there must have been two linen cloths with the image of Christ not-made-by-human-hand in Constantinople. But let us continue our examination of the account of the Mandylion's advent in the imperial city from Edessa on 5 August 944.

It arrived late in the evening, so we are told, while the Feast of the Assumption was being celebrated in the church of St Mary the Mother of God in the Blachernae Palace by the emperor and chief people of Constantinople. The casket containing it was deposited in the upper oratory of this church. The nobles and clergy hailed it from outside 'with reverent adoration. Then with the honour of an armed escort and many lights they took it aboard the royal galley and reached the palace with it.' That is to say it was taken down the northern coast of the peninsula, along the Golden Horn, bearing right into the Bosphorus, and right again into the Propontis to the Bucoleon Gate which faces due south just to the west of the tip of the peninsula, and opposite the imperial palace. The account goes on:

> They set it up there in the holy chapel which is called Pharos.[9] Next day which was the sixteenth of the month, having again hailed it and done reverence to it, the priests and the younger kings (for the old emperor [Romanus Lecapenus] had been left at home on account of his week disposition) with psalms and hymns and ample lights traversed the road down to the sea, and when they had placed it in the royal galley they sailed along close to the city, so that in some way they might give protection to the city by its sea voyage, and anchored outside the west wall of the city. The kings, elder statesmen, the patriarch and the whole assembly of the Church all disembarked and, continuing on foot with a suitable guard, escorted the vessel in which the holy and precious relic was enclosed like a second ark (of the Covenant), or even more precious than that. They walked round the outside of the walls as far as the Golden Gate.

The Golden Gate is part of the Castle of Seven Towers and is about five hundred yards from the southern end of the Theodosian or land wall of the city. A street leads from it direct to the Amastrianon Forum, where it joins the other main street of the city running the length of the peninsula from the Cathedral of Hagia Sofia to the Charisios Gate, near the northern end of the Theodosian Wall.

'They entered the city,' the account continues, 'with high psalmody, hymns and spiritual songs, and boundless lights and torches, and, gathering together a procession of the whole people, they completed their journey through the city centre.' In the course of this long procession many healing miracles are said to have occurred. Eventually ly it reached Hagia Sofia, where it was taken inside the sanctuary, and the Mandylion was laid on the throne of mercy. After another act of worship the procession emerged again with the Mandylion and went to the Bucoleon Palace, where it was placed 'for the time being in what they call the Chrysotriclinios, on the emperor's throne, from which they usually give decisions on the most important matters of state'. After ceremonies had been performed here they took the Mandylion up again 'from there, consecrated and dedicated [it] in the aforementioned chapel of the Pharos on the right side towards the east, for the glory of the faithful, for the protection of the emperor, and to ensure the safety of the whole state and the Christian community'.[10]

If, then, the Mandylion was not the Shroud, is there any evidence by which we can decide whether the casket in which it was kept could in any way be described by a word meaning 'grill' or 'trellis'? The background of the Sainte Face de Laon is a trellis, and the artist has taken care to paint a fringe along the bottom edge of the icon. The style of this painting differs radically from the suspended towel or Veronica style of representation. Up to now most commentators have believed that both these styles derive from a single source – the Shroud – and Ian Wilson goes to some length to explain how the Shroud might have been attached to a board over which the trelliswork cover was placed. This is an ingenious explanation, but the difference in the size of the two sacred cloths and the references of contemporary writers to *sindons* in the plural cannot be ignored. Moreover the identity of size betokened by the use of the words Soudarion and Mandylion demands another explanation. Thus it seems more in line with the evidence to assume that the Veronica representations derive from the smaller cloth, and that the trelliswork representations derive from the larger, although the image of the face was identical, having been created by the single process – whatever that might have been – at the time of death.

Let us therefore look at the evidence and test this hypothesis against it. To start with, there is little doubt that there were two cloths in Constantinople from at least the middle of the tenth century until the city was sacked in 1204. The earliest mention of the burial linens after the Gospels dates from the beginning of the fourth century, when St Nino, a Georgian princess, visited Jerusalem and wrote an account of her visit which is still extant.[11] St Nino had a special devotion to the relics of the Passion but these, though known to be in Jerusalem, were never shown, or, in the case of the True Cross, had not yet come to light. She heard that the Soudarion had been given to Pilate's wife, and that she had taken it to Pontus, the northern part of Anatolia whose chief city was Trebizond. (This tradition persisted, and one of the icons similar to the Sainte Face de Laon is, or was, at Trebizond.) Later it was recovered by St Luke and brought back to Jerusalem. The Shroud, she heard, had been taken by St Peter, but she could not find where it was kept. This story shows that the two cloths were believed to be in Jerusalem at that early date.

Almost a century after St Nino, in 438, the Empress Eudocia, the wife of Theodosius II, went to Jerusalem to look for relics for the church she was building in the Blachernae Palace in honour of the Virgin. A later chronicler writing in the fourteenth century, Nicephorus Callistus, gives a list of the relics she brought back. These include what he calls the *spargana* of Christ. *Spargana* is generally translated as swaddling clothes, but the term is sometimes used to denote funerary wrappings. Some historians have taken this to mean the Shroud, but the term can only be equated to the *othonia*, mainly because there has never been any record of Christ's swaddling bands among the relics. Both *spargana* and *othonia* are used to describe thin strips of cloth, and could never indicate anything as large as a shroud or a head scarf.

Against this must be set the story told by Adamnan of Iona in about 705. He says that Bishop Arculf was shown an eight-foot-long piece of linen bearing Christ's image on it in Jerusalem, which he was told was the shroud of the sepulchre. The same story was told in the eleventh and twelfth centuries by a French monk called Bernard and by Peter the Deacon of Monte Cassino. The latter went to the Holy Land in 1140, and both believed they had seen the authentic shroud. From their descriptions of the ceremony at which it was displayed, this belief was clearly shared by the Jerusalem hierarchy. But we know that the Shroud was in Constantinople in 1150. The cloth these pilgrims saw was only eight feet long, which is identical in length to the Besançon shroud. Were they the same piece of cloth? The Turin Shroud is over fourteen feet long. This suggests that the authentic Shroud was taken to Constantinople at an unknown date, and re-placed in Jerusalem by a copy of the frontal image only, which later came to be thought of as the genuine article. If this copy was later sent to Besançon in the belief that it was genuine, and perhaps in ignorance of the existence of the authentic Shroud in Constantinople, then this goes a long way to explain the scepticism of Bishops Henri and Pierre of Troyes in the fourteenth century. After all, the eight-foot cloth had been venerated in Jeusalem for eight centuries, and the copy, as so often happens, came in time to be taken for the original without any intention to deceive. People are still making mistakes of this kind.

The earliest unequivocal mention by a Western writer of the Shroud dates from 1171, but there remains a slightly earlier reference to what some people believe to be the Shroud, but which, if my hypothesis is correct, must really refer to the Soudarion/Mandylion. It comes in a long list of relics in the imperial treasury made by an English pilgrim, who tells us about the '*Sudarium quod fuit super caput ejus*' (the napkin which was over his head). [12] A few years later an Icelandic pilgrim, a Benedictine abbot, Nicolas Soemundarsson, went to Constantinople. He died in 1159 leaving an account intended to help future pilgrims. He tells us that he saw in Saint Sophia the '*Fasciae cum Sudario et sanguine Christi*' (the bandages with the napkin and the blood of Christ). This blood refers, presumably, not to a separate relic of the Holy Blood in a phial, but rather to stains on the cloth, though the sentence is ambiguous.

In 1201 Nicolas Mesarites, the treasurer or guardian of the Pharos chapel, defended the relics there against attacks by supporters of the usurper, John Comnenus. Among these he lists the burial *sindons* of Christ, using the word in the plural, a sure sign that the Sindon/Shroud and the Soudarion/Mandylion were *not* one and the same. 'These burial sindons of Christ,' Nicolas tells us, 'are of linen, of a quite ordinary weave. They still smell of myrrh, [the Shroud of Turin revealed traces of herbs known to have been used in Jewish burials of the first century when it was submitted to forensic examination by the Swiss criminologist, Dr Max Frei] and are indestructible since they once enshrouded the dead body, annointed and naked, of the Almighty after his Passion.'[13]

In 970 the Mandylion was taken round Constantinople in procession, but it was not publicly shown or taken out of its casket. It was seen in 1058 in Hagia Sofia, but there is no record of the Shroud ever having been exhibited in its full length, as it was when it reached the West.

Finally, we come to the account of Robert de Clari, of the events of 1203 and 1204. He describes his arrival in Constantinople in the army of the Fourth Crusade, and the assault on the city and its subsequent sack. But before these events took place he, along with many other crusaders, visited the city as a tourist, just as many thousand of other soldiers have gone sightseeing while on campaign. Like his successors down the centuries he recorded what he saw, and what he believed he was told. But his knowledge of Greek was limited, maybe non-existent, and he depended, like every other tourist, on guides who explained what they were showing him. With these reservations in mind, his account is extremely valuable, and is to be depended on in broad detail, even if some of the more esoteric things he saw and heard are less accurately reported. Describing the church of St Mary Blachernae, he writes:

'[Here] was kept the *sydoine* in which our Lord had been wrapped, which stood up straight every Good Friday so that the features of our Lord could be plainly seen there.'

There are two points we should notice here: the first is the use of the word *sydoine* which some commentators interpret as *sindon*, but which could equally well be a mis-hearing of the Greek *soudarion*. On the other hand, Robert seems to be referring to the Shroud, when he tells us that the features of Christ could be seen when it 'stood up straight' on Good Fridays. Here again, this could refer to the Mandylion/Soudarion more plausibly than to the Sindon/Shroud, since features is a term usually applied to the face rather than to the whole body. Ian Wilson, assuming that the Shroud of Turin was identical to the Mandylion, sees Robert de Clari's description as confirmation of his

63

theory. But if you read it carefully, it can equally well apply to an exposition of the Soudarion, which would of course have had to be elevated or 'stood up straight' for the congregation to see it at all. On the other hand, there is a great deal of evidence to show that the Sindon/Shroud was likewise made to 'stand up straight' on Good Fridays as well. According to a twelfth-century account of this ceremony inserted in a sermon given by the eighth-century Pope Stephen III, Christ was made to appear 'at the first hour of the day as a child, at the third as a boy, at the sixth as a young man, and at the ninth hour visible in his full manhood in which the Son of God went to his Passion when he bore the suffering of the Cross for our sins'.

This statement echoes the one of Nicolas Mesarites in 1201, when he warned the insurgents not to attack the Pharos chapel of which he was the guardian, proclaiming: 'In this chapel Christ rises again, and the Sindon with the burial linens is the clear proof. . . .'

In order to reconcile all these statements, we must hold to the belief that there were two cloths with the features of Christ upon them, not one. Robert de Clari's evidence alone is ambiguous, and it seems rash to assume that what he describes as taking place in St Mary Blachernae was an exposition of the Sindon/Shroud. Rather it must have been an exposition of the Soudarion/Mandylion. And would it not be strange, given that both cloths were in Constantinople, if only one were exposed on Good Fridays? As the smaller of the two, it seems likely that it was exhibited to a less select congregation at St Mary, but that the other, and larger, was likewise occasionally exhibited in the Pharos chapel. The sermon of Pope Stephen does not reveal exactly in which church this ceremony was performed, so it is not unreasonable to assume that it was in the Pharos rather than in St Mary Blachernae.

Homer uses the word φαρος to indicate a shroud. Much confusion arises from the much better-known use of the word as meaning a lighthouse, of which the Pharos of Alexandria was one of the seven wonders of the ancient world. It is not known whether the lighthouse got its name from the island upon which it stood at the entrance to Alexandria harbour, or for some other reason. It is possible that the island took its name from pharynx (throat), of which Pharos is a diminutive, for it is long and narrow and lies at the mouth of the harbour.

All the evidence, I submit, confirms the belief that there were two sacred cloths in Constantinople, both of which bore the image of Christ not-made-by-human-hand. One of them, the Soudarion/Mandylion, was brought there in 944; the other, the Sindon/Shroud, was brought at some earlier date, but by whom is uncertain. It is less certain that the other funeral linens were among the imperial relics, but there is some reason to believe that copies on cloth of both the Soudarion and the Sindon were made, and that some of them were still in Constantinople when it was sacked. At least one of these copies, the Besançon shroud, found its way to the West. The Veronica of Rome seems to have been a copy rather than one of the original burial cloths, but since both the Veronica and the Mandylion have been destroyed, it is idle to speculate further.

We have seen that the caskets in which the Mandylion was kept, as well as those which housed the Cadouin and Besançon shrouds, could not have been the Grail. Nor could the frame in which the Veronica was exhibited in St Peter's. This leaves the casket in which the Sindon/Shroud was kept in the Pharos church of the Mother of God, but it excludes both the present casket in Turin and the one in which it was kept during the time it belonged to the de Charny family, since that one was stamped with their coat of arms.

It would appear that icons, like the Sainte Face de Laon and those at Spas Nereditsa and Gradac, which show the head of Christ against a trelliswork background, were painted from the Shroud, whereas the suspended-towel type were painted from the Mandylion. We have seen that the word grail derives from the same Latin and French sources as the modern English word grill. The word accurately described the object because it depicted that form of decoration. In other words, the trelliswork background of icons such as the Sainte Face accurately depicts the decoration on the casket in which the Shroud was kept – the Holy Grail.

If this explains how the Grail got its name in its role of the vessel in which traces of Christ's blood and sweat were preserved, it does not explain Wolfram von Eschenbach's definition of it as a thin stone with magical properties. I shall come to this in due course.

Those icons painted before 1260 have several peculiarities which should be noticed. On all of them, with two exceptions, of which the Sainte Face de Laon is one, the head appears in the centre of a horizontal rectangle whose width is greater than its height. This setting is totally at variance with a more or less universal artistic convention whereby a portrait head is set in an upright rectangle whose width is less than its height. Throughout history and in all cultures, artists have almost invariably set the face against a background of an upright rather than a horizontal rectangle, just as when they painted landscapes they did the reverse. There is nothing odd about this: it looks better that way. Besides, to paint a portrait head on a horizontal background is wasteful of space. The appearance of Christ's head on icons of this period in this horizontal fashion suggests, if it does not prove, that the artists were either copying faithfully what they saw in front of them, or they were reproducing from a verbal tradition what they had been told the original looked like. The suspended-towel representations, on the other hand, are equally, if not more, consistent, for in those cases the cloth is shown to be square, which is what one would expect of a cloth or napkin placed over the face of a corpse. This leads me to pose another question: was the Holy Grail a shallow, rectangular box, approximately twice as long as it was broad, with a cover, in whose centre there was a circular space through which the head on the cloth it enclosed could be clearly seen without removing the entire Shroud? If so, how was this achieved?

The clue to the answer to this can be found in the description of the Good Friday Masses in which the Shroud in its entirety was revealed in four stages to represent Christ's childhood, boyhood, young manhood and Passion. In order to produce this dramatic result it was only necessary to fold and then unfold the Shroud in a very simple way, which you can do quite easily for yourself. All you need to do is cut out a photograph of the full Shroud of Turin, showing the frontal and dorsal images. Then fold it in half, and you will have the two images arranged in such a way that the back corresponds exactly to the front. Then fold it in half again, taking care to leave the upper half of the frontal image visible with the head uppermost. This fold shows the frontal image upwards from where the hands cross, leaving the lower part of the trunk and legs hidden. Fold the photograph once more, and you will then find that you are looking at the head and the upper part of the chest in a rectangle which is almost exactly twice as wide as it is deep. You are now looking at what the artist saw when the Shroud was lying in its rectangular casket. By this process you have folded the Shroud into eight thicknesses, which if they were of linen would measure about two or three inches. The other dimensions come to about four feet by two feet. Thus the folded cloth could be accommodated in a shallow, rectangular box not unlike the dress-box you get when you buy a suit or a frock from an expensive tailor.

In order to create the four symbolic stages of Christ's life, it was only necessary to fold the Shroud in the way I have just described, inserting a bar at the mid-point between the frontal and dorsal images, and laying it in the casket. When the casket's lid was removed, chains attached to either end of the bar, running over pulleys above the altar, would then enable the officiating clergy to hoist the Shroud in four separate movements, like a blind, first revealing the head, then the upper part of the body, then the whole frontal image and finally, when held aloft above the altar, the frontal and dorsal images fully visible to those who walk round it. The empty casket, left lying on the altar, must have looked to the congregation, who saw it only from a distance, very much like a dish or tray. It should be noted that it would have been completely impossible to expose the Shroud in this manner if it had been kept then as it is now, rolled round a velvet-covered pole. If it is unrolled you see first the legs, then the abdomen, then the chest and finally the head of the frontal image, and if you continue unrolling it, the dorsal image will appear, but upside down, just as it was seen when exposed for the TV cameras in 1973.

So here we have our new definition of the Holy Grail. It was a shallow box measuring about four by two feet and a few inches deep. It either had a solid top decorated with some kind of grid-like design, or the cover was itself a grid of gold or silver, through which the cloth could be seen beneath. The former is almost certainly the more likely, mainly for security reasons. Had the cover been a grill in the strict sense, the cloth within would have been exposed to the air and to the risk of damage far greater than if it had been kept in a closed casket. It is possible that a circle might have been cut in the lid so that the head beneath could be seen, and that this was covered with glass. On the other hand, it is possible that there was a painted representation of the head on the lid itself. This is pure conjecture. But we do not need to speculate any further. All we need to do is look again at the Sainte Face de Laon, for it tells us all..

Professor Grabar draws our attention to the fringe which most of these early icons have as part of their composition. The artists seem to have some doubt about whether it should be placed at the bottom, as in the case of the Laon icon, or at the sides as in the Novgorod and Alexandria examples. The fringe gives us the clue to the mystery when taken in conjunction with something else on the Laon icon, and with its Slavonic inscription. This other feature consists of two small roundels in the upper left and upper right quarters of the icon. One contains the Greek letters I C and the other X C. These stand for Jesus Christos. It is odd that they should be in Greek characters when the explanatory inscription is written in Slavonic. But there is a good reason for this: the artist has painted exactly what he saw. Other artists have painted what they have been told about the cloth and its casket, but not the artist who painted the Laon icon. How do I know? I mentioned a little while back that the face of the man on the Shroud had been analysed and a number of so-called Vignon characteristics had been detected. The Laon icon contains more of them than any other known icon. This, taken together with the artist's unequivocal statement that the portrait is that of the Lord 'on the cloth', must mean that he was working from the 'life'. If I am correct, then it follows that the rest of the composition faithfully reproduces what he saw, and that the original had the two roundels at the top and the fringe at the bottom. Moreover, the Laon icon is square, another unusual feature, though there are more square portraits than horizontally rectangular ones. This makes it look like a banner, which immediately raises another question: which banner? There is, strangely enough, only one possible answer: the Labarum Constantini, or Imperial Banner of Constantine the Great.

In October 311 Constantine found himself at the gates of Rome ready to attack Maxentius. According to both Eusebius, his friend and biographer, and Lactantius, he had a vision during the night, in which Christ appeared to him, and ordered him to engrave the cross on the shields of his soldiers. Next day he did as he was bidden, inserting above the cross the Greek letters Chi (X) and Rho (P), the first two letters of the name CHRistos, thus: ☧ . The Battle of the Milvian Bridge began, and towards evening Constantine had another vision of the cross in the sky with the words *In Hoc Signo Vinces*' written beneath it. There were many in the army who saw it, and Constantine determined to put this Chi Rho sign on the new imperial standard he created to replace the pagan eagles.

Eusebius describes the new standard, or Labarum, in some detail, and there are numerous representations of it on coins from the reign of Constantine. Eusebius tells us:

> A long spear, overlaid with gold, formed the figure of a cross by means of a transverse bar at the top. At the summit of the whole was fixed a wreath of gold and precious stones, within which the symbol of the Title of Salvation was indicated by means of its first two letters, Chi and Rho ☧ or ⳩ . From the cross-bar of the spear was suspended a square cloth of purple stuff profusely embroidered with gold in the form of a banner or pennant. Beneath the crown of the cross, immediately above the embroidered banner, the shaft bore golden medallions of the emperor and his children.

Once adopted by Constantine as the imperial ensign, it was continued by his successors, with the exception of Julian the Apostate, who reverted to the ancient Roman Eagles. A Greek author writing in 439 affirms that the original Labarum was preserved in his time in the Bucoleon Palace at Constantinople, and Theophanus mentions its existence between 810 and 815.

I have already pointed out that the seventeenth-century Dukes of Savoy regarded the Shroud as a palladium, and that they had it portrayed as a banner coupled with the motto *In Hoc Signo Vinces*.

This shows that they knew of a connection between the Shroud and the Labarum Constantini, and that this tradition had been handed down in their family. They must have received the tradition from the de Charnys, who in their turn must have been told about it by the previous owners.

From depictions of the Labarum on coins it is possible to calculate that the banner measured four feet by four feet. The fringe is usually shown to be on the bottom, but it sometimes appears on the sides as well, though the diminutive scale dictated by the size of the coins makes this and the decoration of the banner itself hard to determine.

Eusebius and Lactantius'tell us that the cloth was 'profusely [or lavishly] embroidered in gold and precious stones' without saying anything about the design itself. Could this have been the trelliswork design of the icons? The artist commissioned by Constantine to embellish his new standard must certainly have been aware of the second Commandment, so he would have chosen some symbol, or motif, to represent Christ. What could have been more appropriate than a pattern of repeated Chi's (Xs), the initial of the holy name? By repeating this letter you achieve this pattern:

in other words, a trellis. Such a design is precisely what we see as the background to the Sainte Face de Laon and other icons.[14]

Here, then, is the solution to one mystery: the casket in which the Sindon was kept was covered while it was in Constantinople by the Labarum Constantini, and the trelliswork pattern on this banner came to be known as the Holy Grill or Grail, and was nothing other than the repeated initial of Christ's name. If the Sindon had been taken to Constantinople by the Empress Eudocia, then it is probable that the person who decided to cover the casket in which it was to be kept would have been her husband, Theodosius II. He may have removed a circle from the centre of the Labarum so that the face on the Shroud could be seen.

This definition of the Holy Grail is consistent with most, but not all, the descriptions of it in the romances. They describe a shallow, rectangular box or casket resembling a dish or a platter, in which are to be found traces of Christ's blood and sweat. These were not in a phial or chalice, but on the cloth in which he was wound at burial – the shroud bought by Joseph of Arimathea for the purpose. But what, you may ask, about that other Grail, Wolfram's *Lapis Exilis* or flat stone?

The anonymous author who wrote the Mandylion's history for the Emperor Constantine Porphyrogenitus in 945 tells us that Abgar V, King of Edessa, who reigned from AD 13 to 50, was a leper. He had heard that Jesus was a miracle-worker from his ambassador, Ananias, who had seen him preaching and healing while on a mission to Egypt. Abgar was so impressed by what Ananias told him that he wrote to Jesus inviting him to come to Edessa to cure him, and asking for his portrait if Jesus could not come in person so that he might look on it and be cured. Abgar sent Ananias back to Palestine with the letter, where he found Jesus preaching to a crowd of people so great that he could get nowhere near him to deliver it. So he sat down as close as he could and began to draw Jesus' portrait for the king. Jesus, realizing that his portrait was being drawn, sent Thomas to bring Ananias to him. Ananias then gave Jesus Abgar's letter, which he read with great attention. He then sat down and wrote a reply declining Abgar's invitation to visit Edessa, but promising to send one of his disciples to cure him. Knowing that Abgar had asked for his portrait, Jesus took a towel, and after washing his face, dried it, and 'in some miraculous fashion' impressed his likeness upon it. He gave the towel to Ananias, telling him to give it to his master so that he might look on it and be cured.

On the way home, Ananias stopped at Hierapolis, not far from Edessa, where he put up for the night just outside the city walls. Near where he pitched his tent was a heap of tiles, under which he hid the sacred towel for safety's sake. During the night a fire broke out, which threatened to destroy the city, and Ananias was arrested on suspicion of having started it. He was at a loss to explain how it had started, but told the authorities that he had hidden a bundle among the tiles from where the flames seemed to have emanated. The place was searched at once and the bundle containing the towel was found unharmed, but on one of the tiles nearby another copy of Jesus' face was found, which the citizens of Hierapolis kept as a talisman. Ananias was set free and went on his way with the cloth. As soon as he reached Edessa, he gave Abgar the letter Jesus had written him together with the towel on which the image of his features had been imprinted. Abgar looked upon it and was immediately cured of his leprosy. He was baptized at once, and a Christian community was established at Edessa.

Abgar put the towel in a niche above one of the city gates for safekeeping, where it was venerated by all who entered that way. After a time many Edessenes relapsed into paganism, though a small

Christian remnant persisted. The Bishop of Edessa at that time took the precaution of bricking up the niche where the cloth was kept, after placing a tile over it to protect it from damp and the ravages of vermin. In this way it was completely hidden and soon forgotten. It might have been forgotten for ever, had not Edessa been attacked by the Persians in 544, and had not one of the Christian priests remembered that Jesus, in his letter to Abgar, had promised to protect the city. A search was made and the cloth was rediscovered. The tile which had been placed over it was found to bear another likeness of Jesus similar to the one on the towel.

The cloth's palladian powers ensured the defeat of the Persians, and Edessa once more reverted to Christianity. A cathedral was built to house the towel and the tile, and Edessa became a pilgrimage centre. In 639, seven years after the death of Mohammed, Edessa was captured by the Moslems, and for many centuries thereafter the Byzantine emperors tried to persuade the Edessenes, who for the most part remained Christian, to let them have the towel and the tile for safekeeping in Constantinople. But they were reluctant to part with them, and it was not until 943 that the emir agreed to let them go. The towel became known as the Mandylion, was brought to Constantinople in great style and installed among the other relics. No doubt it was placed in an elaborate reliquary, for the magnificent traditions of classical Greek and Roman jewellers had been preserved in Constantinople. In the palaces the official costumes were as elaborate and ornate as the combined experience of the silk-weavers and the court jewellers could make them. Reliquaries such as those which housed the Sindon and Soudarion of Christ would have been of the richest possible construction. The Labarum, for instance, must have resembled in its material and decoration a bejewelled and embroidered pallium, a garment which hung down at the back to form a train and which was worn over the long, wide-sleeved dalmatic which nobles and officials wore over silk undergarments. Other reliquaries were encrusted with precious stones, cloisonné enamel and elaborately worked silver and gold filigree.

The tile, known as the Keramion, had by this time been sent to Hierapolis for safety's sake, but it, too, was eventually sent to Constantinople, where in 696 it was installed in the Pharos church of the Mother of God. There is some doubt about this relic's appearance, but it is thought that it may have been a stone or clay head depicting the likeness of Christ in the Parthian tradition of protective deities which were placed over city gates. Examples of these can still be seen at Parthian Hatra. Most likely the Keramion was a Christianized version

71

of one of these. During the reign of Abgar V, when Christianity was tolerated, it had been set up in the conventional manner of the time, but later, when persecution set in, it was removed.

Twenty-five years after the Mandylion had been installed among the imperial relics, the Keramion was brought to join it in the Pharos church, where Robert de Clari describes 'two rich vessels of gold hanging in the midst of the chapel by heavy silver chains. In one of these vessels there was a tile and in the other a cloth. . . .'

Two pictures of the Keramion exist so far as is known: one of them in the Codex Rossianus and the other in a fresco in the ruined church of Dzurdzevi Stupovi in Serbia. They show a thin rectangular tile, but it is hard to detect much detail. Could the Keramion have been Wolfram's *Lapis exilis*? It is at least a possibility. There are, however, two other stones associated with the Passion. One is the Stone of Unction, upon which Jesus' body was laid for annointing and wrapping in the Shroud before burial; the other is the stone rolled in front of the tomb after the body had been laid in it. It is hard to say which – if either – of these stones Wolfram might have had in mind, for neither of them can really be described as thin. The Stone of Unction is usually portrayed as a block, and the Gospels tell us that the one which was rolled in front of the tomb was large. But yet he specifically associates the *Lapis exilis* with Good Friday. Of all the Grail descriptions, this remains the most puzzling, and the one that seems to defy a rational explanation.

Let me now summarize all these facts and definitions. I hope I have been able to show that the Grail was recognized by the poets who first wrote about it as a vessel intimately linked with the Passion of Christ, which contained traces of his blood and sweat. As there is nothing to give us the impression that these poets created the Grail out of their imaginations, we have to look for an historical object which best fits the evidence, and the only one to do this is the reliquary in which the Shroud of Christ was kept. This reliquary must have been a shallow, rectangular box decorated with a pattern of crosses. Such a decoration is to be found in descriptions of the Labarum Constantini, the banner made of purple, embroidered cloth embellished with a trelliswork design made up of the repeated initial letter of Christ's name – Chi, or X. The Shroud with its mysterious image was only vaguely known to these authors, none of whom had seen it, and who therefore depended for their knowledge upon accounts of those who had. The legends of the Grail (or, perhaps, we should call it the Holy Grill) first appeared in eastern France, then the intellectual and cultural centre of Europe, and the men who brought news of the Shroud and of the Grail in which it was kept were members of the Burgundian and Champenois aristocracy. They had learnt about the relics when visiting Constantino-ple during the crusades. Then came the Fourth Crusade and the sack of Constantinople, after which the Shroud and the Grail, the Mandylion and Keramion, all vanished: the first, for a century and a half, the others completely. Gradually the memory of these relics faded until the succeeding generation of poets and writers had forgotten what the Grail really was. Wolfram von Eschenbach believed he had special knowledge and thought it was a thin stone; others, remembering that the Grail had preserved traces of Christ's blood and sweat, and misin-terpreting the word itself, thought of it as a cup, but more precisely as the Chalice of the Last Supper. This is attributable to the similarity of the Latin words for trellis and chalice, which in ancient Latin were *cratis* and *cratus* or *crater* respectively, and which in medieval Latin became *gradalis* and *gradella*.

I have sketched the history of the Shroud from the mid-fourteenth century to the present day, and established its connection with the Grail, and I have shown that the former's history is well documented. Scientific examination of the Shroud beginning with Secondo Pia's first photograph of it in 1898 down to the present year has failed to prove it a medieval forgery. I have traced its history from the sixth century to 1204 and the history of the Mandylion and Keramion from the tenth century. I have shown that medieval eye witnesses speak of two cloths bearing the image of Christ not-made-by-hands in Con-stantinople, and identified these as the towel or Soudarion, which was placed over Christ's face and head, and the Sindon or Shroud in which his body was wrapped before burial. I believe that the former may have been irrevocably lost, unless it can be positively identified with the Sudarium Christi of Oviedo, while the latter still survives in Turin.[15]

RULING MONARCHS 1125–1451

Date	England	France	Hungary	Empire	Champagne	Duchy of Burgundy (d)	County of Burgundy (c)	Savoy	Constantinople
1125					Theobald II				
1135	Stephen								
1137		Louis VII							
1138				Conrad III					
1144						Eudes II			Manuel I Comnenus
1148							Beatrix		
1152				Frederick I	Henry I				
1154	Henry II								
1162						Hugh III			
1173			Bela III						
1176									
1180		Philip II						Thomas I	Alexius II Comnenus
1181					Henry II				
1183									Andronicus I Comnenus
1184							Otto I		
1185									Isaac II Angelos
1189	Richard								
1190				Henry VI					
1192									
1195						Eudes III			Alexius III Angelos
1196			Imre						
1197				Otto IV	Theobald III				
1198					Theobald IV				
1204			Ladislas I						Alexius IV & Baldwin I
1205			Andrew II						Henry of Flanders (Reg.)
1206									Henry
1208									
1212				Frederick II					
1216	Henry III								Peter de Courtenay
1218						Hugh IV			

Year	England	France	Hungary	(Hohenstaufen)	Navarre	Burgundy	(Bavaria / Otto)	Savoy	Constantinople
1221									Robert de Courtenay
1223		Louis VIII							
1226		Louis IX St							
1228								Amadeus IV	Baldwin II
1235									
1235									
1248							Otto II / Adelheid		
1250				Conrad IV					
1253					Theobald V				
1254				Conradin					
1261									Michael VIII Palaeologus
1267				d. of Conradin					
1270		Philip III	Stephen V						
1271					Henry III				
1272	Edward I		Ladislas IV			Robert II			
1274									
1279									
1282							Otto V		d. of Michael VIII
1285		Philip IV			Jeanne Inc. to France				
1290			Andrew III Anjoy Dynasty						
1301									
1303							Robert		
1306						Hugh V			
1307	Edward II								
1308				Henry VII					
1314		Louis X							
1315		Philip V				Eudes IV			
1316							Jeanne Inc. to France		
1318									
1323		Charles IV							
1327	Edward III								
1328		Philip VI						Aymon	
1344								Amadeus VI	
1350		John II				Philip I Inc. to France			
1361									
1364		Charles V							
1377	Richard II								
1380		Charles VI							
1383								Amadeus VII	
1391								Amadeus VIII	
1399	Henry IV								
1451								Louis I	

LIST OF POPES: 1159–1458

Alexander III (Roland Bandinelli)	Sept. 1159–Aug. 1181
Lucius III (Ubaldo, Bishop of Ostia)	Sept. 1181–Nov. 1185
Urban III (Uberto Crivelli)	Nov. 1185–Oct. 1187
Gregory VIII (Alberto di Morra)	Oct.–Dec. 1187
Clement III (Paolo Scolaro)	Dec. 1187–Mar. 1191
Celestine III (Hyacinth)	Mar. 1191–Jan. 1198
Innocent III (Lothario di Segni)	Jan. 1198–July 1216
Honorius III (Cencio Savelli)	July 1216–Mar. 1227
Gregory IX (Card. Ugolino)	Mar. 1227–Aug. 1241
Celestine IV (Geoffrey Castiglione)	1241 died before consecration
Innocent IV (Sinibaldo Fieschi)	June 1243–Dec. 1254
Alexander IV (Rinaldo, Bishop of Ostia)	Dec. 1254–May 1261
Urban IV (Jacques Pantaleon)	Aug. 1261–Oct. 1264
Clement IV (Guy Foulquois)	Feb. 1265–Nov. 1268
Gregory X (Tebaldo of Liege)	Sept. 1271–Jan. 1276
Innocent V (Pierre de Tarentaise)	Feb.–June 1276
Hadrian V (Cardinal Ottobuoni)	July 1276 died before consecration
John XXI (Peter the Portuguese)	Sept. 1276–May 1277
Nicholas III (Giovanni Orsini)	Nov. 1277–Aug. 1280
Martin IV (Simon de Brion)	Feb. 1281–Mar. 1285
Honorius IV (Giacomo Savelli)	Apr. 1285–Apr. 1287
Nicholas IV (Gerolomo di Palestrina)	Feb. 1288–Apr. 1292
Celestine V (Pietro Morrone)	July–Dec. 1294 resigned – died May 1296
Boniface VIII (Benedetto Gaetani)	Dec. 1294–Oct. 1303
Benedict XI (Nicolo Bocasi)	Oct. 1303–July 1304
Clement V (Bertrand de Goth)	June 1305–Apr. 1314 in Avignon
John XXII (Jacques d'Euse)	Aug. 1316–Dec. 1334 in Avignon
Benedict XII (Jacques Fournier)	Dec. 1334–Apr. 1342 in Avignon
Clement VI (Pierre Roger)	May 1342–Dec. 1352 in Avignon
Innocent VI (Etienne Aubert)	Dec. 1352–Sept. 1362 in Avignon
Urban V (Guillaume Grimoard)	Oct. 1362–Dec. 1370 in Avignon
Gregory XI (Pierre Roger, nephew of Clement VI)	Dec. 1370–Mar. 1378 in Avignon

THE GREAT SCHISM

ROME	AVIGNON
Urban VI Apr. 1378–Oct. 1389	Clement VII Sept. 1378–Sept. 1394
Boniface IX Nov. 1389–Oct. 1404	Benedict XIII Sept. 1394–1423
Innocent VII Oct. 1404–Nov. 1406	Clement VIII 1424–1429 resigned
Gregory XII Dec. 1406–July 1415	Felix V (Amadeus VIII, Duke of Savoy) Elected Nov. 1439 by Council of Basle. Resigned Apr. 1449.

In June 1409 the Council of Pisa deposed both Gregory XII and Benedict XIII (though they both refused to acknowledge its authority) and elected:

Alexander V (Pietro di Milano)	June 1409–May 1410
John XXIII (Balthasar Cossa)	May 1410–May 1415 deposed

In 1415 the Council of Constance deposed John XXIII, induced Gregory XII to resign and elected:

Martin V (Otto Colonna)	Nov. 1417–Feb. 1431
Eugenius IV (Gabriel Condulmier)	Mar. 1431–Feb. 1447
Nicholas V (Tommaso di Sarzana)	Mar. 1447–Mar. 1455
Calixtus III (Alfonso Borgia)	Apr. 1455–Aug. 1458

CHAPTER 3

THE IDOL OF THE TEMPLARS: 1274–1307

———•———

When I began research for this book I was living in Périgord. As mentioned earlier, I had been invited to investigate French sources of the Arthurian legends, and a conversation with Ian Wilson, in which we discussed the possible connection between the Turin Shroud and the Templar 'idol' set up a new train of thought and suggested a new area of research.

Tony Kildwick, a young research student from Cambridge and a fellow motorbike enthusiast, joined me on a tour of France in the course of which my ideas began to take on coherent shape. I said in my introduction that the supposed adherence of the Templars to Catharism was nonsense. This belief is to some extent based on the erroneous identification of Bertrand de Blanquefort, a Templar Grand Master, with a Cathar nobleman called Bertrand de Blanchefort. It is true that both names appear as 'Blancafortis' in Latin texts, but the Templar came from Guyenne, not Languedoc, and had nothing whatever to do with the Cathars. In any case, there are three towns in France called Blanquefort and one called Blancafort, apart from the Blanchefort from which the Cathar took his title. Since French noblemen were invariably known by the names of their estates and not by hereditary surnames, nothing can be deduced from the coincidence of two men with similar names.

Montpellier was a good place to begin my examination of the Templars' history. It is not only an ancient university city but nearby St Gilles was for nearly a century the chief Templar house in southern France, and was linked to another important preceptory in Montpellier itself. A glance at the map of the Mediterranean will tell you why St Gilles and Montpellier were so important. They stand at a crossroads and at a point of embarkation for the Holy Land for those coming from northern Europe and Spain.

The Military Order of Knights of the Temple of Solomon, to give the order its formal title, was established in 1118 or thereabouts with its headquarters in the Temple area of Jerusalem. The crusaders mistakenly identified the Moslem Dome of the Rock with Solomon's Temple. Their first duty was to protect the road to Jerusalem, but it was not long before they assumed the role of a volunteer police force. According to William, Archbishop of Tyre:

> certain noblemen of knightly rank, devoted to God, professed a wish to live in chastity, obedience and without property in perpetuity, binding themselves in the hands of the lord patriarch to the service of Christ in the manner of secular canons. Among these, the first and most important were the venerable men, Hugues de Payns and Godefroi de Saint-Omer. Since they did not have a church, nor a settled place to live, the king [of Jerusalem, Baldwin II] conceded a temporary dwelling to them in his palace, which he had below the Temple of the Lord, to the south side.[1] The canons of the Temple of the Lord, under certain conditions, conceded a courtyard which they had near the same place, to be used for the functions of the Order. Moreover, the lord king with his nobles, as well as the lord patriarch with his prelates, gave to them certain benefices from their own demesne, some in perpetuity, some on a temporary basis, from which they could be fed and clothed. The first element of their profession enjoined on them for the remission of their sins by the lord patriarch and the other bishops, was that they should protect the roads and routes to the utmost of their ability against the ambushes of thieves and attackers, especially in regard to the safety of pilgrims.

Hugues de Payns and Godefroi de Saint-Omer gathered about nine companions, as well as gaining the support of important princes like Hugues, Comte de Champagne, and Fulk V, Comte d'Anjou, but they did not expand fast until after the Council of Troyes in 1128, which gave the new order the church's official blessing and commissioned St Bernard of Clairvaux to draw up a Rule for them.

This Rule consists of seventy-two articles which outlined the order's basic structure. Initially there were two classes: knights and sergeants, or serving brothers, corresponding to the professed monks and lay brothers of non-military monastic orders. Entrant knights had to be old enough to bear arms, of noble and legitimate birth; sergeants had likewise to be old enough to bear arms, and to be of legitimate birth, though not all were noblemen, indeed, the vast majority were the vassals of noblemen. There were to be no associate houses for women, and this total rejection of women was symbolized by the white surcoat the brethren wore over their armour. Sergeants wore a black or brown mantle, reflecting their more lowly social status. Married brothers were allowed affiliation to the order, but they were not permitted to wear the white habit, though marriage did not prevent them attaining the very highest rank in the order, and, indeed, there was more than one grand master who had been married and begotten children earlier in his life. Such men had either dissolved their marriages, their wives entering nunneries, or they were widowers when they joined the order. The order, like other monastic orders, owned houses, lands, retainers and serfs for its support. Grants of land from pious wellwishers soon established a solid economic background, which in time grew to vast proportions.

Templars embodied many of the cherished beliefs of the age. Many were men of little education with no aptitude for the contemplative life, whose main skill was fighting. They were attracted by the prospect of action leading to eternal salvation. They were irrevocably tied to the crusading movement, and when that movement's impetus was lost, their usefulness and *raison d'être* ended. It is no accident that the order was dissolved within twenty-five years of the fall of Acre and the final defeat of the crusading enterprise in the East.

By the middle of the twelfth century the order had not only acquired vast estates but also much liquid capital. Soon the fighting knights were outnumbered many times over by a large body of officials, bailiffs, craftsmen and other associates. The brethren began to finance lay crusades, and in a surprisingly short time the order took on the role of European banker-in-chief. This was the logical consequence of the order's military and international character. Monasteries had traditionally guarded valuables for the laity and had lent money on their security. The Templars had the added advantage of owning numerous strongholds, not only in the West but in the Holy Land, where the massive remains of their huge fortresses bear witness to their strength. Here they could keep cash, bonds and deeds in safety, and when it was necessary to move them around, men were on hand to protect them. Within eighty years of its foundation the order had become an international corporation, and by the middle of the thirteenth century it was managing the financial affairs of kingdoms.

The order's possessions were divided into eight langues or linguistic regions according to nationality, and ten provinces which ignored state boundaries, especially in France. The chief house of each langue was called a grand priory, and was directly subordinate to the grand master. The langues in order of seniority were Provence, Auvergne, France, Italy, Aragon (which comprised Navarre, Catalonia, Roussillon and Sardinia), England (including Scotland and Ireland), Germany (a highly complex langue made up of Upper and Lower Germany, Hungary, Bohemia, Poland, Denmark and Sweden) and Castile (made up of León, Portugal, Algarve, Granada, Toledo, Galicia and Andalusia). The ten provinces mentioned in the French Rule, which had been drawn up in 1140 to supplement St Bernard's Rule, are listed as Jerusalem, Tripoli in Syria, Antioch, France, England, Poitou, Anjou, Portugal, Apulia and Hungary. Each province had its own master and commander who headed the local hierarchy of commanders of individual houses. France was divided into five commanderies or grand commanderies. These were the Grand Commandery of France (the area around Paris known as the Ile de France) with its headquarters at the Temple in Paris; Champagne with headquarters at Voulaine-les Templiers near Châtillon-sur-Seine and in the diocese of Langres (in an enclave of Champagne surrounded on all sides by Burgundian territory); Poitou and Aquitaine governed from Poitiers; Auvergne governed from Angoulême; and Provence-Languedoc from St Gilles-du-Gard and Montpellier. Germany had two grand commanderies and one commandery with headquarters at Mainz, Magdeburg (later moved to Halberstadt), and Trier respectively. Hungary was a province on its own, but closely associated with the German commanderies because it was part of the same langue.

Ordinary chapters met weekly, the quorum being four. Provincial chapters met when there were important matters to discuss concerning the province or langue. General chapters consisted of the grand master's council, and were made up of baillis, or heads of langues, Sub-baillis, commanders of all kinds and a certain number of knights elected by the others. Each province had its own master or commander, who headed the local hierarchy of commanders or preceptors of the individual houses. During the thirteenth century the post of Visitor of the Order was created, second only to that of the grand master himself.

When a grand master died, a special chapter was held to elect a successor in accordance with detailed and complex rules. The marshal of the order organized the funeral ceremonies and informed the commanders of provinces, ordering them to attend a council to nominate a temporary grand commander. On the day fixed for the election of the grand master, the temporary grand commander assisted by several dignitaries appointed two or three brothers, from whom the council elected an electoral commander. The council appointed him an adjutant, with whom he spent the rest of the day and the night discussing the election.[2] The next day at midday the commander and his adjutant called two other brethren to join them, and these four elected two others until there were twelve of them, symbolizing the apostles. They then elected a chaplain to symbolize Christ. This elective body presented itself to the chapter and then retired to deliberate. The grand master was chosen by a simple majority and the thirteen electors returned to the chapter to announce their decision.

In the early days general chapter meetings were held in Jerusalem; weekly chapters were compulsory for the brethren in local preceptories, where general business and matters of discipline were dealt with, so long as they were of a minor nature. Serious offences such as sodomy, simony, heresy, treason or the revelation of chapter secrets were submitted to higher authority.

The admission of postulants took place at weekly chapters. If a majority of the brethren agreed, the candidate was brought into the chapter to be examined by two or three senior brothers. If his answers were satisfactory, which meant that he was a free man, noble, fit and of legitimate birth, he was brought before the master where he then vowed obedience, chastity and poverty; to follow the usage and custom of the house; and to help to conquer the Holy Land. After this he was formally admitted to the order, and the white mantle was placed on his shoulders. The brother-priest then spoke Psalm 133: '*Ecce quam bonum et quam jocundum habitare fratres in unum* – Behold how good and how pleasant it is for brethren to dwell together in unity. It is like the precious ointment upon the head, that ran down upon the beard, even Aaron's beard: that went down to the skirts of his garments; as the dew of Hermon, and as the dew that descended upon the mountains of Zion: for there the Lord commanded blessing, even life evermore.'

Then the master or preceptor raised him up by the hand and kissed him on the mouth, followed by the priest and the rest of the brethren present.

Much has been made of the supposed obscenity of the Templar Initiation and of the kissing that formed part of it. In fact it differed very little from the everyday practice of the time whereby the bond between lord and vassal was affirmed by the ceremony of homage. Here the vassal knelt, placed his clasped hands within those of his master, and declared: 'Lord, I become your man', and took an oath of fealty. The lord then raised him to his feet and bestowed on him a ceremonial kiss. The vassal was thenceforth bound 'to love what his lord loved and to loathe what he loathed, and never by word or deed do aught that could grieve him'.

The second-in-command of the order was the seneschal. Not much

Exposition of the Shroud at
Turin, 1931.

Geoffrey II de Charny.
From his tombstone (now
destroyed) in the Abbey of
Froidmont, near Beauvais.
(*Bibliothèque Nationale*)

Painting of the Besançon Shroud.

'Lamentation at Nerezi', 1164, showing Christ wrapped in a shroud decorated with a trelliswork pattern.

Resurrection at
Mileševa, *c.* 1235,
showing a folded
Shroud.

16th-century Shroud
painting by Giulio
Clovio.

'Women carrying oil to the Sepulchre', 15th century. The Sindon and Sudarion are shown folded on a rock. (*Russian Museum, Leningrad*)

Nottingham alabaster entitled 'John the Baptist'. (*Burrell Collection, Glasgow*)

Mont–Saint-Jean: (*above*) the
Church and Castle; (*right*) a
Calvaire.

Former Templar Preceptory of Bure-les-Templiers, Burgundy.

Templar Church of Thoisy-le-Désert, Burgundy.

Château de Montfort where the Shroud was kept between 1418 and its transfer to St Hippolyte-sur-Doubs, and perhaps between 1307 and its transfer to Lirey.

The 19th-century Church at Lirey.

The Church of
Akheiropoeitos,
Salonika: the
interior.

The Shroud
Chapel.

The 19th-century
Epitaphioi.

is known about the holders of this office because, like vice-presidents of the United States, they held it as deputies for the grand master, into whose shoes they often stepped.

The marshal was responsible for discipline. He held the black and white Templar banner in battle, was responsible for the horses, armour, harness, arms and general military equipment. He took care of the booty and bought all the supplies for the house or commandery. He could hold chapters when both the master (or grand master) and seneschal were absent, or during the time before a grand master had been appointed. After taking the advice of the brethren he could appoint the gonfanonier, or standard bearer and the sub-marshal, who were always brother sergeants.

Next in the hierarchy came the treasurer of the order, who in the early days always held the post of Commander of the Terre de Jerusalem, but later that of Commander of France. From the beginning of the thirteenth century the Trésor Royal of the King of France was already administered by the Temple, an arrangement which lasted for more than a century, and which made of the Templar treasurer an officer of the French state. Up to 1227 Frère Aymard was a financial adviser much listened to by Philip Augustus, Louis VIII and the young Louis IX (Saint Louis). From 1228 the treasurer was Jean de Milly, who retained the post till 1236. The treasurer was not only responsible to the order, but as the king's chief financial adviser he was a royal servant too.

By 1179 the order's wealth and power had increased to the point where Pope Alexander III thought it necessary to legislate to restrict its privileges and against the abuses which arose from them. Between 1199 and 1210 Innocent III several times warned that violence was not to be done to the Templars, their men or their property, and condemned the order at the same time for its pride and its abuse of the privileges it enjoyed. None of this would have been necessary had the brethren been universally popular, or behaved in a way that did not provoke resentment against them. By 1265 it was necessary for the pope to remind the grand master that if the Church ceased to protect the order from prelates and princes, it could not sustain their attacks, and he went on to suggest that the brethren display more humility.

Throughout the latter part of the thirteenth century there was a growing disenchantment with the crusading movement, brought about to a large extent by the onset of economic collapse which came to a head in France in the middle of the following century. When the Templars were driven out of the Holy Land in 1291 no one saw this as the final demise of the crusading effort, though in fact that is what it was. The ever-increasing wealth of the order, combined with the King of France's ever-increasing need for money, spelt the doom of the order. Suddenly in the early hours of Friday 13 October 1307, the Templars of France were arrested on the orders of King Philip the Handsome in the name of the Inquisition. Their property was taken over by royal agents, and they were charged with heresy, indecent and unnatural sexual practices, blasphemy and idolatry. In the course of the following six weeks the arrested brethren, who included, of course, all the order's senior officers, were tortured and then confessed their guilt almost to a man. The only senior member to escape arrest was the Commander of the Paris Temple who was also the senior officer of the Province of France, Gérard de Villiers. The efficiency of the royal government was demonstrated by the simultaneous arrest of nearly all the Templars in France during that October night. No modern dictatorship could have done better. Pope Clement V, a Frenchman, won a few face-saving concessions, since the order was directly responsible to the papacy, and hence outside the royal jurisdiction.

Philip the Handsome had expelled the Jews and confiscated their wealth in 1306, and was now looking around for a new source to plunder. He had tried the age-old trick of devaluing the currency, but that failed, as it usually does. In fact the suppression of the Templars did not provide the answer he was looking for because the bulk of their wealth was based on mortgaged land, and they had very little portable wealth in the shape of gold or movable assets.

Most Arthurian scholars say that the association of the Templars with the Grail and the Knights of the Round Table is no more than guesswork, in spite of the fact that Wolfram von Eschenbach describes the Grail knights as *Templeisen*. This is the German translation of the Latin word *Templarius*, which can be found in many thirteenth-century documents, but which by the fifteenth century had come to mean Knight of the Order of the Temple. Earlier usage, as in Wolfram's day, was more general, and the word could stand for a servant or any official having to do with a temple, and by extension, with a church. The word *templum* in the twelfth century meant both a temple and a church, and in certain contexts, of course, the Temple of Solomon in Jerusalem. So in Wolfram's time, namely within eighty or ninety years of the order's foundation, it is by no means clear whether he wished to indicate that the Grail knights were Templars or merely servants of the Church. Having said that, it is, perhaps, more significant that Wolfram's Grail knights, like the historical Templars, are described as wearing white surcoats on which were red crosses. If

Wolfram meant his knights to be considered as Templars, and if he was basing his story on historical facts, then the Templars must have been the owners or guardians of the Grail, and hence of the Shroud, before the time Wolfram wrote his poem: in other words before about 1205. All the evidence shows that they could not have been, for these relics were safe in Constantinople until April 1204. So on balance I concluded that the Arthurian scholars are right, and that Wolfram is not writing about the Templars when he calls his Grail knights *Templeisen*.

On the other hand, Ian Wilson believed that the Templars did own the Shroud before it passed into the hands of the de Charnys, and if so, then they probably owned the Grail casket in which it was kept. This raised a lot more questions. How did they obtain it? When and where did they obtain it? Did they obtain the Shroud without the Grail? Was the Shroud the mysterious 'idol' they were accused of worshipping? If they owned the Shroud at all, why was the fact not better known? Could the 'idol', which was sometimes described as a 'head', be the Soudarion and not the Sindon/Shroud? Was there any evidence that the Veronica which I identified as the Soudarion, and which was in Rome at least until the fifteenth and sixteenth centuries, had reached there through the agency of the Templars?

I found the answer to one of these questions in Montpellier, after spending a week combing the Archives Départmentales and reading accounts of the trial of the Templars.[3]

In the early autumn of 1307 King Philip the Handsome stayed two weeks at his favourite abbey, Maubuisson, a few miles north of Paris. He had with him a number of close advisers with whom he discussed his plans to suppress the order. He encountered some opposition from the Archbishop of Narbonne, Gilles Aycelin, who pointed out that it was in the power of the pope alone to act against the Templars. The king's lay advisers were more subtle. They said that he could proceed against the French Templars as individuals, and this advice he accepted. Accordingly an order was signed about 23 September 1307 for the arrest of every Templar in France, and instructions were sent in the strictest secrecy to all the seneschals of France telling them to move against the order in the early hours of Friday 13 October and to seize everything of value in its houses.

Earlier that year the king had met the pope and compelled him to agree to the overthrow of the order. But before complying with the king's request, the pope played for time and demanded proof of the crimes with which the king was accusing the Templars. Such 'proof' was cooked up so that the pope could support the king with a clear conscience. The Templar habit of keeping its ceremonies secret gave rise to fantastic rumours, and these had increased both in number and fantasy in proportion to the order's ever-increasing wealth and power. The Templars' unpopularity was inevitable, and arose from the way in which the order had become wealthy. In order to get round the Church's ban on usury, the brethren advanced money on the security of estates and other realizable valuables, such as jewels and relics. Borrowers did not pay any interest on the money they were lent, but they had to transfer their property to the order, which in turn allowed them the use of it for life; the order only took possession of it on the borrower's death. This had the effect of dispossessing heirs, who were not unnaturally resentful. As large numbers of kings, princes and noblemen had raised money in this way to finance their crusading endeavours, and had not returned to their native land, their sons and heirs suddenly found themselves at best tenants of their ancestral estates, at worst dispossessed of them altogether. In such circumstances it is hardly to be wondered that the worst possible construction was put on any real or imagined scandal in which the order might be involved. The most sensational of these scandals concerned a mysterious 'head' or 'idol' the brethren were accused of worshipping, and before which they would throw themselves to the ground with shouts of 'Yallah'.

It shows how hostile public opinion towards the Templars had become that no one thought fit to ask what manner of 'head' it might be that the brethren worshipped. Although the order had been created for the defence of Christian pilgrims and had been inspired by a special devotion to the person of Christ, such was now its unpopularity that people did not hesitate to accept the most improbable explanations.

The trial took place during the years following the mass arrests of 1307, and its proceedings have survived. It must not be forgotten, however, that the answers the brethren gave were obtained after torture and that many of them were in reply to leading questions. One thing is clear: statements given to the Inquisition do not give the impression of being in any way false or designed to mislead. The brethren told the truth so far as they knew it, when it came to the question of idolatry. In assessing the value of these answers to the enquiry I was making, I had to bear in mind the standing of the knight in question. In a strictly hierarchical order, the knowledge of a recently professed brother sergeant, for instance, would be far less than that of a preceptor or master. Furthermore, in an order whose houses were scattered all over western Europe as well as in Cyprus and the Holy Land, only a very small number of knights could have seen the so-called idol, although many might have seen copies of it. Consequently I had to look into the background of each brother before I could come to any conclusions about the nature and whereabouts of the idol. On matters such as this depended my ability to say whether it was the Grail, the Sindon or the Soudarion, or something else altogether.

Take the evidence of Brother Jean Taillefer of Genay, for example. He was received into the order at Mormant, one of the three preceptories under the jurisdiction of the Grand Priory of Champagne at Voulaine. He said at his initiation 'an idol representing a human face' was placed on the altar before him. Hugues de Bure, another Burgundian from a daughter house of Voulaine, described how the 'head' was taken out of a cupboard, or aumbry, in the chapel, and that it seemed to him to be of gold or silver, and to represent the head of a man with a long beard. Brother Pierre d'Arbley suspected that the 'idol' had two faces, and his kinsman Guillaume d'Arbley made the point that the 'idol' itself, as distinct from copies, was exhibited at general chapters, implying that it was only shown to senior members of the order on special occasions.

Among those who confessed nothing, and who were steadfast in their denial of any irregularities in the manner of receptions or in the conduct of religious ceremonies, were Jean de Châteauvillars, Henri de Hercigny, Jean de Paris and Lambert de Thoisy, all of whom came from houses in Burgundy under the jurisdiction of Voulaine. Jean de Châteauvillars, like the others, was a young man – in his case aged thirty – and a knight (and so a nobleman), who had been received at Mormant four years before. (See Appendix B.)

Brother Pierre-Regnier de Larchent said that although he had never seen the 'idol' (he came from a house in the diocese of Sens outside the jurisdiction of Voulaine) he believed it was always kept in the custody of the grand master, or the brother who presided at general chapters, usually the seneschal in the absence of the grand master. This evidence indirectly confirmed the statements of other brethren who said they had never seen the 'idol' because they had never attended a general chapter. Brother Jean-Denis de Tavernay said that Guillaume de Beaujeu, who was grand master from 1273 to 1291, and Hugues de Pairaud, who was seneschal of the order from 1291 (and later master of England for several years, and who narrowly failed to be elected grand master in 1292) were the first to hold special chapters at which the 'idol' was exhibited.

The treasurer of the Paris temple, Jean de Turn, spoke of a painted head in the form of a picture, which he had adored at one of these

87

chapters. Since all who attended them agreed without dissent that they were held shortly before dawn, it is hardly surprising that their descriptions, given the dim light in the chapels in which they were held, are somewhat vague. In the prevailing gloom it would have been very difficult to see the face on the Shroud (always assuming that the 'idol' and the Shroud were one and the same) or indeed the features of a painting. But it struck both Tony Kildwick and me that the timing of these ceremonies was significant, for it suggests that the rising sun was linked symbolically with Christ rising from the tomb. While such symbolism would have had great meaning for those in the secret of the 'idol's' identity, it is not hard to see why those who were not might have regarded the whole business with grave suspicion.

There was another point which I missed, but which Tony spotted. When the moment came for the postulant to take his vows, he was required to place his hand not on the Bible, which was the usual practice, but on the Missal open at the point in the Mass where the body of Christ is mentioned. Several brother priests, such as Bertrand de Villers and Etienne de Dijon, both from the diocese of Langres, said that at the point in the Mass where the Host is consecrated they were told to omit the words *Hoc est enim corpus meum*. Could this, Tony asked, be because the Shroud was thought of as being the officiating priest, thus rendering the human priest superfluous? In other words, was it Christ offering his body, the Host, to the communicants?

Finally there was the apparently absurd accusation that the 'idol' was the head of a bearded woman. Nearly all the brethren agreed that the head was bearded and had long hair, and the Templars, like the majority of their contemporaries, regarded long hair as effeminate, so the length of the 'idol's' hair was remarkable for this, if for no other reason. The head of the man on the Shroud has not only long hair and a longish beard, but the dorsal image shows that he wore a pigtail. There is something curiously modern about this, when one recalls the outrage of the conventional, when young men began to wear their hair long in the 1960s and 1970s.

The charges against the order were listed under seven broad headings. Those concerning the 'idol' are worth quoting in full, for they helped to point us in the direction we later followed, and go some way to explain the answers I have just quoted.

1. That in each province the order had idols, namely heads, of which some had three faces and some one, and others had a human skull.
2. That they adored these idols or that idol, and especially in their great chapters and assemblies.

3. That they venerated (them).
4. That (they venerated them) as God.
5. That (they venerated them) as their Saviour.
6. That some of them (did).
7. That the majority of those who were in the chapter (did).
8. That they said that the head could save them.
9. That (it could) make them rich.
10. That it had given the order all its riches.
11. That it made the trees flower.
12. That (it made) the land germinate.
13. That they surrounded or touched each head of the aforesaid idols with small cords, which they wore around themselves next to the shirt or the flesh.
14. That in his reception, the aforesaid small cords or some lengths of them were given to each of the brethren.
15. That they did this in veneration of an idol.
16. That they (the receptors) enjoined them (the postulants) on oath not to reveal the aforesaid to anyone.

These were clearly not random charges, but a deliberate attempt to play on the prejudices and superstitions of contemporaries. It is completely in line with countless political and religious trials since. Although they are grotesque in many respects, these charges can be partly explained by reference to the Shroud/Sindon. When asked to describe the 'idol' some said the head was black, others white, and some that it was silver or gold. One brother described the eyes as 'flamboyant like carbuncles'; another saw two faces; yet another described three heads. Some thought it had two legs, others said two parts of legs, and one even went so far as to say it resembled a cat. Indeed the brownish tinge of the Shroud is not very different from the colouring of a ginger tom. There were some brothers who thought the 'idol' was a carved statue, others a painting, one that it represented Christ, another Mahomet or Baphomet, yet another thought it represented John the Baptist.

Surely this evidence suggests that copies of the head, perhaps some of them not unlike the Sainte Face de Laon, others of carved stone or alabaster, such as those of the Nottingham School of the fourteenth and fifteenth centuries, were widely distributed throughout the order's houses. This would at least explain why nothing resembling a pagan idol was found after the brethren had been arrested, and why none of the pictures found in their chapels raised so much as an eyebrow. The Nottingham alabaster images are still entitled St John the Baptist because the nimbus behind Christ's head resembles a dish.

Many of them combine the head with a much smaller image of the upper part of Christ's body emerging from a shallow, rectangular box, and some have a third, even smaller image, above the central head. A complex carving like this, seen in the gloom of a chapel lit only by candles, could easily have been mistaken for an 'idol' by the ill-disposed. Though these English alabasters date from a period after the Templars were disbanded, there were continental versions of an earlier date. If such devotional carvings had been thought to be in any way out of the ordinary, the royal authorities, not to mention the ecclesiastical, would have produced them as evidence against the order, for it is inconceivable that all of them were hidden or destroyed before the king's men carried out the arrests on 13 October 1307.

Although these ceremonies were held at night and in the greatest secrecy, there is no evidence for believing that they were in any way heretical, but they may have differed in minor ways from those of other monastic orders. On the other hand, the very fact that they were surrounded by so much secrecy made everyone highly suspicious of them. Far from being satanic, the Templar head was something so sacred that the secrecy surrounding it can only be explained by recognizing the order's need to protect it at all costs. There is certainly nothing extraordinary in surrounding sacred objects with secrecy; it is done all the time to this very day.

So far I have only discussed the evidence of fairly junior members of the order. When we came to look at what its leaders had to say, all doubts about the identity of the 'idol' were put to rest.

In November 1307, about six weeks after the attack on the order, three senior brethren were interrogated after undergoing grievous torture. They were the Grand Master, Jacques de Molay, the Seneschal, Hugues de Pairaud, and the Preceptor of Normandy, Geoffrey de Charny. Questioned about the 'idol', Hugues de Pairaud had this to say:

> He had seen, held and touched it at Montpellier at a chapter there, and that he and the other brethren had adored it. . . . Required to declare the place where it is now, he said that he sent it to Pierre Allemandi, Preceptor of the House of Montpellier, but that he did not know if the king's men found it. He said the 'head' had four feet, two on the front side of the figure and two on the back.[4]

Hugues de Pairaud's evidence was the first breakthrough we had achieved up to that time. Here was a piece of evidence which linked the Shroud to the Templars, for it is an accurate description of the cloth when it is hanging over a bar at the point where the frontal and dorsal images meet. Imagine to yourself what the fully unfolded

Shroud looks like. Suspended in the manner I have just described, as it must have been when it was exposed for veneration during the Good Friday Masses in Constantinople, it is indeed a head 'with four feet, two on the front side of the figure and two on the back'. Nothing could be a more accurate description of it. Yet described as a head with four legs, it takes on an almost obscene character. Hugues de Pairaud, though, was telling the precise truth, but those who had never seen the Shroud, or who were wilfully intent on defaming the order, interpreted his answer in such a way as to conjure up this obscenity. To laymen totally ignorant of the Shroud, this was damning evidence. The Inquisitors who probably knew the truth did nothing to disabuse them.

But this vital piece of evidence did more than confirm that the Templars' 'idol' was really the Shroud: it told us when the relic was at Montpellier. All we had to do now was discover when and how it came there, and when and where it went next.

The Templars of Montpellier were particularly compromised in the eyes of the Inquisitors on account of the 'idol's' presence there. After the fall of Acre in 1291, and due to its geographical situation, Montpellier became briefly the *de-facto* headquarters of the order, and the site of the important general chapter of 1293. The evidence of brethren who were stationed there consequently became more significant. Brother Bernard de Selgues, head of the preceptory of nearby St Gilles, and thus a senior member of the order, said that he had taken part in many provincial chapters, and that at one of them held at Montpellier, which assembled at night 'according to custom' '*on y exposa un chef ou une tête*'. The use of the word *chef* in this context is interesting. Its usual meaning, of course, is chief or head, but it can also mean a reliquary, and it is not unreasonable to translate Brother Bernard's statement as 'they exposed there a reliquary or a head', which the brethren had adored.

Brother Raoul de Gise confirmed Hugues de Pairaud's evidence, but added that the 'idol' had a terrible countenance, and that when they were shown it they all prostrated themselves on the ground and pulled their cowls over their heads. No wonder they were unable to describe it precisely. Brother Raimond de Fabre de Montbazon said he had attended about ten general chapters of the order at Montpellier, which were usually attended by senior brethren from far and wide. He mentioned one in particular, held on 9 May 1284 and attended by Pierre Allemandi, who was then commander or master of the province of Provence. The general chapter of 1293 was held under the chairmanship of the Grand Master, Jacques de Molay, and the last one he had attended was in 1305 under the then Master of Provence, Guige d'Adhemar.

Because of its geographical situation, Tony and I guessed that the Templars had brought the Shroud to Montpellier from Constantinople. We were wrong, as it turned out, but at that stage of our search it seemed the most plausible explanation. The evidence we had found so far amounted to this: When Acre fell in May 1291 the order had been expelled from the Holy Land. The grand master at that time was Guillaume de Beaujeu, who had died bravely defending the city against the infidels. Brother Jean-Denis de Tavernay had said that it was de Beaujeu who was the first to hold special chapters in honour of the 'idol'. Since he was elected in May 1273, we had a date before which it might have been in other hands. What clues did his career offer us? Guillaume de Beaujeu was the fourth son of Guichard de Beaujeu, Seigneur de Montpensier et Montferrand (see Table 3). His maternal grandmother was Elisabeth de Mont-Saint-Jean, Dame d'Ancy-le-Franc, through whom he was a second cousin of Geoffrey de Charny, Porte Oriflamme de France, the Shroud's owner in 1353. Like many other of the order's leaders he was a Burgundian. His uncle, Humbert de Beaujeu, was Constable of France, and his cousin, Guichard IV, was the French ambassador to England.

Before his election as grand master, Guillaume de Beaujeu had been Commander of the Province of Apulia in southern Italy. In May 1274 he attended the Council of Lyon, whose chief purpose was the reunification of the Eastern and Western Churches, but whose secondary was the preaching of a new crusade. Between 1275 and 1283 he was in the East. He spent little more than a year in France after his election, so assuming that his institution of the special chapters for the 'idol' took place while he was in France, this must have been during 1274. On the other hand, if the Shroud/'idol' was in Acre at the Templars' headquarters there, then these chapters must have been instituted between 1275 and 1283. At that stage of our search there seemed to be no way of deciding.

Thibaud Gaudin, Beaujeu's successor, was elected grand master in Cyprus in August 1291. His tenure of office was brief and spent entirely in the East. After the fall of Acre Thibaud embarked with the remnants of the knights, the archives and the holy vases and retreated to the castle of Sayette, where his election took place. By April 1292 he was dead.

Jacques de Molay, twenty-third and last Grand Master of the Templars, was born about 1244. He was received into the order by Amaury de la Roche, Master of France and Commander of the Terre

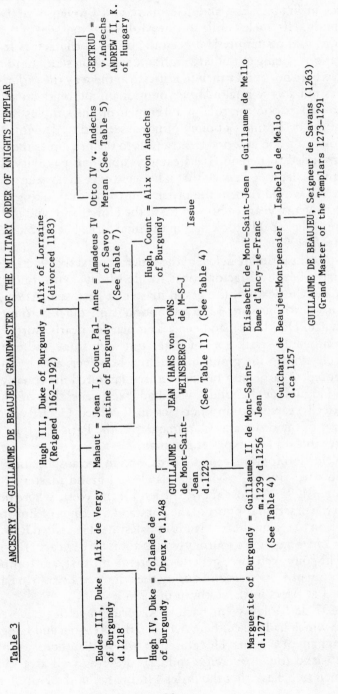

Table 3   ANCESTRY OF GUILLAUME DE BEAUJEU, GRANDMASTER OF THE MILITARY ORDER OF KNIGHTS TEMPLAR

Eudes III, Duke = Alix de Vergy
of Burgundy
d.1218

Hugh III, Duke of Burgundy = Alix of Lorraine
(Reigned 1162–1192)   (divorced 1183)

Hugh IV, Duke = Yolande de
of Burgundy   Dreux, d.1248

Mahaut = Jean I, Count Pal-   Anne = Amadeus IV
              atine of Burgundy   of Savoy
                                                     (See Table 7)

GERTRUD =
v.Andechs
ANDREW II, K.
of Hungary

Otto IV v. Andechs
Meran (See Table 5)

Hugh, Count = Alix von Andechs
of Burgundy

Issue

GUILLAUME I   JEAN (HANS von
de Mont-Saint-   WEINSBERG)
Jean   (See Table 11)
d.1223

PONS
de M-S-J
(See Table 4)

Marguerite of Burgundy = Guillaume II de Mont-Saint-
d.1277   m.1239 d.1256   Jean
                                        (See Table 4)

Elisabeth de Mont-Saint-Jean = Guillaume de Mello
Dame d'Ancy-le-Franc

Guichard de Beaujeu-Montpensier = Isabelle de Mello
d.ca 1257

GUILLAUME DE BEAUJEU, Seigneur de Savans (1263)
Grand Master of the Templars 1273–1291

93

de Jerusalem, and by Humbert de Pairaud, Visitor General of Temple Houses in France, England, Germany and Provence, at Beaune in Burgundy. His uncle Guillaume de Molay was marshal of the order at the time, and his family had been the order's benefactors for several generations. Being a trained knight, he was soon sent out to the Holy Land, where he found much to criticize in the way the order was run. He was not a very imaginative young man, although an active one, and he understood the role of a Templar on the simplest level only. Guillaume de Beaujeu's policy of peace seemed to de Molay to be at best cowardly and at worst treacherous to the principles the order had been founded to defend. De Beaujeu's apparent passivity disgusted him, and he let it be known that if he were ever to have any say in the matter, he would reform the order to his way of thinking. He spent the first twenty years of his service in the Holy Land, and in 1285 was in Acre and probably took part in the final futile but heroic defence of the city in 1291.

Despite the ultimate defeat of the order, the last six years in Palestine must have been satisfactory ones for de Molay, with much military action and the death of the grand master he despised. After Thibaud Gaudin's death in April 1292 promotion came quickly to men of his experience. De Molay had been a Templar for nearly thirty years by then, and could speak convincingly and with some authority.

His election to the grand mastership, however, was by no means unopposed. A large number of brethren favoured the equally experienced Hugues de Pairaud, who had been seneschal of the order for sixteen years, and another faction favoured Gérard de Villiers, treasurer of the order and Commander of the Paris Temple, a rather younger but no less experienced man.

The election took place in Cyprus, and in the absence in France of his two chief rivals, de Molay was elected grand master in the late autumn of 1292. Almost at once he left for the West, where he set out to gain the practical support of the pope and the kings of Europe for an expedition to regain the lost lands in Palestine. He visited Italy, Spain, France and England, a journey which took three years. During that period he convoked three general chapters – the first, at Montpellier in the autumn of 1293, a second during the winter of 1295–6 in Paris, and the third at Arles in the autumn of 1296.

In 1297 de Molay went back to Cyprus to settle, if he could, a dispute which had arisen there between the brethren and King Henry II (Lusignan) of Cyprus. He refused to believe that there was no room on the island for a sovereign military order as well as a king, and continued to believe that the order's future lay in the Holy Land. He

94

decided, therefore, that it should remain in Cyprus until it had regained some portion of the mainland, and to this end he organized a feeble expedition to capture an island off Tripoli which he envisaged as a base for further operations. It was a catastrophic failure.

De Molay's was a greatly mistaken policy, and the brethren looked in vain for the reforms they had expected. But the strange difference between de Molay's words as a young knight and his deeds as grand master was due entirely to his somewhat limited intelligence. His earlier criticisms sprang more from a lack of imagination and narrowness of character than from any deep understanding of the problems facing the order. When he became grand master, he found out too late how much easier it is to criticize than to act constructively. As he grew older his intolerance and youthful energy gave way to bigotry and conservatism. One of his contemporaries described him as *ladre* (stingy), for he was essentially small-minded in matters of money and unwilling to spend it when it could have been of lasting advantage, preferring always to economize and take the short-term view. Worst of all, he was incapable of compromise or of making any concessions to his critics.

This, then, was the man Pope Clement V summoned to Europe in 1306: an elderly, old-fashioned martinet, who had spent all his adult life soldiering; a man of simple ideas, narrow-minded, who saw little need to change the organization of which he was the head, and whose notions of reform were limited to cheese-paring economies and a demand for blind obedience. He would have found himself completely at home on the French General Staff of the 1930s.[5] When he arrived in France late in 1306 or early in 1307, Jacques de Molay did not consider that there was anything fundamentally wrong with the order or with the way he governed it.

The pope had asked de Molay to visit him incognito and with as small a retinue as possible. The grand master thought otherwise, arriving with sixty knights and a baggage train of gold and jewels. Did he also bring the Shroud? Ian Wilson thought so, and so did I. In the light of evidence we had amassed so far, it seemed likely. But we were wrong, for although there is no direct evidence to tell us what happened to the relic at this time, later discoveries pointed strongly in other directions.

Clement V was at Poitiers when the grand master landed in France. But confident of a good reception from the pope, de Molay went first to Paris to seek support for another crusade from King Philip the Handsome. With his knights and his treasure safely installed in the Paris Temple, de Molay went to see the king. It was probably the first time they had met, and the parsimonious old Templar was well aware of the extravagant king's constant need of money, and felt that he and his order, holding as they did the royal purse strings, were in the stronger position in any negotiations which might take place. Philip, for his part, received the grand master with the honour due to his office, but speedily realized that, for all his age and experience, de Molay was a naïve old man who accepted things at face value. The interview ended to the satisfaction of both men. The wily king had learnt all he needed to know about the man who commanded the order, and de Molay went off to Poitiers blithely unaware that relations between the king and the Templars would be anything but of the most cordial. For more than a century the French royal treasury had been housed in the Paris Temple, and as recently as 1304 the king had confirmed all the order's rights and privileges. With papal support, let alone the privileges enjoyed by men of the Church, what had the order to fear? During his long absences overseas de Molay was sublimely confident that his seneschal, Hugues de Pairaud and the order's treasurer and Commander of the Paris Temple, Gérard de Villiers, had maintained harmonious relations with the Crown and the royal Court. He was deeply mistaken.

Hugues de Pairaud was about the same age as Jacques de Molay, and had been received into the order in 1265 by his uncle, Humbert de Pairaud, the then visitor general, who had also been one of de Molay's receptors. Hugues de Pairaud had risen quickly in rank, and by 1269 had been Preceptor of La Rochelle. Soon after he was appointed Master of the London Temple, and by 1291 had become seneschal of the order, an office he held in addition to his Mastership of England. In de Molay's absence, he had virtually governed the order on both sides of the Channel, and had conducted many receptions and held frequent chapters. He had received fifteen knights personally in the last twenty-two years, and no other leader was so closely connected with the reception ceremony as he. In the course of his career, he had visited many houses in his official capacity, which accounts for the testimony of many witnesses who said that at chapter meetings over which he presided he had brought in a 'head' for worship. But each witness's description of this object differed from the others. Philip the Handsome had appointed him receiver and warden of the royal revenues and he was an intimate of the French Court. His failure to be elected grand master in 1293 was not only a misfortune for the order, but also from his own point of view. He attributed it to intrigues on de Molay's behalf by the powerful faction who had seen service in the Holy Land, and who were mistrustful of the brethren who had remained in Europe. After the election de Pairaud had overtly obeyed de Molay, but privately he had gone his own way. In August 1303, for instance, he had signed a personal agreement with the king of mutual defence and support and specifically against Pope Boniface VIII, whom de Molay had helped to elect, and who was Philip's bitter enemy. The grand master was completely unaware of this when he went to see Pope Clement at Poitiers in May 1307. This pope was cast in a very different mould from his predecessor. A Frenchman, by name Bertrand de Goth, he had been Archbishop of Bordeaux before his election (as a result of pressures brought to bear by King Philip on the College of Cardinals) who, during the nineteen months of his pontificate, had already submitted time and time again to the imperious will of the French king. He was prepared to knuckle under again now that the king had decided to attack the Templars and to confiscate their wealth, though not unconditionally.

Before de Molay went to see the pope, Clement and Philip had had a meeting at which the king had given the incredulous pontiff a long list of horrendous accusations against the order, which he had demanded the pope investigate immediately. They were of such a fantastic nature that only two interpretations seemed possible to Clement: either the king was off his head, or the Templars were greater traitors than Judas Iscariot. This placed the pope in a serious dilemma, for if the charges could be substantiated, the king's power over the Church and the papacy would be supreme: if, on the other hand, the knights were exonerated it would be their triumph, not the Church's, and they would almost certainly launch a war of revenge against the French monarch. In that event the unscrupulous king, whose hands were not entirely innocent of the blood of one pope, would fight as viciously as a cornered animal.

When Pope Clement told de Molay what had transpired at his interview with the king, the grand master was outraged. He returned to Paris more puzzled than alarmed, however, secure in the belief that the order would not be attacked since it enjoyed the special protection of the papacy – a sad misapprehension in the circumstances. He summoned a general chapter, which met in Paris on 24 July. It took place as usual in strict secrecy, so no report of its proceedings exists, but soon afterwards a circular was sent to all the preceptories in France forbidding any brother to speak of the order's rites and practices to any outsider as the Rule laid down: a sure sign that the accusation of idolatry – and hence, indirectly, the position of the Shroud in Templar worship – must have been discussed. Soon after the general chapter, Hugues de Pairaud was heard to say that any Templar who had reason to leave the order should do so swiftly, for a frightful calamity was impending, which shows that he, at least (and almost certainly others) took the threat seriously.

In the light of subsequent events, it seems certain that the safety of the Shroud, in the event of an attack by the king, must have been discussed, and plans made for its removal to a place of safety. It is not known who attended the chapter, but it is probable that apart from the grand master and the seneschal, others would have included the Treasurer and Master of the Paris Temple, Gérard de Villiers, the Preceptor of Normandy, Geoffrey de Charny, possibly the Marshal, formerly the Commander of Etampes, Jean de la Tour, and the commanders of Champagne, Burgundy and Auvergne. I did not then know in what way the Preceptor of Normandy might be related to his namesake, the Geoffrey de Charny in whose church at Lirey the Shroud appeared nearly fifty years later, but the evidence given at his trial gave me some clues for further research.

Geoffrey de Charny[6] was received into the order at Etampes, near Paris, in 1269 or 1270 by Amaury de la Roche, who had been one of de Molay's receptors. At the time of his interrogation by the Inquisition he was fifty-six years old. He was therefore of approximately the same age as de Molay and de Pairaud, and a man with a lifetime's experience in the order. Was it merely coincidental that he had been received into the order by a member of the de la Roche family? And was Amaury de la Roche a collateral ancestor of Humbert de la Roche, Comte de Villersexel, the husband of Marguerite de Charny who gave the Shroud to her kinsman, the Duke of Savoy? As a genealogist I knew that only a study of the families of these men could answer such questions, and I hoped that it would reveal much else that was at present obscure.

By now I felt sure that the Templar's 'idol' was none other than the Shroud of Turin, and that it had been kept in a reliquary which might have been the Holy Grail. It had been produced on special occasions of great solemnity – which was only natural – such as general chapters, and was consequently only seen by senior members of the order, and then only rarely. Clearly copies of both the head and body of Christ had been made and distributed to the major preceptories. Some of these must have been paintings, but others were three-dimensional carvings. The latter had portrayed the head of Christ surrounded by a large disc, which was in reality a representation of the halo, but which could be mistaken for a dish, and hence the head thought of as that of St John the Baptist on its charger. Some of these paintings and sculptures might have represented the Shroud suspended above its casket, the Grail, and when incorporated with the larger head, could be easily mistaken by uninitiated and unsophisticated brethren as an object with more than one head or face, and with more than one set of limbs. In keeping with the artistic style of the time, some of these stone images would have been painted and gilded. All this could account, I felt, for the apparent contradictory evidence given by the brethren – evidence which an ill-disposed examiner could twist to make it sound sinister, heretical and idolatrous. Ian Wilson had drawn attention to one such painted head found near Templecombe in Somerset; the Sainte Face de Laon and paintings of the Veronica image were known to originate during the time of the Templars' greatest power and wealth. Some of them might, indeed, have been commissioned by the order. If they had been, this would explain why, when the preceptories and their chapels were attacked by the royal agents, they found nothing remarkable there, for they were in no way unorthodox.

Hugues de Pairaud had told the Inquisition that he had sent the 'idol' to Montpellier during Pierre Allemandi's term of office. This lasted from 1265 to 1304, and the only recorded general chapter to be held at Montpellier during this time was the one ordered by Jacques de Molay in the autumn of 1293. Since nothing like the Shroud was found in the Montpellier Temple in 1307 (or elsewhere, for that matter) it follows that its sojourn in Montpellier must have been brief. It might have been exposed at the general chapters in Paris during the winter of 1295–6 and in July 1307, but if it was, it seems odd that de Pairaud should have mentioned only the occasion when he adored it at Montpellier fourteen years before.

The order did not feel itself threatened in 1293, so it is probable that the 'idol' was kept somewhere central for use at general chapters. The most obvious place was the Paris Temple, but we could find no evidence for this belief at that stage of our search. De Pairaud said in evidence that he did not know if the king's men had got the Shroud or where it was when he was interrogated. He seems to imply that it might still be in Montpellier, but on the other hand, if there had been a plan to hide it from the royal attack, then he might genuinely not have known. Certainly it was not in Paris in October 1307. We know what de Pairaud did not: the plan to save the Shroud *was* successful, for otherwise it would not be in Turin cathedral today.

But when did the Shroud reach France, and had it come into the possession of the Templars in 1204 immediately after the sack of Constantinople? Ian Wilson thought it had, and if he were right, then it would almost certainly have been taken to the order's headquarters in the Holy Land, then at Acre. But was Ian right? I began to think not, after I had read the evidence of Brother Jean-Denis de Tavernay, who said that Guillaume de Beaujeu was the first grand master to expose the 'idol' at special chapter meetings.

Guillaume de Beaujeu was elected grand master in 1273, nearly seventy years after the sack of Constantinople. His term of office lasted until 1291, so if the Shroud had been in the Templars' hands for all that time, why was it kept hidden for so long? On the other hand, it was possible that the holy cloth had been sent directly to France in 1204: if so where had the Templars kept it, and once again, why did it have to wait till de Beaujeu's time before being shown? Of course, Brother Jean-Denis was not a very senior member of the order, and he could have been mistaken. On the other hand, he was another Burgundian (he came from near Autun) and his evidence suggests that he had seen the 'idol' itself rather than a copy.

The secrecy with which the royal attack was launched against the order was such that only a handful of knights escaped arrest. There is no doubt that de Pairaud guessed what was afoot, even if he wasn't sure when the attack would come. Gérard de Villiers was the only senior member of the order not to be arrested. I felt convinced that those who planned the rescue were led by de Villiers, and that de Charny must have summoned help from his kinsman, Jean de Charny (I was only much later able to say with some confidence that Jean and Geoffrey were brothers). All this suggested to me that the Shroud must have been sent to a Templar house in Burgundy or Champagne during the period following the general chapter of July 1307, even if it had not already been sent there after the 1293 chapter in Montpellier.

I decided as a consequence of this that the next stage of my investigation should take place in Burgundy. I would trace the de Charnys' ancestry and examine the history of the Templars in that part of France.

CHAPTER 4

THE PLOT TO SAVE THE SHROUD: 1307

———————•———————

After a long day's ride from Montpellier, Tony and I fetched up at Saulieu and found a comfortable Logis de France there with pleasant rooms and excellent food and wine. The countryside reminded us of Somerset, but on a grander scale; its rounded, wood-covered hills rising to about eighteen hundred feet were friendly and welcoming. It seemed an appropriate setting to be looking for traces of the Holy Grail, for we were not more than twenty-five miles from Autun – the Roman Augustodunum – said by the chronicler Geoffrey of Monmouth to have been the place where King Arthur heard of Guinevere's infidelity and Mordred's treachery. This is what he has to say:

> In the skirmish near Autun, the Romans suffered heavy losses, but Lucius Hiberius bore these disasters well. . . . He swayed this way and that, for he could not make up his mind whether to engage in a full-scale battle with Arthur or to withdraw inside Autun and there await reinforcements. In the end he let his misgivings take the upper hand. The next night he marched his troops into Langres, on his way to the city of Autun. This was reported to King Arthur, who made up his mind to outmarch Lucius. That same night he by-passed Langres on his left and entered a valley called Saussy, through which Lucius would have to pass.[1]

The knights taking part in this battle included Gawain, the king's nephew; Sir Kay, the seneschal; Sir Bedevere, the cup-bearer; and many others. As soon as Arthur had won the battle of Saussy he spent the following winter in this locality, When summer came he made ready to set out for Rome, when news came that his nephew Mordred had placed the crown on his own head and was living adulterously with Queen Guinevere.

Coincidence? Probably, but there was much evidence to suggest that Chrétien de Troyes and the other twelfth-century troubadours of

101

Champagne and Burgundy had not only read Geoffrey of Monmouth's account of the life of King Arthur and the account of his campaigns in Burgundy, but that they had seen in Geoffrey's history a parallel with the Templars of their day. But if my theories were correct, they had written the Grail into the Arthurian stories nearly a century and a quarter before the relic itself came to Burgundy. The enigma was becoming more obscure.

We awoke next morning to another warm, sunny day and left Saulieu by the main road to Arnay-le-Duc. In about three miles we branched off to the left along a minor road which led towards Pouilly-en-Auxois, which brought us to Thoisy-le-Berchère, with its renaiss-

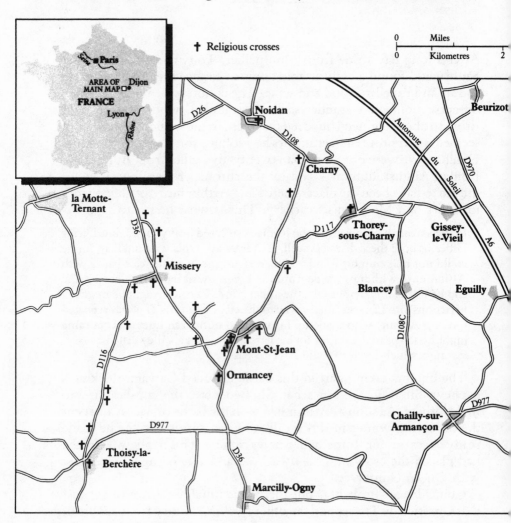

ance château set in a small, compact park on the edge of the village. We had parked the bikes by the churchyard wall, in which we noticed a handsome stone cross of a design more sophisticated and simpler than the usual ugly ones you see in French graveyards. Its slender octagonal shaft and arms were terminated in carved stone rosettes, but instead of the body of Christ crucified there was a small, enshrined statue of the Virgin. As the château was not open to the public, we remounted our bikes and rode out of the village towards the line of hills on the eastern edge of the valley in the direction of the village of Charny. At Ormancey, which lies at the foot of the escarpment below Mont-Saint-Jean, we came upon another stone cross of the same design as the one in Thoisy churchyard standing on a little green; half a mile further on we came across a third, this time without its arms and top, at a crossroads. At the entrance to Mont-Saint-Jean a road joined ours at a sharp angle from the right. It led under shady chestnut trees up to the ruins of the castle gateway, and there, halfway along it, under the shadow of the castle walls, was a fourth cross, similar in every way to the others, except that its base, instead of being a circular drum, resembled a carved stone altar.

We rode into the castle precinct and drew up outside the church which stands on a flat terrace within the castle enceinte, from which the dungeon itself is separated by a dry moat. The view from here was superb, for the castle and church dominated the valley across which we had just ridden, and looked out westward to the Morvan hills in the distance. There was nothing remarkable about the architecture of either building, which together occupied less than half the enclosed, fortified area. Beyond them, to the north, we could see the village astride the crest of a spur jutting out from the main ridge, which rose another hundred feet or so beyond. It was a good defensive position of no special significance, and similar to thousands of others to be found all over France. We were told that the castle had been recently bought and restored by a Parisian judge, and that it was not open to the public. The church key was kept by the curé, who lived in another village, so we had no alternative but to be on our way. On entering the village from the castle ramp we came upon a fifth stone cross like the ones we had already seen, but with a much-worn inscription which read in part 'EREXERAT D.T.....P 1366 REPARUIT C.I.M.P. 1769'. In fact the first date was extremely difficult to read, and might have been 1166, 1266, 1366 or 1466, the second digit being almost totally obscured.

At the further end of the street, where it forked, there was yet another cross of similar design. On its base was carved 'IN HOC SIGNO VINCES. 1894'. On the outskirts of the village we found yet two more crosses; one, a little more elaborate than the rest, stood at the entrance to what had once been a priory, but to which order it belonged we were not able to find out. On leaving Mont-Saint-Jean for Charny, we passed a ninth cross at the top of the hill, called on the map La Croix de St Thomas, likewise restored – in this case in 1825. In Thorey half a mile further on we found a tenth, and yet another in the village of Charny itself. Altogether we found twenty-four crosses that afternoon, all clustered round the hill – La Grande Montagne – on which Charny and Mont-Saint-Jean were situated.

Charny was much smaller than Mont-Saint-Jean, consisting of no more than a dozen not very old houses and an ugly nineteenth-century church. The castle, on the other hand, was much larger than the one at Mont-Saint-Jean. It had been demolished, so I learnt later, on the orders of Louis XIII, and the demolition men had done a thorough job. What is left stands, like its twin, on the edge of an escarpment, but in this case one that dominates the valley of the Armançon, tributary of the Yonne. In its heyday it must have been almost impregnable to judge by the remains of its massive walls and towers. Together the castles of Charny and Mont-Saint-Jean, but three miles apart from each other, on the northern and southern flanks of the plateau, must have presented a formidable obstacle to any attacking army, no matter from which direction it might approach.

But what, we asked ourselves, could the presence of so many wayside crosses mean? In Brittany they are the stages at which pilgrims stop to say prayers on their way to the shrine of some saint. They are found throughout Catholic Europe at crossroads where the wayfarer may make his devotions and fulfil his religious obligations. In most of France such a concentration is exceptional, and indicated to me, at any rate, the erstwhile presence of a shrine or place of pilgrimage. There was a tradition that Mont-Saint-Jean had been such a centre of pilgrimage in the Middle Ages, but this tradition was linked with St Pelagia, a patron saint of youth. These calvaires differed from ones I had seen in Brittany in their utter simplicity. Admittedly most of them had been restored, but it was clear that while the crosses themselves may have been torn down by the Revolutionaries at the end of the eighteenth century, most of the bases were original, and clearly of medieval origin. When later I plotted their position on a large-scale map it was easy to see how they were sited on all the roads leading to the Plateau of Charny–Mont-Saint-Jean. Was this the sanctuary to which the Shroud had been brought in 1307? It was hard to say, but the crosses were a grain of circumstantial evidence in favour of the idea.

The next step in the search was clear: we would see what the

Archives Départmentales of Côte d'Or in Dijon had to tell us about the *calvaires*, and I would trace the ancestry of Geoffrey de Charny and try to find out all I could about the Templars and their houses in Burgundy. This took much longer than either of us anticipated, and it was only after several months and two more visits to Burgundy that I was able to formulate any coherent theory.

Although Geoffrey de Charny was the first owner of the Shroud in modern times, if the relic had formerly belonged to the Templars then I had to find out how it came into his family's possession some forty-five years or more before he built his church for it at Lirey in 1353. Geoffrey himself was certainly not more than ten years old when the Templars in France were dissolved in October 1307. The first step was to study the events of the summer and autumn of that year and to find out which member or members of Geoffrey's family might have obtained the relic; how they got it, and who were the men who plotted to wrest it from under the nose of the greedy king, Philip.

Geoffrey's father Jean, Sire de Charny, married as his first wife Marguerite de Joinville, in about 1294. Her father was Jean de Joinville, the biographer of his king and friend, St Louis. Jean de Joinville was Seneschal of Champagne, an office hereditary in his family, and consequently the man to whom the king's order to arrest all the Templars in Champagne would have been sent. In 1307 he was about eighty-three years old, and in no position to act personally, so he must have deputed this unwelcome order to an underling. Geoffrey's widow, Jeanne de Vergy, played an important part in the decision to exhibit the Shroud at Lirey. Her exact year of birth is unknown, but she was much younger than her husband. She was the daughter of Guillaume de Vergy, Seigneur de Mirebeau, Fontaines-Françaises and Bourbonne, Lieutenant-General of Dauphiné (see Tables 4 and 2). Guillaume's father, Jean de Vergy, Seneschal of Burgundy, was living in 1263 and died in 1310, so he, like his fellow seneschal de Joinville, was also an old man in 1307 when he received the king's orders. He, too, must have deputed the duty of arresting the brethren to a younger man.

Jean de Charny had two brothers, the Templar Preceptor of Normandy, and Dreux de Charny, Seigneur de Savoisy, and a sister, Jeanne de Charny, the wife of Jean de la Fauche, all of whom were living in 1307. In addition to the Templars I have already mentioned as perhaps taking part in a plot to save the Shroud, there were two other men who might have played a part, albeit a minor and negative one. They were Duke Hugh V of Burgundy and Robert, Count-Palatine of Burgundy (now Franche-Comté). By 1307 the county of Champagne

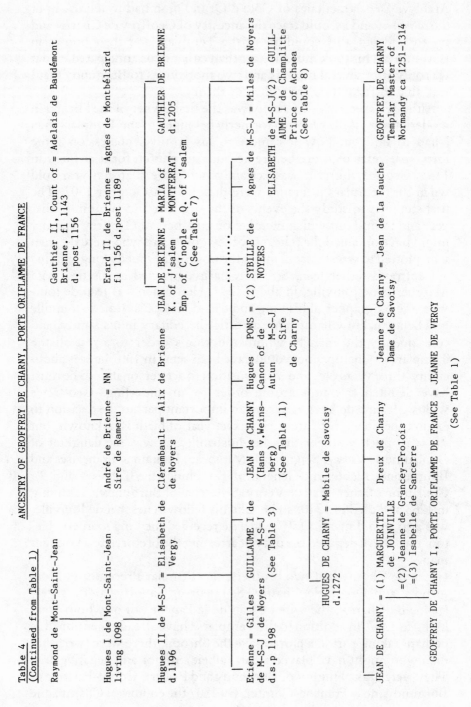

Table 4
(Continued from Table 1)

ANCESTRY OF GEOFFREY DE CHARNY, PORTE ORIFLAMME DE FRANCE

had been united to the Crown of France through the marriage of Philip the Handsome to Jeanne, the only child of the last Count of Champagne, Henri III. Hugh V, Duke of Burgundy, Count of Auxonne and Châlon, Chamberlain of France, Titular King of Thessalonica (see Table 3) succeeded his father Duke Robert II in 1306 and reigned till 1315. He was betrothed to Catherine de Valois in 1302, but the marriage never took place, and in 1313 he made over his rights to the kingdom of Thessalonica to his brother Louis, soon after the latter's marriage to Maud of Hainault.[2] Count Robert was only a child when he succeeded his father, Count Otto V, in 1302, and like Duke Hugh he too died in 1315. Whatever knowledge they may have had of a plot to rescue the Shroud, they took no action to prevent it, even if they did nothing much to support it. The Duchy of Burgundy was quasi-independent, and the County-Palatine formed part of the Holy Roman Empire at that date.

A study of the Templars of Burgundy was, as it turned out, more complicated than at first I had thought. The term 'Burgundy' is applied indiscriminately to the ancient Kingdom of Burgundy which ended in the eleventh century; to the County of Burgundy of Outre-Saône – the future Franche-Comté; and to the Capetian Duchy of Burgundy, which though technically a province of France because its duke owed allegiance to the French king, was for all practical purposes independent. But the boundaries of these territories presented at this period a patchwork of enclaves which is extremely difficult to disentangle without the help of a good map. The Counts of Champagne, Auxerre-Nevers and Châlon were vassals of the 'Duke of Dijon', but only for some of their lands. The County of Macon was tightly bound to the Duchy of Burgundy, and as for the region of Langres, the bishops there exercised a power, later reinforced by the acquisition of the County of Langres in 1179, which entitled them to be included among the Peers of France. I concentrated on the history of the Templars in this imprecise region comprising the duchy, the counties governed by the duke's vassals, and the episcopal lordships of the region from Troyes in the north to Macon in the south and from Langres in the east to the Nivernais in the west.

My first discovery was that the Templar Commandery of Burgundy (the term commandery and preceptory are more or less interchangeable) corresponded almost exactly with the county, which in turn corresponds with the Archdiocese of Besançon. To the south the Commandery of Macon did not correspond so much to the feudal principality as to an ecclesiastical district (not even a diocese). But perversely, all the Templars in the Duchy of Burgundy came under the jurisdiction of the Grand Prior of Champagne, whose houses were situated in the dioceses of Langres, Autun and Châlon. The grand prior's residence was at Voulaine-les-Templiers in the diocese of Langres, some ten miles east of Châtillon-sur-Seine in the valley of the Ource. In 1163 the brethren who had been established for thirty-six years at Bure, about seven miles away, were given the church of Voulaine by Bishop Geoffrey of Langres, together with the village and the neighbouring parish of Leuglay. Although adjacent villages, Leuglay and Voulaine were situated in different provinces, the former in Champagne and the latter in Burgundy. In 1175, Duke Hugh III gave the Templars the lordship of Voulaine, which differed from the church and its lands. This donation was increased by further gifts from Guillaume de Joinville, Bishop of Langres, in 1208 and 1237. The Seigneur de Leuglay owed allegiance to the Count of Champagne, which led to the Grand Priory of Voulaine taking the title of Grand Priory of Champagne after the union of the two estates.[3]

The lordship of Voulaine consisted of the Commanderies of Mormant, Epailly and Bure, of which the grand prior was the patron and overlord. The Commandery of Epailly, eight miles north-east of Châtillon-sur-Seine, stood near the Roman road from Langres to Auxerre. It had several farms and houses attached to it as well as a beautiful chapel and pretty gardens of which some traces can still be seen. It also had a large cellar, and several chapters are known to have been held there.

The Commandery of Bure, between Voulaine and Beneuvre, was the stock from which all the other houses in the district, even Voulaine itself, had sprung. As such, in recognition of its seniority, it enjoyed certain privileges over the Grand Priory of Voulaine. The Commandery of Mormant was much younger, having been founded in 1300.

The Commandery of Thoisy-le-Désert, which like all the others came under the jurisdiction of Voulaine, was the recipient of lands given by Fromond de Villiers in 1202, by André de Pouilly in 1221, by Odo de Bure in 1243 and at various times by the seigneurs of Mont-Saint-Jean. The castle there, together with much of the surrounding land, belonged to the lords of Charny and Mont-Saint-Jean. It was a strong fortress with a turreted entrance gate, a vaulted room similar to those one can see in surviving commanderies, and with a chapel. At the end of the last century the then owner recalled a family tradition about the discovery of a cellar where eight skeletons had been found, two shields and an iron coffer full of rings. In 1849 some stone coffins were unearthed in the neighbouring château of St Sabine, but all of these may have been deliberately planted, in much the same way as the notorious casket of the Duc de Blacas was planted at Essarois, near Voulaine, to lend spurious antiquity to certain secret societies, such as the Rosicrucians and Freemasons, who sought to claim descent from the Templars.

These, then, were all dependencies of the Grand Priory of Champagne at Voulaine, and it was to one of them that I felt sure the Shroud must have been taken some time between July and October 1307, assuming that it had not already been sent there directly after the general chapter of Montpellier in 1293. A careful analysis of their location, importance and security enabled me to reduce a list of nearly fifty properties to one of less than a dozen. Finally, this dozen was reduced to about four or five possible hiding places. Highest on my list, of course, was Voulaine itself, for reasons I shall describe shortly. I could not rule out entirely the houses at Bure, Epailly and Châtillon, because they all possessed chapels, cellars or other buildings in which the relic might have been hidden. Nor could I ignore Thoisy-le-Désert, because of its geographical and other associations with the de Charny and Mont-Saint-Jean family, and because it owned a strong castle. Less probable, but at the same time possible, were the houses in the neighbourhood of Charny, Montfort and Mont-Saint-Jean. These were Avosne, Semur-en-Auxois, Uncey-le-Franc, Normier, Busy-le-Grand, Lucenay-le-Duc and Sombernon. I did not, at first, entirely rule out the houses nearer Dijon, the most likely of which seemed to be St Philibert, near Vergy, and La Romagne, near Champlitte. I thought it unlikely that the Templars would have sent the Shroud to Dijon itself, for if they had, the duke, or perhaps the de Vergys, rather than the de Charnys, would have taken care of it. As an outside possibility there was Ruetz, a commandery near Joinville, which had for a long time been under the especial patronage of the Seneschals of Champagne.

Apart from Châtillon-sur-Seine, Dijon, Beaune, Châlon-sur-Saône and Auxerre, all the other Templar establishments were thickly concentrated round Voulaine, which continued to be the focal point in this region even when the Hospitallers succeeded to the Templars' property after the dissolution. There were almost twenty of them, and their rich lands and forests, their large communities of brethren, lay-brethren, sergeants and servants ensured that they exercised a wide influence in the province. Their complete loyalty to Jacques de Molay, whose brother was Dean of Langres, and whose family were of Burgundian origin, gave them an importance so disquieting that when it came to the imposition of penalties after the trial, Philip the Handsome ordered much fiercer ones for the Burgundians than for those from other provinces. But was this his only reason, I felt bound to ask? Did the king know that in truth the Templars' 'idol' was none other than the Shroud? And was the fact that the Burgundian knights had successfully spirited it away from under his nose the true reason for his animosity? Was Duke Hugh V's ready compliance with the king in despatching one hundred and forty-nine Burgundian knights to Paris likewise motivated by resentment that he had not got the relic? He was a thoroughly weak man, and seems to have collaborated more readily with the king's agents than might be expected. Of these one hundred and forty-nine, seventy-five belonged to Voulaine and its daughter houses.

Let us, then, look a little closer at the Grand Priory of Voulaine. Its influence and power were great throughout Burgundy, and the grand prior himself was the senior commander or preceptor in the order. This was due to the historical accident of the order's having been founded in Champagne, and from its earliest days, Champagne had enjoyed supremacy over all other provinces and grand priories. He exercised control over thirteen commanderies in Burgundy, seven in Lorraine, and as many in Champagne; he had been endowed, over the lifetime of the order, by the general chapter with the income from the commanderies of Bure, Mormant and Epailly, and with the castle of Voulaine itself. A sixteenth-century description of this fortress has luckily survived, for not one stone of it remains standing upon another today. This splendid castle was demolished in 1825.

The stronghold was surrounded by a massive wall strengthened by ten towers each measuring fifty by fifty paces. This wall was surrounded by a moat. In front of the entrance were a barricade and a bridge at the end of which stood a dovecot, a forge, stables and cattle shed, and also a pavilion containing the rooms of the captain of the guard. In the middle of the courtyard stood a strong, square dungeon, its front facing the entrance.

On the ground floor of the front of the dungeon there was a vaulted chapel forty-eight feet long and twenty-four wide. The living quarters of the grand prior were in the middle of this front, with a small room in each turret. At the end of the grand prior's lodging was the treasurer's room, with a small room in a turret shut by an iron door, where the charters, papers, title deeds and bonds and the house's treasures were kept.

If the Shroud was not kept at Voulaine itself, Epailly was a possible alternative. Not only did it have a beautiful church, but from the evidence given at the trial by Brother Guillaume de Bissey, the grand master's chaplain, the preceptor of Epailly was Hugues de Villiers, a

110

kinsman of Gérard de Villiers, the order's treasurer. Hugues de Villiers was also almoner to the Duke of Burgundy, and he might have been privy to the plot to rescue the Shroud. Montmorot was another possibility. The Templars had built a castle there and a chapel, but all that remains now is a farmhouse, and there is no description of the buildings which have been destroyed. In 1293 Hugues de Pairaud was preceptor of this house and was responsible for several exchanges of land in Montmorot and Fraignot. It was remote and lay not far off the most direct route between Voulaine and Charny.

La Romagne, five miles from Champlitte, was one of the most richly endowed houses in the Grand Priory of Champagne. It was situated on the boundaries of the Duchy and County of Burgundy and the County of Champagne. It possessed a strong moated castle surrounded by thick, turreted walls, which enclosed a dungeon and chapel as at Voulaine. It was within easy reach of the seat of the Lords of Champlitte, who, as I was later to learn, had played a not insignificant part in the history of the Shroud during its 'missing' years. The list of its properties is a long one, consisting of twenty-four estates and dependencies in the départements of Côte d'Or, Haute-Marne and Haute-Saône.

There was one more scrap of evidence I thought it worth taking into consideration; it concerned Jacques de Molay's place of origin. It is well known that he was a Burgundian, and most historians have thought that he came from Molay in Franche-Comté, a village near Dôle, and that he may have been born in the neighbouring château of Rahon, one of the sons of Jean de Longwy, Seigneur de Rahon. Unfortunately there is no evidence that Jean de Longwy had more than one son, whose name was Mathieu. One of the Templar properties in the Commandery of Auxerre, part of the Grand Priory of Voulaine, was a farm and mill at Molay, a village five miles northwest of Noyers. Jacques de Molay underwent his noviciate in the Temple at Beaune, another daughter house of Voulaine. Now, admittedly Beaune is not more than thirty miles from Molay in Franche Comté, whereas the Molay near Noyers is seventy-five miles away, but there is a third Molay, near Gray, which belonged in the thirteenth century to Henri de Vergy, Seigneur de Mirebeau, Autrey, Fouvent, Champlitte and Fontaines-Françaises, Seneschal of Burgundy. Henri had no more than three sons, the eldest of whom had no issue; the second, Jean, inherited his father's lands, and became Seneschal of Burgundy, a post he held at the dissolution; and Henri d'Autrey, who was a canon of Langres, where de Molay's brother was dean. The pedigree of the de Noyers family does not reveal a son named Jacques,

111

who might have held the title of Sire de Molay, but since all the extant pedigrees are incomplete, and because of the tiresome habit the French nobility had of taking their names from their estates, it is exceedingly hard to discover to which of these three families the last grand master might have belonged. But that he belonged to one of them there can be very little doubt. Consequently any plot to save the Shroud in the event of an attack by the king would have had his support if it meant housing it at Voulaine, which at the end of all my investigations remained by far the most probable place for it to have been.

It was now time to look at the events of the summer and autumn of 1307 a little more closely. The evidence I have set out so far suggests that the senior Templars who attended the general chapter in July had some idea of the threat facing them, even though they might not have guessed when it would materialize, or that it would be so efficiently carried out when it did. If the Shroud was not already at Voulaine, then it would have been no more than common prudence to send it there in July to avoid it being taken by the king. The fact that the overwhelming majority of the brethren were arrested during the night of Friday 13 October testifies to their unawareness of the date of the king's attack and to the secrecy with which it was planned and carried out. The number of those arrested is in dispute. Some authorities speak of a figure around five thousand, whereas others speak in hundreds only. Certainly the number of people dependent on the order must have run into thousands, but I was not concerned with them. Only a very few senior knights of Burgundian origin, or belonging to the Grand Priory of Voulaine, either as resident brethren, or as preceptors of daughter houses, knew anything about the Shroud or what was planned in the event of a royal attack. Because we know what happened subsequently, it was easy to eliminate large numbers of men and places because the plot to save the Shroud must have been carried out secretly and efficiently, and must have involved only those who needed to know about it. The participants must have been acceptable to and trusted by Jean de Charny, which indicated that his brother Geoffrey de Charny must have been a member of the plot, acting on behalf of his family within the order. The leader who undertook the actual rescue had to be a man of age and experience, and someone who could be sure of carrying it off successfully. Such a man was Gérard de Villiers. The timing of the rescue must have depended upon a precise knowledge of when the king would attack; this meant that the collaboration of the Seneschals of Burgundy and of Champagne – Jean de Vergy and Jean de Joinville – was essential. Both were elderly men, who must have delegated this unpleasant duty, which meant the arrest of men who were their friends and kinsfolk, to younger, more active underlings, who were almost certainly unaware of the plot.

The care of Templar houses in Europe before the loss of the Holy Land was left to knights and sergeants unfit for military service on account of wounds or age. To these was left the responsibility of looking after the order's lands, banking activities and the administration of its estates. In the sixteen years between the fall of Acre and the dissolution, the number of young and active knights domiciled in Europe rose, but the constitution of the general chapter of July 1307 was elderly. The supreme authority of the order was not the grand master but the chapter. From the earliest days the grand master possessed only representative power, all authority residing in the assembly of brothers. In the July 1307 chapter, therefore, de Molay had no more than one vote. He had been warned by the pope of the accusations the king was likely to make against the order, so the matter of the Shroud must have been discussed. Why, I asked myself, did the order not pre-empt the issue and demonstrate to the king and the pope the true nature of the so-called 'idol'? It seemed to me that there were two reasons: first because it was generally believed that the authentic Shroud of Christ was at Besançon, where it had been sent by Otto de la Roche, Duke of Athens, a century before. No one had questioned its authenticity, so how could the Templars now claim that theirs was the authentic one? No one would have believed such a claim. Their second reason was more complex. They would have had to explain how and when they had acquired the relic, and why people should consider theirs authentic and the Besançon shroud false. To do this would have meant disclosing secrets they were not on any account prepared to divulge, since they concerned the confidentiality of their financial dealings. Like modern bankers – Swiss ones especially – the Templars maintained the strictest secrecy about such matters, which nothing would induce them to betray.

It follows, therefore, that plans for the Shroud's safety must have been made after lengthy deliberation, and that this must have taken place at the general chapter of July 1307. The circular issued after it ended, forbidding the brothers to discuss with outsiders the order's rites and practices, seems to bear this out.

There is some confusion over whether the king signed the order for the arrests on 14 or 27 September. Whichever date it was signed, the instructions to the seneschals would not have reached them much before the beginning of October, allowing them about two weeks to make the necessary preparations. The royal orders required the seneschals and baillis to take all the brethren into custody – knights, sergeants and novices alike. It is uncertain whether servants were to be arrested, but if so, then more than five thousand men were to be arrested throughout France.

On the day of the arrests the royal officials should have been accompanied by the leading men of the district, to whom an explanation of what was happening should have been given under an oath of secrecy. Jean de Vergy and Jean de Joinville as Seneschals of Burgundy and Champagne were responsible for carrying out these orders. Since Voulaine, although the Grand Priory of Champagne, was situated in Burgundy, it would have fallen to Jean de Vergy to arrange for the arrest of the brethren there. But just then he had other things to attend to. On 18 October 1307, five days after the arrests, his cousin Blanche, the sister of Duke Hugh V of Burgundy, was to be married at Montbard to Edward, Count of Savoy, the son of the reigning Count Amadeus V. Obviously he could not have carried out all the arrests personally, but he could very easily have warned Jean de Charny. On the other hand, Jean de Charny's wife was Marguerite de Joinville, so the warning could have come from the aged Seneschal of Champagne.

The commander of the rescue operation was almost certainly Gérard de Villiers. He alone among the leaders was never caught, and according to the surviving records, only sixteen other knights escaped arrest. Brother Gérard was a kinsman of both seneschals and a fellow Burgundian. The others were junior knights, but all noblemen. Two of the sixteen were abroad, one in England and one in Germany. Of the remainder, most were Burgundians and kinsmen of each other or of the de Charny, de Joinville and de Vergy families. They included Hugues de Châlon, a nephew of Hugues de Pairaud, the seneschal of the order; Pierre de Modies, a nephew of Hugues de Châlon; Falco de Milly, a kinsman of a former Grand Master, Philip de Milly, and of a former Treasurer, Jean de Milly. I was later to discover that the de Milly family played a significant part in the history of the Shroud (see Tables 5 and 6). Jean de Chailly came of a family whose estates were at Chailly-sur-Armançon, a village two miles from Charny. If not a kinsman of Jean de Charny, he was certainly a close neighbour. The rest were Richard de Montcley, who fled to Franche-Comté, of which he was a native, but was recaptured near Montbéliard later; Clérambault de Conflans, who fled with Brother Richard, and who came from near Champlitte; Brothers Renaud de la Foillie, Guillaume de Lins, Hugues d'Aray, Adam de Wilancourt and Brothers Barans and Geraudon, whose second names are not known. Brother Jean de

Châlon, Hugues' brother, was captured later and said in evidence that Gérard de Villiers had had prior warning of the arrests.

That one of those who escaped arrest was related to the men who knew the secret of the Shroud might be thought coincidental, but that five were is quite a different matter. According to the evidence of a lay brother who was captured later, Hugues de Châlon was said to have fled '*cum toto thesauro fratris Hugonis de Peraudo*' and that Gérard de Villiers had fled '*cum quinquaginta equis*'. Could the treasure of Hugues de Pairaud be the Shroud and the Grail? And could the fifty horses (and presumably their riders) be its escort? In the light of what we know today, the answer must surely be Yes. These men certainly had the motive to undertake such a risky task, and they knew that if they were successful they could count on the protection of powerful friends. Duke Hugh V had no reason to betray them, and Count Robert of Burgundy, assuming he was in the secret, likewise kept silent. Jean de Joinville, whose admiration for St Louis was only matched by his disapproval of that king's grandson, Philip the Handsome, had no reason to divulge the secret. The same goes for Jean de Vergy, whose son Guillaume had recently married a cousin of Jean de Joinville. But in any case, once the shock of the arrests had worn off, criticism of the king's action was widespread, since the Templars were men of the Church, and as such their arrest was a direct contravention of ecclesiastical rights of immunity. In Paris, where the king's chief minister, Guillaume de Nogaret, had summoned the leading members of the university to a meeting in the chapter house of Notre Dame, it was easy to stun potential opponents into silence by the enormity of the accusations. But in Dijon, and Troyes, and Auxerre and other provincial cities, disbelief gained hold of men's minds. It took less than a fortnight of constant questioning under torture for the arrested leaders to confess to all the crimes laid at their door. Jacques de Molay wrote an open letter to his brethren exhorting them to confess all their evil practices as he had done. Even Hugues de Pairaud, to whom the events of the past two weeks did not come as a complete surprise, made a sweeping confession, though a close examination of what he actually said – or is reported to have said – shows that he was affirming his true belief when he said that the 'idol' brought the order all its worldly power and wealth, that it caused the trees to flower and the earth to bring forth fruits and that it gave salvation to those who worshipped it.

But apart from anything else, everyone knew the Inquisition and its methods, and everyone knew that King Philip's confessor happened to be the Inquisitor General of France. Not for nothing were its

directors, the Dominicans, known as the *Domini Canes* – the Dogs of
the Lord. Today we call their methods of extracting confessions
brainwashing, and confessions obtained by such methods can be
spotted without the slightest difficulty – the technique and its results
are, alas, all too familiar to us. Our fourteenth-century ancestors were
no more fooled by such confessions than we are. So when it came to a
choice between saving Christ's Shroud which bore the image of his
tortured body upon it, or of handing it over to the king, these men did
as their consciences bade them, especially since the king in question
had kidnapped one pope and had had his own nominee elected in his
place. They kept silent about the plot to save the Shroud, and feigned
ignorance when asked. The majority of Frenchmen might be fooled
by the barrage of propaganda put out by Guillaume de Nogaret, but
sophisticated men like Jean de Joinville and Jean de Vergy were not
taken in for a moment. When on 27 October Pope Clement V plucked
up courage to write a letter to the king protesting against the arrests
as a breach of his own rights in the matter, they felt that their dis-
obedience of the king's orders was completely justified.

> These acts [wrote the pope] are the occasion of astonishment and sadness to
> us . . . you have perpetrated these attacks upon the persons and goods of
> men directly subject to the Roman Church, and in this action of yours so
> unlooked for, everybody sees, and not without reasonable cause, an insult-
> ing contempt for us and for the Church of Rome.

When, in December, the pope at last obtained direct access to
Jacques de Molay, Hugues de Pairaud and more than sixty other
senior brethren, they revoked their confessions made under torture.

Two more scraps of circumstantial evidence deserve mentioning.
The cross in the centre of Mont-Saint-Jean, unlike all the others, was
inscribed with the words which Constantine the Great read in the sky
before the Battle of the Milvian Bridge, and which he had inscribed on
his Imperial Standard, the Labarum: IN HOC SIGNO VINCES. Coincidence? Possibly. But when I read in Courtépée's *History of the Duchy of
Burgundy* that 'several relics, of which some were richly enshrined' had
been brought from the East by the Seigneurs of Mont-Saint-Jean at the
time of the crusades, I asked myself whether these could have included
the Shroud and the Grail casket which was covered by that self-same
Labarum Constantini.

After the trial (which ended in 1311 to all intents and purposes) of
those Templars who were released, some joined other orders, some
married, and in the empire, of which Franche-Comté formed a part,
some joined the Teutonic Order. In Germany Hugo von Salm, the

Templar Commander of Grünbach and Visitor of Germany, accompanied by twenty knights fully armed, forced an entry into the Synod of Mainz. The Bishops of Mainz and Trier, who were presiding, heard their protestation of innocence. Then, with utter disdain, the Templars turned their backs on the bishops and left as free men.

Forty-seven years elapsed before Geoffrey de Charny, the nephew and namesake of the martyred Preceptor of Normandy and the grandson of Jean de Joinville and grandson-in-law of Jean de Vergy, deemed it safe to bring the Shroud to light. A generation and more had gone by, and there was no further danger from the King of France. During this period the Shroud was kept either at Mont-Saint-Jean, or more likely at Charny or Montfort. All three were secure refuges for the relic, and of the three, Montfort seems the most likely, since it was here that Geoffrey's granddaughter Marguerite de Charny kept it before making it over to her kinsman, Duke Louis of Savoy.

I had now taken the history of the Shroud back a further eighty years, to about 1274. It was time to turn my attention to the Fourth Crusade and to the seventy years that followed the sack of Constantinople in April 1204.

CHAPTER 5

THE REAL QUEST FOR THE HOLY GRAIL: 1171–1222

———•———

In 1157 the twenty-year-old brother of King Baldwin III of Jerusalem, Amalric, Count of Jaffa, married Agnes de Courtenay, the daughter of Joscelin III, Count of Edessa. It was not a happy marriage. She was several years older than her husband, and had been a widow for eight years, though not an inconsolable one, for she was a nymphomaniac and a termagant. Five years later, and after the birth of a son, Baldwin, and a daughter, Sibylla, Amalric succeeded his childless brother as King of Jerusalem. But his accession was not without difficulty, for the patriarch refused to recognize his wife as queen. This refusal was less on account of her morals, to which the barons took stronger exception than the patriarch, but because she was her husband's third cousin, and thus forbidden under canon law, on account of consanguinity, to be his wife. Barons and patriarch united to demand the dissolution of the marriage, to which Amalric not unwillingly agreed, provided the rights of his son and daughter were recognized (see Table 5).

Amalric was a big, handsome man with a shock of fair hair and a thick blond beard. If his wife's private life had been scandalous, his own was not altogether blameless, but a great deal was forgiven him, as much for his good looks as for his clever statesmanship. He was the last Christian King of Jerusalem of whom it could be said that he was worthy of the throne. Having divorced Agnes, he was in no hurry to rush once more into matrimony, and it was not until 1167 that he took as his second wife Maria Comnena, who was not only young and pretty, but also the daughter of the Emperor Manuel I Comnenus of Constantinople. Early in 1171 King Amalric decided to pay a personal visit to his father-in-law, in pursuit of his policy of close alliance with the Eastern Empire and of his need for financial and military support

Table 5   COURTENAY OF EDESSA/MONTFERRAT/LUSIGNAN/HENNEBERG/MILLY/BRIENNE/HOHENSTAUFEN/ARPAD of HUNGARY

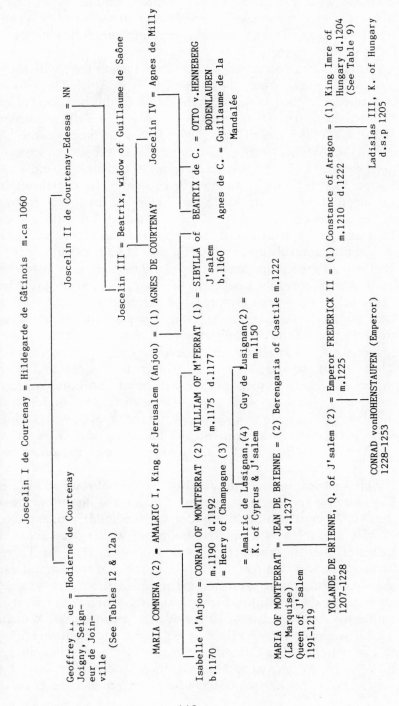

119

from the West. He left Acre on 10 March, sending ahead Philip de Milly, the recently elected Grand Master of the Knights Templar, who now resigned his office on his appointment as the king's ambassador to the emperor.

At Gallipoli Amalric was met by his father-in-law, who escorted him to the capital, where they arrived early in April. The visit made little impact on the Byzantine public, but it established good relations between the Imperial Court and the Court of Jerusalem. According to William, Archbishop of Tyre, who was a member of the king's entourage, Manuel Comnenus received his distinguished vassal with great courtesy. The visit lasted two months, and the king and his party left on 15 June. Amalric was invited to enter the city through the Bucoleon Harbour Gate – an honour reserved for the most distinguished guests only – and spent the first part of his visit in the vast Bucoleon Palace, which occupied the greater part of the south-eastern area of the peninsula upon which the city of Constantinople is built. William of Tyre tells us that the emperor showed his son-in-law all the most secret parts of the palace, the sanctuaries it contained, the basilicas and their treasures. 'Nothing,' he tells us, 'was hidden. Nothing sacred which had been placed in the hidden places of the sacred rooms from the time of the blessed Emperors Constantine, Theodosius and Justinian but was familiarly revealed to the king and his companions.' The emperor ordered all the relics of the saints to be exposed as well as the 'most precious evidence of the Passion of Our Lord, namely the cross, nails, lance, sponge, reed, crown of thorns, sindon (that is the cloth in which He was wrapped) and the sandals. . . .' During the latter part of the visit, Amalric and his party moved to the more intimate atmosphere of the Blachernae Palace at the other end of the city.

This visit is important in the history of the Shroud and the Holy Grail for two reasons: first, because Amalric and his entourage were the first Westerners to see the Sindon and the Soudarion, and second, because it enabled William of Tyre to tell Walter Map about these treasures when they met at the Lateran Council in 1179–80. There can be little doubt that the first that people knew of the Shroud and its grill-like casket in the West stems from this visit, and that its consequences for the literature, painting and sculpture of the West were enormous. Like tourists of all periods and nationalities, William of Tyre was carried away by the marvels he was shown during his visits to Constantinople, and these increased in wonder in the telling. On the other hand, there were those who took a more sober view of what they had seen, but one which likewise acted as an inducement to those

120

whom they told to see the relics of Constantinople for themselves, and if possible to bring some of them back to the West. The quest for the Holy Grail can be said, therefore, to have begun during King Amalric's visit to the Emperor Manuel in 1171.

Among those who accompanied the king was one of his first wife's kinsmen, Robert de Joinville;[1] Philip de Milly, his ambassador (who unhappily died during the visit); and Philip's brothers, Guy and Henri de Milly. The de Milly brothers were the sons of Guy de Milly, a nobleman whose origins were in Picardy, and of his wife, Stephanie of Flanders. Philip was born there in 1120 and went to the Holy Land as a young man. In 1161 he was given the Seigneurie of Outrejourdain in exchange for that of Nablus, after his marriage to Isabella, the only daughter and heiress of the Seigneur of Montréal and Outrejourdain. On Isabella's death, which took place about 1165, Philip renounced all his rights and properties in favour of his daughter Stephanie, and joined the Templars. On the death of Bertrand de Blanquefort, the seventh grand master, Philip de Milly was elected to succeed him. His tenure of office, as we have seen, was very brief, lasting no more than a year at most. Philip's daughter Stephanie had been married and widowed twice by 1174 and had, by then, married (as her third husband and his second wife) Reynald of Châtillon, the de facto Prince of Antioch.

Reynald's career falls into two parts, separated by fourteen years in a Moslem prison. He was the younger son of Geoffrey, Comte de Gien-sur-Loire, taking his title from the family's property at Châtillon-sur-Loire. He came to the East in the reign of Baldwin III and made the misalliance of the century by marrying the king's widowed cousin, Constance, Princess of Antioch. While he was in prison his wife died and his stepson became Prince of Antioch, which left Reynald landless. Yet in 1174 his captors demanded a huge ransom (which his friends paid), for during his incarceration his stepdaughter had become the Empress of Constantinople and his daughter, Agnes, had married King Bela III of Hungary; finally, he was a cousin by marriage of King Baldwin IV of Jerusalem. In 1174 Amalric I was succeeded by his son, Baldwin IV, who was a leper. His death was thought to be imminent; he could not marry and father an heir, and his closest male kinsman was unpopular with many of the barons and with the leper-king's mother, Agnes de Courtenay. Agnes found in her brother, Count Joscelin III of Edessa and in Reynald of Antioch, both of whom had been released from prison in 1176, men to whom the duties of governing might be entrusted. Joscelin was appointed seneschal of the realm and Reynald, as I have already mentioned, was

Table 6   MILLY/COURTENAY/HENNEBERG-BODENLAUBEN/CHATILLON/ARPAD OF HUNGARY

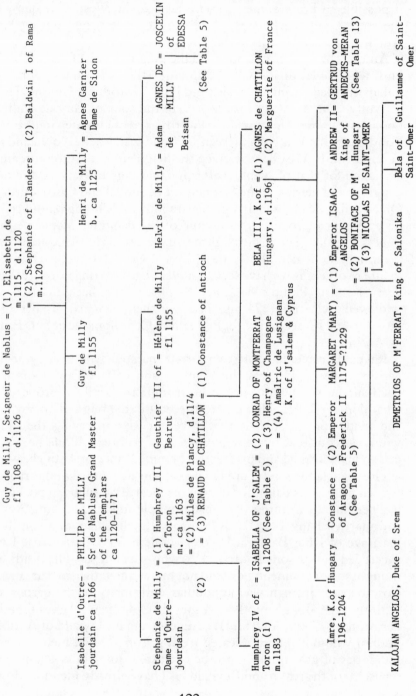

122

married to the greatest heiress of the kingdom, Stephanie de Milly, Dame d'Outrejourdain (see Tables 5 and 6).

In 1177 William of Montferrat, the husband of Amalric I's elder daughter Sibylla, died, leaving his wife pregnant with the future Baldwin V. The king wished on account of his health to appoint a regent, and Reynald of Antioch was chosen; for the next five years he held a paramount position in the kingdom after the king himself. In 1175 Reynald's daughter, Queen Agnes of Hungary, gave birth to a daughter, Margaret, who was destined to become at the age of ten, the year before her grandfather died, the wife of the Emperor Isaac Angelos. In later life she became a key figure in the history of the Shroud and the Holy Grail.[2]

Philip de Milly's youngest brother, Henri, nicknamed the Buffalo, was the father of three daughters, the second of whom, Agnes de Milly, was the wife of Count Joscelin III of Courtenay-Edessa. It is not known exactly when Joscelin and Agnes married, but as he was released from prison at the same time as Reynald de Châtillon, it is reasonable to assume that it was about 1174. A year later the elder of Joscelin's two daughters, Beatrix de Courtenay, was born. She, like her cousin the Princess Margaret of Hungary, also became a key figure in the history of the Shroud and the Holy Grail.

The Grail literature, apart from its religious aspect, expressed the ideals of courtesy and courtly love – ideals strangely at odds with current social practice. The noble lady's lover, by definition not her husband, was mighty in battle, and in her presence was witty, well-washed and well-dressed. He composed and sang love songs for her, and was always scrupulous to defend her honour. All this was an expression of a wider entity we call chivalry, and which regulated the behaviour of a knight according to fixed moral principles. Its perfect representative was the chaste, loyal warrior for religion, the defender of a lady's honour, of which Sir Galahad and Perceval were the supreme examples. The proper medieval gentleman was generous, especially when it came to bequeathing land and money to the Church. He was sincerely religious, respectful of Church authority, which meant his chaplain, his bishop, and the monks of his locality, and faithful to his military and religious duties.

The men and women who had either seen the Shroud in Constantinople, or knew of its precise nature and where it was kept, were the sons and daughters, grandsons and granddaughters of noblemen who had been brought up in this moral tradition. They could justify acts which we might today regard as immoral, by reference to this courtly and religious code of behaviour. The decision to divert the Fourth

Crusade to Constantinople is one such act. Modern historians are well-nigh unanimous in condemning it as one of the worst acts of Western barbarism ever to have been perpetrated. But though there were many who deplored the wanton vandalism and destruction of life and works of art, there were just as many – including churchmen – who justified it on moral grounds.

All through the ages folk had dreamed of Byzantium, the incomparable city, radiant in a blaze of gold. To bring it within the fold of Rome, and thus to unite the divided Church of Christ, was a legitimate religious objective. Certainly one of the most important factors leading to the diversion was the arrival in the West of Prince Alexius Angelos, son and heir of the deposed and blinded Emperor Isaac Angelos. To restore him and his father to the throne of Constantinople, of which they had been ruthlessly deprived, was politically and religiously permissible. There does not, however, seem to have been a premeditated conspiracy among the Latin leaders to do this. The attack on Constantinople, while not contemplated when the idea of a crusade was first mooted at the council of Compiègne in 1200, coincided nevertheless most conveniently with the interests of Venice, of Boniface of Montferrat, of Philip of Swabia, and – to the extent that it placed a Roman Catholic prince and a Roman Catholic prelate on the imperial and patriarchal thrones of Byzantium – of Pope Innocent III as well. Although the pope, to give him his due, was appalled at the destruction and vandalism occasioned by the attack on Constantinople, he was not particularly sorry that it had taken place.

Apart from these politico-religious considerations, there is good evidence for believing that another major factor to influence the decision to divert the crusade to Constantinople was the cult of relics. Of all the cities in the East, without excepting those of the Holy Land, Constantinople was regarded by the Latins as the richest in relics. But not only relics: while it was the sacred relic inside its case which gave the object its value in the eyes of the crusaders, the reliquary itself was more often than not a marvellous work of art. If this was true of the reliquaries containing the remains of comparatively minor and obscure saints, how much more was it true of the Holy Grail which contained the very Shroud of Christ? Everyone knew that the Greek emperors had collected relics from the days of Saints Helena and Pulcheria. Western imagination had been stirred by the pious riches of the imperial city in the *Journey of Charlemagne to Jerusalem*, which until the sixteenth century was considered to be perfectly authentic, and was reckoned in good faith as the first of all the crusades. It was to Charlemagne that were attributed from the tenth century all the distinguished relics of Eastern origin, and thus everything that came from Charlemagne passed for having been brought by him from Constantinople on his return from the Holy Places. The influence of this legend must explain the renown which Constantinople enjoyed even before the twelfth century among pilgrims to the Holy Land. The imperial city was one of the Holy Places included in their itinerary. They went there to venerate all the material souvenirs of the Passion. Some of them must have heard, even if they did not understand, the Byzantine hymn to the Shroud:

> How can we with mortal eyes contemplate this image, whose celestial splendour the host of heaven presumes not to behold? He who dwells in heaven condescends this day to visit us by his venerable image. He who is seated with the cherubim visits us this day by a picture which the Father has delineated with his immaculate hand, which he has formed in an ineffable manner, and which we sanctify by adoring it with fear and love.

But there was another important factor: it came from the influence exercised by the legends of the Holy Grail on the nobility of Europe. The most famous *chanson de geste* (song of heroic exploits) was 'The Song of Roland', composed in about 1100 by an unknown troubadour and the archetypal romance of chivalry. It was a story of adventure and love, glorifying the aristocratic way of life, exalting women, the institution of courtesy, a code of morals and ideals for gentlemen. Stories of Charlemagne and his Court were not the only inspiration for chivalric romances; tales of old Rome and, for the courtiers of the Plantagenet Kings, Henry II and Richard Coeur de Lion, the legends from the Celtic fringes of Wales, Brittany and Ireland in which King Arthur and the Knights of the Round Table were the leading characters. To these Walter Map and Chrétien de Troyes grafted on the quest for the Holy Grail. Chrétien was not slow to see parallels in the political situation in the France of his day with the Arthurian legends. Perceval, the hero of the Arthurian cycle, was the son of the widow of Anjou. So was the young Prince Arthur of Brittany, who, on the death of his uncle Richard Coeur de Lion, became the heir to the Angevin Empire of his grandparents, Henry II and Eleanor of Aquitaine. In 1199 this fourteen-year-old lad, the son of Richard's dead brother Geoffrey of Anjou, Dúke of Brittany, was Richard's heir, though in fact he became a pawn in the power struggle between his two uncles, John Lackland of England and Philip Augustus of France. John seized the throne of England, which of rights should have been Arthur's, and then the person of the young prince, whom he ordered to be murdered soon afterwards.

King Henry II had found it politic to foster these tales of ancient

British glory to rival the splendour which Charlemagne's exploits shed on his descendants, the Kings of France. And so the Grail and the Shroud, historical objects of immense religious and political significance, began to occupy the minds and inspire the aims of some of the leaders of the Fourth Crusade. Religion and mysticism had always been closely linked to the military purposes of the crusades. The ancient theme of the quest was brought up to date and began to parallel the actual aims of men like Boniface de Montferrat, Otto de la Roche, Guillaume de Champlitte, Robert and Geoffrey de Joinville, Pons de Mont-Saint-Jean de Charny, and many other leading noblemen of Burgundy and Champagne. Inspired to undertake their quest, as modern youngsters are inspired by what they see on TV, to emulate their heroes, these knights embarked on the crusade with the deliberate intention of seeking, and if the opportunity arose, of capturing the real Grail and the holy burial cloths of Christ.

The cult of relics generally, such as those of the Passion, and especially the True Cross, seemed to have been the premise and corollary of the mission accepted on 28 November 1199 by those who took part in the Tournament of Ecri-sur-Aisne, which is generally regarded as the genesis of the crusade. As physical objects divorced from a specific milieu, relics are entirely without historical significance. Unlike other objects, they carry no fixed code or sign of their meaning as they move from one period to another: all relics, that is, with two possible exceptions – the Sindon and the Soudarion. Being representational objects they carry an intrinsic code comprehensible to those who see them. All others, most of which were bits and pieces of saints – what Chaucer's Pardoner dismissed as 'pigges bones' – are eminently capable of fraudulent creation. After the sack of Constantinople the traffic in relics became such a scandal that a formal decree was issued by the Fourth Lateran Council in 1215 forbidding such transactions as sacrilegious and simoniacal.

The symbolic value of a relic is only the reflection of the value assigned to it by the society that honours it. But relics were the main channel through which supernatural power was available for the needs of ordinary life. Ordinary men and women could see and, sometimes, handle them; yet they belonged not to this transitory life but to eternity. Among all the objects of an unintelligible world, they alone were both visible and full of beneficent power. For the Templars and those who had seen it the Sindon, with its inexplicable image of Christ crucified, fulfilled these criteria beyond all peradventure. It did indeed make the earth bear fruit, the grapes to ripen and the deserts to run with milk and honey. For the people of Edessa and Constantinople these relics had palladian virtues which could protect them from their enemies. People of all classes saw in the veneration of relics their best hope for deliverance from trouble. Finally, if, as the physical remains of saints, relics were understood more easily than the more abstract elements of Christianity; if, indeed, the relics *were* saints, how much more the sacred cloth in which Christ the Saviour himself was buried in the tomb? Here in the presence of the Shroud you were in the presence of Christ.

Those who attended the Tournament of Ecri, and who knew about the Shroud and the Grail which enshrined it, kept their own counsel and said nothing. Like every other crusader, they all hoped to recoup their expenses and make a profit during the campaign itself, for a streak of realism ran strongly through their temperaments; but with the benefit of hindsight it is possible to deduce that these special relics figured prominently in the minds of some of the leaders. Certainly the hope of looking upon the religious treasures of Constantinople, and perhaps of taking possession of all or some of them, was strong enough to bring about the adherence of the military men and prelates to the project to divert the crusade from the Holy Land to Constantinople, if only to preserve them from the infidel and the schismatic Greeks.

Every crusade was in some sense a pilgrimage, and every crusader a pilgrim. Constantinople, as the most important repository of relics in Christendom, was a legitimate goal for pilgrims. As early as the eighth century the Venerable Bede had included Byzantium among the Holy Places on account of the large piece of the Cross which was preserved there, and pilgrims had never ceased to stop to venerate it on their way to the Holy Land, especially during the period of the crusades. Historians of the time took care to note the abundance of sacred treasures preserved there, and how the inhabitants of the imperial city were as proud of them as they were of their beautiful churches and palaces.

Genuine supernatural faith, popular credulity, love of the marvellous, as well as material interest all combined to play their part in medieval piety, of which crusading was only one facet. To reverence the tangible remains of Christ and the saints is perfectly legitimate in principle. Knights, and Templars in particular, carried relics in the pommels of their swords or in sachets round their necks. And why not? The practice is far from dead today – it is only that the objects of veneration have changed. After all, the majority of crusaders were little more than armed pilgrims, though they called themselves soldiers. Ever since the days of ancient Rome the share-out of booty after a town had been taken by storm was, by definition, one of the rules of war. It is, therefore, certain that the acquisition of relics figured large among the motives behind the diversion. Indeed, in March 1204, before the city was attacked and captured, the leaders of the crusade drew up a treaty specifying the way the empire and its spoils were to be shared out. The relics almost certainly formed part of this, but since at the time the treaty was negotiated no one knew for certain how many relics there were, nor their precise nature, it was decided that Bishop Garnier de Trainel of Troyes (see Table 2) should make an inventory of them so that their respective values could be measured with an eye to an equitable distribution. The Shroud and the Grail were not included in this inventory. In any case it became, in the event, a free-for-all once the city had been captured. Though a few men were hanged for looting, things got so completely out of hand that there was nothing the leaders could do to prevent the seizure and destruction of those relics and ecclesiastical treasures which took the fancy of the rampageous soldiery.[3]

Devotion to relics can decline into idolatry and even fetishism, but it is doubtful if Philip the Handsome and the Inquisitors were worried about this when they accused the Templars of it. If a church or monastery owned a wealth of relics it could be sure of drawing crowds: and no stone was left unturned by some in order to obtain them. The most popular were naturally relics of Christ himself.

No one guaranteed the authenticity of these relics, especially those which consisted of skulls, bones and bits of saintly flesh, so that both laymen and clerics were often fooled. On the other hand the Church strongly disapproved of such frauds and follies, and denounced the traffic in bogus relics, forbidding the veneration of any object without express permission. Ignorant soldiers, be they barons, knights or simple archers, were alike guilty (if, indeed, guilty is the right word in the circumstances) of falling into this trap.

The crusaders' zeal for 'liberating' relics had its greedy aspect, of course, but the factor distinguishing the knight, the churchman and the merchant from one another was only what they considered to be of value. The feudal baron desired land, the priest and monk a hoard of sacred souvenirs and the merchant commercial advantage.

When Innocent III learnt, several weeks after the event, what had taken place in Constantinople on the days following the capture of the city by the crusaders, he protested vigorously. By sacking the city instead of liberating Jerusalem, the Franks had shown that they preferred earthly loot to heavenly riches, even if the earthly loot included sacred relics of the Passion. The division of the relics was, said the pope, utterly detestable, one of the worst crimes of which the crusaders were guilty, and which laid them open to excommunication and interdict. No wonder those who had taken possession of the greatest relic of all, the Sindon of Christ, kept their mouths shut.

But the theory behind the crusade was at variance with pontifical politics. No one dreamt of excusing the sacrilege, but if the systematic expropriation of goods conquered in battle was not illegal, the pillage of relics did not seem to be any more of a misdemeanour. One could think of worse crimes.

But the crusaders could justify their actions in another way. In a letter listing the relics in Constantinople, which he wrote to Count Robert I of Flanders at the beginning of the previous century, Alexius Comnenus invited the crusaders to seize the city rather than let it fall, with its vast collection of holy relics, into pagan hands. Many contemporary writers, like Geoffrey de Villehardouin, Robert de Clari, Otto de Saint-Blaise and others, quoted this letter in justification of what took place in April 1204. There is no doubt, therefore, that the seizure of relics was an important, if not primary object of the crusade, and that it was wholly justified in the eyes of contemporary laymen and clerics, even if we today regard it with abhorrence.

The best-known and most important relic to be 'rescued' was the True Cross, and from this period dates the setting up of wayside crosses and *calvaires* such as Tony and I had seen in such numbers round Charny and Mont-Saint-Jean. Moreover, it was easier to carve small pieces of wood from it than to snip strips off the Sindon or Soudarion, for to have done so would have destroyed the cloths completely, whereas it could be said that cutting up the True Cross and distributing pieces of it far and wide was to save it from falling into infidel hands. Had the cloths been cut up in this way the strange evidence of the images they carried would have gone for ever, so other methods were sought to tell the world about them. One method was to include descriptions in popular poems and stories, which resulted in the legends of the Holy Grail; another was to reproduce them in paintings and sculptures, and I shall discuss this at greater length in the last chapter. The cutting up of the True Cross accounts for the relatively large number of fragments surviving to quite recent times in the West. But above all, the True Cross was considered as the most valuable relic of them all, the glory and the defence of Christians more sure than any army of soldiers.

The popular preacher Fulk de Neuilly, who had preached the Fourth Crusade, had sought to purify society because only through such purification could the crusade succeed and the heavenly

Jerusalem be won. Exactly the same sentiments were expressed, though in semi-fictional form, by Chrétien de Troyes, Wolfram von Eschenbach, Walter Map and the other writers of Grail stories. Society's values were changing, and Fulk was only carrying on where Bernard de Clairvaux had left off. The suffering Christ offered a key to Fulk for the purification of the Church and the idea of the crusade. For those who had seen it the Shroud bore witness, even more than the Cross itself, to the suffering of Jesus, for on it could be seen the traces of his precious blood and the wounds inflicted by the crown of thorns, the nails and the vicious flagra.

Eschatology had a part to play not only in the idea of the crusade but in the Grail legends too. The last days were to be preceded by the coming of Antichrist, whose advent required the conversion of the world to Christianity. Towards 1200, just as now, towards 2000, millennial movements were again announcing the destruction of civilization and the coming of the reign of Antichrist. Antichrist could only be defeated by a united Christendom: the Moslems and Cathars – even the Greeks – stood in the way of this unity. It is small wonder that the crusaders proceeded with such zeal against these foes. Once Christ had triumphed an eternity of bliss would follow, the earth would bring forth its fruits, and starvation, sickness and poverty would be at an end. This is exactly what the Templars were affirming when, at their trial, they made such claims about their 'idol', which they knew to be none other than Christ himself.[4]

It is easy to conclude that the cult of relics contributed to the military success of the crusade, and that devotion to the True Cross occupied a particularly important place in the minds of the crusaders. The Sindon and Grail occupied just as important a place in the minds of the comparatively small number of crusaders who knew about them or had seen them. These men were determined to preserve the cloth and the secret it concealed for a select few. To some extent this has remained the policy of the Shroud's owners into the present century, for it has never been given the kind of publicity which attended the Crown of Thorns in the Sainte Chapelle in Paris, or the True Cross. To preserve these relics for Christendom, all that was needed was the capture of the city.

In April 1195 the Emperor Isaac II Angelos of Constantinople was toppled from his throne by his brother Alexius, thrown into prison with his son and heir, and his eyes put out. Ten years earlier he had married, as his second wife, the ten-year-old Princess Margaret of Hungary, daughter of King Bela III and Agnes de Châtillon. The emperor's daughter, Irene (by his first wife), had married Philip,

Duke of Swabia, the Hohenstaufen King of the Romans (or more precisely, King of Germany). These events made little impact in the West at the time, but they were to exercise a profound influence on the course of the Fourth Crusade and, ultimately, on the history of the Shroud.

Four and a half years later, in November 1199, the twenty-two-year-old Count Thibault of Champagne and his cousin, Count Louis of Blois, vowed to lead a crusade. Among his closest supporters were Geoffrey V de Joinville, Seneschal of Champagne; Garnier de Trainel, Bishop of Troyes; Count Gauthier de Brienne; Gauthier de Montbéliard; Geoffrey de Villehardouin, Marshal of Champagne and the leading chronicler of the enterprise; and his namesake and nephew, Geoffrey de Villehardouin the younger; and many other worthy knights and noblemen.

On Ash Wednesday the following year, 1200, Count Baldwin of Flanders and Hainault took the cross, together with his wife, his brother, Henry and his nephew, Thierry of Flanders. A little later Count Hugh of Saint-Pol took the cross together with a group of his followers, and soon after that Count Geoffrey of Perche.

At the conference of Compiègne the barons agreed to send envoys ahead to make all arrangements for their transport to the Holy Land. Two were appointed by Count Baldwin, two by Count Thibault and two by Count Louis. Geoffrey de Villehardouin was one of those chosen by Thibault. The leaders having agreed to set sail from Venice, the envoys duly departed and reached there in the first week of Lent, 1201.

I do not propose to describe the terms of the treaty the envoys made with the Venetians, beyond saying that they overestimated the number of men, horses and material to be transported, with the result that the Venetians built too many ships and those who eventually arrived to board them were too few to pay the total cost due for their construction. This gave rise to prolonged arguments and to an agreement under which the crusaders undertook to capture Zara for Venice from King Imre of Hungary by way of compensation for the money laid out by the Venetians on the unwanted ships. This act of aggression against the Hungarians undoubtedly coloured the attitude towards the Venetians of the Hungarian Empress Mary-Margaret.[5]

Having signed an agreement with the Venetians, Geoffrey de Villehardouin and his fellow ambassadors made tracks for home. At Piacenza in Lombardy Villehardouin left the others and went straight to France, probably by way of Montferrat, where he almost certainly reported the outcome of the recent negotiations to its ruler, the

131

Marquis Boniface. As he was crossing the Mont Cenis pass he happened to meet Gauthier de Brienne, who was on his way to Apulia to recover some lands belonging to his wife. With him were a number of other crusaders including Gauthier de Montbéliard and Robert de Joinville. On hearing from Villehardouin what arrangements had been made in Venice, Gauthier and his companions expressed their appreciation of what had been done, but as things turned out they failed to join the main body of the crusaders in Venice and made their own way to the East.

When Villehardouin arrived back in Champagne he found Count Thibault seriously ill; he died a few days after the marshal's return. It then fell to Geoffrey de Joinville and Geoffrey de Villehardouin, as seneschal and marshal respectively, to find another leader for the crusade. They approached Duke Eudes II of Burgundy, but he was unwilling to accept, whereupon Geoffrey de Joinville was asked to make a similar approach to the Count of Bar-le-Duc, a cousin of Count Thibault's. He also refused. Finally the Marquis Boniface de Montferrat was invited and he accepted. This appointment was distinctly unwelcome to Pope Innocent III, for Boniface and his family were faithful adherents of the Hohenstaufen Emperors, with whom the papacy was waging a bitter struggle for power, both spiritual and political.

The Montferrat family had important links with the East, having been closely connected with the Latin kingdom of Jerusalem. Boniface's brother, Rainier, had married a daughter of the Emperor Manuel I Comnenus (1143–80), had received the title of 'Caesar' and an 'estate' or kingdom in Thessalonica. Conrad of Montferrat had also married into the Byzantine Court, but had been badly treated and had fled to Syria. Rainier, on the other hand, had been murdered, so Boniface had cause for resentment against the Greeks, which might in some degree be satisfied if he could reclaim his brother's lands in Greece and Thrace (see Table 7).

Boniface himself had married Elena di Busca, a daughter of Duke Thomas I of Savoy, in about 1171, by whom he had a son Guillaume, who had married a daughter of Frederick Barbarossa. She died before 1200 and Guillaume had married again in 1201, Herta di Clavesana, by whom he had a son, Boniface the younger. He later married Margaret of Savoy, a daughter of Amadeus IV. This was but one of four marriages between members of the Houses of Savoy and Montferrat between 1170 and 1320. It resulted by the seventeenth century in the inclusion of Montferrat in the Duke of Savoy's long list of titles.[6] Boniface's brother Guillaume was the husband of Princess Sibylla, the

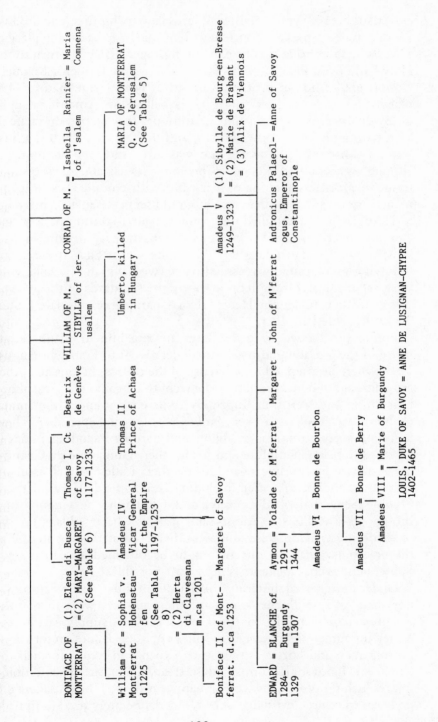

Table 7   <u>MONTFERRAT/HOHENSTAUFEN/SAVOY/COMNENUS/ANJOU(JERUSALEM)</u>

BONIFACE OF = (1) Elena di Busca
MONTFERRAT   =(2) MARY-MARGARET
               (See Table 6)

Thomas I, Ct = Beatrix
of Savoy   de Genève
1177-1233

WILLIAM OF M. = Isabella
SIBYLLA of Jer-   of J'salem
usalem

Rainier = Maria
       Comnena

CONRAD OF M.

MARIA OF MONTFERRAT
Q. of Jerusalem
(See Table 5)

William of = Sophia v.
Montferrat   Hohenstau-
d.1225   fen
           (See Table
           8)
     = (2) Herta
        di Clavesana
        m.ca 1201

Amadeus IV
Vicar General
of the Empire
1197-1253

Thomas II
Prince of Achaea

Umberto, killed
in Hungary

Boniface II of Mont- = Margaret of Savoy
ferrat. d.ca 1253

Amadeus V = (1) Sibylle de Bourg-en-Bresse
1249-1323   = (2) Marie de Brabant
            = (3) Alix de Viennois

Margaret = John of M'ferrat

Andronicus Palaeol- =Anne of Savoy
ogus, Emperor of
Constantinople

EDWARD = BLANCHE of
1284-   Burgundy
1329   m.1307

Aymon = Yolande of M'ferrat
1291-
1344

Amadeus VI = Bonne de Bourbon

Amadeus VII = Bonne de Berry

Amadeus VIII = Marie of Burgundy

LOUIS, DUKE OF SAVOY = ANNE DE LUSIGNAN-CHYPRE
1402-1465

elder daughter of King Amalric I of Jerusalem by his first (and unsatisfactory) wife, Agnes de Courtenay. This marriage had taken place in 1172, when the bride was fifteen, after King Amalric's return to the Holy Land from the visit to his father-in-law, the Emperor Manuel I Comnenus.[7] Another brother, Conrad of Montferrat, had in 1190 married Sibylla's younger half-sister, Isabella, King Amalric's daughter by Maria Comnena, in spite of rumours that he had one wife in Constantinople and another in Italy and the fact that she had a husband, Humphrey de Toron, who was alive and well at the time, although generally reckoned to be homosexual and consequently unsuitable for the begetting of heirs. Notwithstanding these impediments – more apparent than real, it would seem – Isabella's marriage to Humphrey was annulled on grounds of non-consummation, and Conrad's overlooked in the interests of dynastic pragmatism. In 1191 Isabella bore Conrad a daughter, Maria, known as La Marquise. The following year Conrad was assassinated; two days later Isabella, with what seems unbecoming haste even by the standards of those days, was betrothed to Count Henry II of Champagne, the late Count Thibault's eldest brother.

Boniface, after receiving the letter inviting him to assume command of the crusading army, immediately went to France in August 1201, where he attended a conference of the counts, barons and other crusaders at Soissons. From there he went to Cîteaux, the great abbey near Dijon and Vergy in Burgundy, where he attended the annual chapter which took place every Holy Cross Day in September. There he found a great number of abbots and barons, including Eudes le Champenois de Champlitte and his brother, Guillaume de Champlitte; Richard de Dampierre and his brother, Eudes; as well as many other Burgundian noblemen, including Guillaume de Vergy, later to become Seneschal of Burgundy; and Guillaume de Champlitte's brother-in-law, Pons de Mont-Saint-Jean et Charny. Plans for the forthcoming crusade were doubtless discussed at this chapter. Was the possibility that the Shroud might be obtained also discussed? Subsequent events make it seem at least possible.

Under the terms of the treaty Villehardouin and his fellow ambassadors had made with the Venetians, the crusaders were to pay the Republic 85,000 marks for their transport and supply, while the Venetians agreed to provide fifty galleys of a special design for transporting men and horses at their own expense in return for half the conquests. Innocent III confirmed the treaty under certain conditions, with which the Venetians were unhappy, provided the crusaders did no harm to other Christians, unless they deliberately tried to impede

Table 8   SEIGNEURS DE CHAMPLITTE, PRINCES OF ACHAEA/BURGUNDY (IVREA)/HOHENSTAUFEN/JOINVILLE

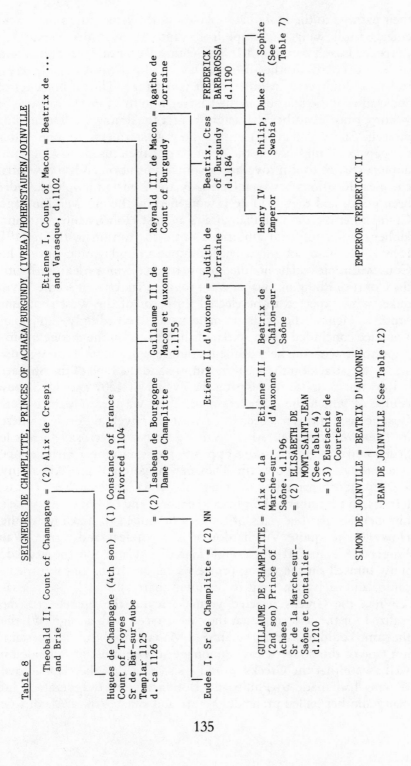

135

their passage to the Holy Land. At about the same time a new factor emerged following the escape from captivity of Prince Alexius, the Emperor Isaac's son, in 1201. The young Byzantine prince had gone to the court of his brother-in-law, Duke Philip of Swabia, and there he had met Boniface of Montferrat at Christmas. The family interests and claims of the marquis in the East led him to adopt the cause of the young prince. Another character to enter the drama was Duke Philip himself. Embroiled in a struggle for the Western empire, opposed by the papacy, Philip saw in the diversion of the crusade to Constanti-nople a chance to improve his diplomatic position and to thwart his enemies. Relations between Germany and Constantinople had never been good, and these had been worsened by the intervention of the Comneni emperors in Italian affairs against Hohenstaufen interests. Hohenstaufen imperial ambitions came to fruition in the mind of Henry VI, who sought world domination and would have taken Constantinople had he not died prematurely. Prince Alexius' flight to the Court of Philip of Swabia was providential, or so it seemed to the duke, who expected to be elected Emperor of the West should his brother, Henry, die without male issue. Accordingly, Philip and Boniface concluded a pact to establish Alexius on the throne of Con-stantinople with the help of the crusading army. The scene was now set for the attack on the Eastern Empire and the rape of the Shroud.[8]

I do not propose to describe the events of 1202 and 1203 in the course of which the crusaders made their way from Venice to the Bosphorus, for this has been done most effectively by Ernle Bradford in *The Great Betrayal*. All I need say is that the crusaders reached Scutari on the Asiatic shore opposite Constantinople in June 1203, where they set up their camp. They put the young Prince Alexius into a galley, accompanied by the Doge of Venice and Boniface of Mont-ferrat, and a number of knights and barons, and rowed over to parade him beneath the sea walls of the city he hoped to make his capital. However, to quote Villehardouin: 'Out of fear and terror of the Emperor Alexius [III] not a single man of that land or in the city dared show himself on the young prince's side. So the barons returned to camp, and each man went to his own quarters.'[9]

When the Greeks rejected young Alexius the French crusaders realized for the first time that they were faced with a siege. Whether the same could be said of the Shroud Mafia is doubtful. It is certainly not true of the doge, whose espionage service must have made him well aware that the Greeks would resist, and that the claims young Alexius had made to Philip and Boniface were exaggerated. Like many another exiled pretender before and since, Prince Alexius was under the illusion that his name would evoke an immediate response from the people. His complete failure to elicit any such response must have led the lesser barons to ponder deeply on what had (or had failed to) happen.

The next day plans were made for an assault on the city by seven divisions, of which the Burgundians formed the sixth under the command of Eudes and Guillaume de Champlitte, Otto de la Roche and others. The siege of Constantinople lasted just under two weeks, from 5 to 17 July 1203, at the end of which the usurper Alexius III collected as much money and treasure as he could carry away, and taking with him those who wished to go, fled and abandoned the city. The inhabitants were utterly astonished. They went to the prison where the Emperor Isaac was confined, clothed him in the imperial robes and carried him, now aged and blind, to the Blachernae Palace, where they set him on the throne and swore allegiance to him. Then, with Isaac's agreement, messengers were sent to tell Prince Alexius and the crusaders that the usurper had fled and that the people of Constantinople had re-established Isaac as their rightful ruler.

As soon as the young prince heard this news he sent for Boniface of Montferrat, who immediately summoned all the barons together, and the next day messengers came out of the city and confirmed all that had taken place within it. The crusaders, suspicious of a trap, sent envoys to seek the Emperor Isaac's confirmation of the covenants his son had made to them. One of the envoys was Geoffrey de Villehardouin.

On entering the Blachernae Palace the envoys found the old emperor seated on his throne with the young and beautiful Empress Mary-Margaret beside him. They asked to speak to the old man in private on behalf of his son and the crusaders. Isaac rose and gave his hand to the empress, who led him into another room where they were joined by the envoys, the chancellor and an interpreter. Here they learnt the crusaders' terms.

After the conference the envoys returned, and in due course the young prince was brought to his father, the Greeks opening all the gates to admit the crusaders who escorted him. Villehardouin writes: 'Many of our men went to visit Constantinople, to gaze at its many splendid palaces and churches, and to view all the marvellous wealth of a city richer than any other since the beginning of time. As for the relics, these were beyond all description. ...' One thing that must have impressed the crusaders, no matter what their rank, was the culture and education of the Byzantines. While even important nobles such as Villehardouin himself were barely literate (it is almost certain that he dictated his account of the capture of Constantinople), for the skills of reading and writing were left to priests, their Byzantine opposite numbers were conversant with the Greco–Roman culture upon which their civilization was based.

Princess Margaret of Hungary was only ten when she had married Isaac Angelos. As Villehardouin and others bear witness, she was still a young and beautiful woman of under thirty. She had borne the emperor several children, of whom the eldest, Kalojan Angelos, is the only one to concern us. Although a daughter and sister of Hungarian kings, she was half-French by birth and closely related by blood and marriage to many of the Frankish leaders. Her experiences in Constantinople had done little to endear to her the Greeks over whom her husband and stepson now ruled. The events of the next eight months were to do nothing to endear them to her any more (see Tables 6 and 9).

On 1 August 1203, Prince Alexius was crowned co-emperor with his father. The young Alexius IV found it impossible to fulfil the promises he had so blithely made to Boniface and Duke Philip. He partly solved the problem by melting down church and imperial plate and by levying huge taxes on his political opponents, which only served to antagonize his subjects further and to heighten the crusaders' suspicions, especially when they found that he was quite incapable of controlling his government or of carrying out his pledges. Within the city matters went from bad to worse. Towards midnight on 4 February 1204, when the young emperor was asleep in his room, Alexius Murzuphlus and others who ought to have been guarding him snatched him from bed and, leading him away prisoner, flung him into a dungeon. Then, with the help and approval of the other Greeks, Murzuphlus made himself emperor and had himself crowned in Saint Sofia.

On hearing that his son had been taken prisoner the Emperor Isaac was so overcome by fear that he had a heart attack and died. Less than a week later young Alexius was strangled by Murzuphlus himself, who gave out that he had died from natural causes. The unfortunate young man was buried with much pomp and circumstance as befitted an emperor but the truth quickly leaked out. The Latin clergy pointed out to the barons and to the other crusaders that anyone guilty of murder was unfit to rule, while those who consented to the crime were his accomplices. The excuse they had been waiting for had arrived. Assured by the clergy that an attack on the city was fully justified, since its aim would be to avenge the murder of the Lord's annointed, Alexius IV, they now saw their chance to place the

Table 9   ARPAD OF HUNGARY/ANDECHS-MERAN/HENNEBERG

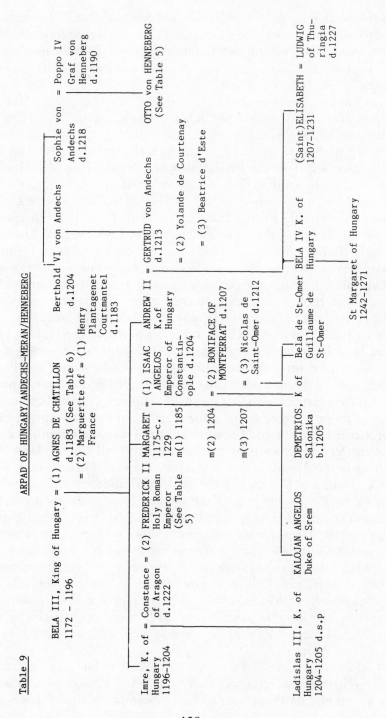

139

Byzantine Empire and Church under obedience to Rome. Moreover, it had to be done at once, for the crusaders were in a desperate situation; they could expect no supplies and no protection from the new regime within the city. Even to escape would be difficult. There was no choice but to fight or perish.

Let me pause here to remind you of the city's geography, for it is important to bear it in mind when considering the events of the following weeks. The city of Constantinople occupies a peninsula roughly triangular in shape, with slightly curving sides. The land walls stretched from the Blachernae Quarter on the Golden Horn on the north to the Studion Quarter on the Sea of Marmora on the south, a distance of some four miles or so. The sea walls along the Golden Horn were slightly shorter and ran in a gentle curve from Blachernae to Acropolis Point, the most ancient part of the city, now known as Seraglio Point, which faces northward up the Bosphorus. From the Acropolis to Studion was about five and a half miles. The sea walls went round the blunt apex of the peninsula, facing the entrance to the Bosphorus, then in a slightly concave curve along the Marmora shore. The current ran too fast round the apex of the city for landing-craft to come up easily under the base of the sea walls on the Golden Horn side. In order to launch a successful attack from this direction it was necessary to control the harbour, and this the Venetians and Franks made sure of doing prior to the attack on Blachernae on 6 April.

Ten days earlier the barons had held a conference to determine their plan of action. Accordingly on the morning of Friday 9 April the fleet approached the city and began to attack. The assault continued, fast and furious, in more than a hundred places till round about three o'clock in the afternoon. But it was unsuccessful. That evening, about six o'clock, the barons and the doge held another conference in a church on the further side of the Golden Horn, near their encampment. They decided to spend the next day and the whole of Sunday repairing the damage done to their ships and equipment, and to renew the assault on the Monday. This was successful: three city gates were forced and the crusaders streamed in. Horses were brought across the Golden Horn, some knights mounted them and rode towards the part of the city where Murzuphlus had his headquarters. As soon as his men saw the knights charging towards them on horseback, they turned and fled. Murzuphlus himself beat a hasty retreat to the Bucoleon Palace.

Unlike their Latin brethren, the Greeks were far more tolerant of other religions and sects, even allowing Jews, Cathars and Moslems their own places of worship. The very existence of the Mosque of the

Saracens, which stood a little to the north of Hagia Sofia on Acropolis Point, was a source of affront to the bigoted crusaders. When some fanatics attacked it and set it on fire, they started a conflagration which decimated a huge area of the city. Spreading south across Mese Street right across to the Marmora and almost as far as the harbour of Eleutherius, it left an area of devastation some three miles square. The fire lasted eight days and destroyed countless habitations, mainly of the poor; even the marble of Hagia Sofia was scorched and cracked by the heat. But there is no evidence to show that the churches within either the Blachernae or Bucoleon Palaces were harmed, so the theory that the Shroud and Mandylion perished in the conflagration cannot be sustained.

Meanwhile Count Baldwin took over Murzuphlus' headquarters, while his brother Henry settled in front of the Blachernae Palace. Boniface of Montferrat and his men remained near the most densely populated parts of the city. Thus the whole of the army was stationed in and around the imperial capital.

The attackers rested quietly on the first night, during which Murzuphlus, taking advantage of the invaders' weariness, made for the Golden Gate in the Studion Quarter and escaped from the city, unbeknown to the crusaders.

During that night of 12–13 April another fire broke out which spread rapidly through large areas of the town, causing immense damage. Next morning the crusaders left their quarters early, fearing to find stronger opposition than they had encountered the previous day. But to their astonishment they found none. Boniface rode straight to the Bucoleon Palace, which surrendered to him at once, on condition that the lives of all the people in it should be spared. Among these he found the Empress Agnes, sister of the King of France and the widow of the Emperor Alexius IV, now the wife of a Byzantine nobleman, Theodore Vrancas, and the Empress Mary-Margaret, together with a number of other noble ladies. In the same way the Blachernae Palace surrendered to Count Henry of Flanders. Villehardouin tells us that huge stores of treasure were found in both palaces, and that the Marquis of Montferrat and Count Henry each garrisoned the palace surrendered to him and set a guard over the treasure. In the Blachernae was kept the Soudarion/Mandylion and in the Bucoleon was kept the Sindon.

The great imperial palace of the Bucoleon is really a misnomer for it was a huge complex of buildings occupying most of the south-eastern apex of the city beneath the Acropolis. It can be compared to the Moscow Kremlin and was a city within a city, for indeed the Kremlin was inspired by it. It was bounded on one side by the fourth-century Hippodrome, a vast oblong arena nearly five hundred yards long, and on the others by the curving sea walls. Within this large enclosed area were a dozen major halls, bath complexes, a senate house, audience chamber, a barracks and offices of state together with as many churches and chapels, all of them scattered in park-like surroundings. The complex of buildings in which the sacred relics of the Passion were kept was on a terrace overlooking the sea at the south-eastern tip of the palace area, dominated by a tall lighthouse – the Pharos. This complex was made up of three inter-connected churches dedicated to the Prophet Elias, the Virgin and St Demetrios.

Nearby was the small gate giving on to a quay through which the Emperor's most favoured guests entered the palace. It was through this gate that Amalric I had entered in 1171.

Here, in this vast complex of halls and palaces, basilicas and churches, the French and Hungarian empresses found themselves alone, deserted by their Greek consorts, on the morning of Tuesday 13 April when the Marquis Boniface of Montferrat came to take possession of it. In the absence of a crowned emperor, constitutional practice lodged sovereignty with the crowned empress. Consequently from the moment Murzuphlus fled until Baldwin was crowned in Saint Sofia on 16 May, the Empress Mary-Margaret, as the senior of the two, held supreme authority in Constantinople. It was therefore her responsibility, insofar as she was able to exercise it under the circumstances, to guard the relics in both palaces. For those in the Blachernae she could do nothing, but those in the Church of the Virgin of the Pharos were under her eye, and whatever happened to them was done with her knowledge and, one presumes, her approval.

Immediately after taking possession of the Bucoleon, Boniface, as commander-in-chief, issued a general order to collect and hand over all the booty. Some obeyed, others did not, even though they were threatened with excommunication if they disobeyed the order. There is no gainsaying the appalling damage that was done in the course of 13 and 14 April, but most of it was to buildings in the city itself. The city was very large, and gangs of ignorant soldiery ran amok through its streets unhindered by the inhabitants, who were powerless to prevent them doing as they wished. The restoration of public order, therefore, was of the highest priority.

The next step, therefore, was to elect an emperor, and an electoral college of twelve was appointed. After some deliberation Baldwin of Flanders was chosen and his coronation was fixed for 16 May. The previous day Boniface married the Empress Mary-Margaret, and both did homage to the new emperor as their lord. After the coronation Baldwin was escorted to the Bucoleon where he settled down to attend to the business of governing his new empire. Boniface now requested Baldwin to give him possession of the lands across the straits and in Greece which had belonged to his brothers Rainier and Conrad, but Baldwin hesitated, thus arousing suspicions in Boniface's mind that the new emperor was not going to fulfil his promises. This was to have far-reaching consequences.

It is extremely unlikely that the Sindon and Grail left the Pharos church until after 13 April. On the other hand, it was in the power of Mary-Margaret during the brief interregnum, and in both her power and Boniface's after they married, to do with it what they wished. There would have been a brief period around the second half of May when both Boniface and Baldwin were living in the Bucoleon Palace, before they set out in different directions to consolidate the victory they had won in capturing the city. We have no evidence at all of what discussions took place between them concerning the Shroud, but it is reasonable to believe that the subject must have been discussed, and that when it came to dividing the relics according to the agreement made in March, Baldwin was allocated the True Cross and the Crown of Thorns. We can infer this because there is documentary evidence to show what subsequently happened to them – they went to Paris and were installed in the Sainte Chapelle which was specially built for them. It is inconceivable that the Sindon was simply ignored, and all the evidence points to an agreement by which Boniface received it.

Let us look, for a moment, a little more closely at the evidence, meagre though it undoubtedly is. Robert de Clari tells us that the Sindon was used in a special Mass and in particular on Good Friday. He first visited the city in August 1203, soon after the crusaders arrived at Scutari: Good Friday in 1204 was on 23 April, ten days after the city fell to the crusaders. Villehardouin tells us that little or nothing was looted in the Bucoleon and that the Blachernae was surrendered to Count Henry on the same conditions. These two palaces were about four miles apart – rather more than the distance between the Tower of London and Buckingham Palace – and the rioting and looting took place in the city itself which lay between – as it might be in Holborn and Tottenham Court Road. The palaces therefore escaped the worst of the violence, and were completely unaffected by the fires that had ravaged parts of the city in the course of the fighting. There were in these circumstances no reasons for cancelling the Good Friday ceremonies, which almost certainly took place as usual in the Bucoleon and Blachernae churches, so it could well have been one of these ceremonies that Robert de Clari describes. There is no reason for thinking that the holy cloths were removed before 15 May, the day on which Boniface and Mary-Margaret were married. There is no evidence to suggest that they were taken by Murzuphlus or any of the Greek nobles or clerics who went with him on 11 and 12 April. If any of them had taken it, it is inconceivable that its recapture would have gone unrecorded, for in order for it to be in Turin today, this is what would have had to happen.

Almost immediately after the coronation Baldwin left the city with an army in pursuit of Murzuphlus, leaving only a small garrison to ensure the safety of the city. This garrison was under the command of Count Louis of Blois. Conon de Béthune was left in charge of the Blachernae and Bucoleon palaces, together with Geoffrey de Villehardouin and one or two other barons. We can be sure that Villehardouin had nothing to do with the fate of the Shroud, for it is impossible to believe that he would have said nothing about it if he had. Villehardouin's loyalty was to the French King, his supreme overlord, whereas Boniface's was to the Western Emperor who, he hoped, would soon be Philip of Swabia. He knew that Pope Leo III had granted temporal authority to Charlemagne, and that this was symbolized in two mosaics the pope had set up in the Lateran, in which on the one hand Christ was seen giving the keys to St Peter and the Labarum to Constantine, and on the other St Peter giving the pallium to Leo and the Labarum to Charlemagne. Having been thwarted of the imperial crown, Boniface would have had both the motive and the opportunity to take the Labarum/Grail and the Shroud it contained with every feeling of justification.

The new Latin emperor made for Mosynopolis, a Thracian city some two hundred miles west of Constantinople, where he expected to find the deposed Emperor Alexius III (the usurper brother of the late Emperor Isaac), who had fled there before his advance. Baldwin now declared his intention of staying in Mosynopolis to wait for Boniface, who had not yet arrived in the imperial camp. This was because he was bringing his wife with him, and had not been able to travel as fast as the emperor. This seems to suggest that Boniface and Mary-Margaret left Constantinople at the end of May or beginning of June. Did they bring the Shroud with them? Almost certainly, for at that stage Boniface and Baldwin had not quarrelled, and there can be no doubt that the former had every intention of claiming his kingdom of Thessalonika as of right, and that Salonika – the second city of the empire – was his destination.

The day after he arrived in Mosynopolis, Boniface went to see

Baldwin to ask permission to go on to Salonika, but Baldwin refused. Boniface was extremely angry and the two men quarrelled and parted company on unfriendly terms. Baldwin himself went on to Salonika with all his attendants, while Boniface turned back with his wife and his men, among whom were Guillaume de Champlitte and Graf Berthold von Katzenellenbogen.[10] Guillaume's wife was Elisabeth de Mont-Saint-Jean, the sister of Pons de Mont-Saint-Jean et Charny and the great-aunt of Jean de Charny. Berthold von Katzenellenbogen was the commander of the not inconsiderable German contingent and a kinsman of Otto von Bodenlauben-Henneberg, of whom more later. Once more we have to consider the fate of the Shroud. If they had brought it with them from Constantinople, it seems certain that they would have continued to guard it with the greatest care. When Boniface retired to the great fortress of Demotika, seventy miles north of Mosynopolis, Villehardouin tells us that the Greek garrison 'surrendered it because his wife, the former Empress, was known to them. Then the Greeks began to rally to his side and to come in from all the country around . . . to acknowledge him as their lord.' Baldwin meanwhile having reached Salonika, both men began to prepare to fight each other.

Back in Constantinople the Doge of Venice, Count Louis of Blois and the rest of the barons were greatly perturbed by the news that the emperor and the marquis had fallen out. At their request Geoffrey de Villehardouin, who was on good terms with both, was asked to go and put an end to the quarrel. He agreed and set out for Adrianople, where Boniface was besieging the emperor's men. As soon as Boniface heard of Villehardouin's approach he went to meet him, taking with him Jacques d'Avosnes, Guillaume de Champlitte, Otto de la Roche and Hugues de Coligny. Villehardouin succeeded in patching up a truce between the two antagonists, and then went back to Constantinople. Boniface, for his part, returned to Demotika where he had left Mary-Margaret.

Once more we have to fall back on circumstantial evidence to support our theory. Guillaume de Champlitte and Otto de la Roche were two of Boniface's closest friends and advisers. Both men were ancestors or kinsmen of people who a century and more later were closely associated with the Shroud. I have already discussed Monsignor Barnes' account of how the Shroud came to France: he believed that Otto de la Roche sent it to his father in Franche-Comté, and that Pons de la Roche entrusted it to the Archbishop of Besançon. I do not agree. Otto was a direct ancestor of Humbert de la Roche-St Hippolyte, Count of Villersexel, Marguerite de Charny's husband.

Table 10   MONTBÉLIARD/KATZENELLENBOGEN/BURGUNDY (COUNTS)/BRIENNE/ANDECHS/JOINVILLE

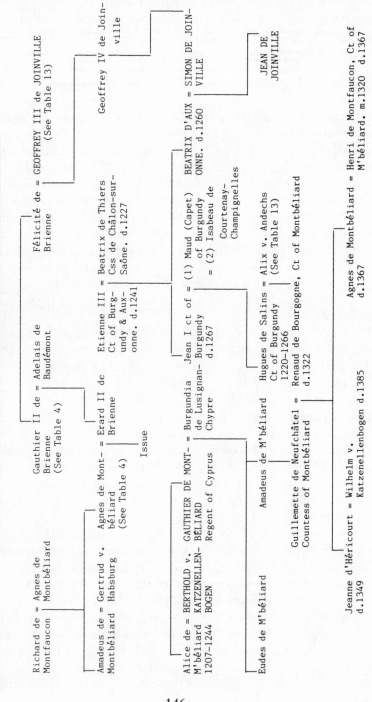

146

'The Sainte Face de Laon', showing the background trellis pattern.

'Entombment of Christ', 15th century, showing the body wrapped in the Sindon and Othonia. (*Tretyakov Gallery, Moscow*)

'Veronica', late 13th
century, School of
Rostov-Suzdal. (*The
Tretyakov Gallery,
Moscow*)

'Veronica and "Weep not
for me, Mother"', 17th
century. (*The Russian
Museum, Leningrad*)

(*Above left*) the Abbey Church of Frauenroth, showing fresco Charny/Weinsberg arms (*above right*), and the tomb of Otto and Beatrix von Henneberg (*below*).

The Krak des Chevaliers.

The Mass of St Gregory: (*right*) showing Christ emerging from a box-like casket/Grail with his hands in the Shroud position, *c.* 1490; (*below*) Christ emerging from a chalice-like Grail, *c.* 1360. (*The German National Museum, Nuremberg*)

Sepulchre Chapel frescoes at Winchester Cathedral.

The Psalter of Landgrave Hermann of Thuringia, *c.* 1211/13, illustrating the earliest example of the three-nail type of crucifixion.

Heilsbronn Minster,
Franconia: (*right*)
painting of Christ 'The
Man of Sorrows', (*below*)
the South Portal.

The 'Grail' casket of Charlemagne. (*The German National Museum, Nuremberg*)

Guillaume de Champlitte shared his seigneurie with his namesake, Guillaume de Vergy, who was an ancestor of Jeanne de Vergy, Marguerite de Charny's paternal grandmother, and thus her ancestor too. I have already pointed out the close relationships between the Montferrat and Savoy families.

There can be little doubt, therefore, that the acquisition of the Shroud and its Labarum-covered casket was a carefully planned family undertaking. Its capture must have been the prime motive of men like Guillaume de Champlitte, Otto de la Roche and Berthold von Katzenellenbogen, not to mention Boniface of Montferrat himself and others whose loyalties were towards the Hohenstaufens, who joined the crusade in 1199 and 1200.

At the end of August Baldwin was persuaded to accept the arbitration of the doge and Count Louis. Envoys were therefore chosen to fetch the marquis and take him to Constantinople, one of whom was that veteran diplomat Geoffrey de Villehardouin. They reached Demotika where they found Boniface with Mary-Margaret and a great number of 'people of good standing'. After some discussion Boniface agreed to return with them, and they were back in the capital by the beginning of September. Boniface and Baldwin reached an agreement by which the former received Salonika in exchange for Demotika, which was placed under the command of Geoffrey de Villehardouin until Boniface was in possession of his kingdom. Boniface and Mary-Margaret thereupon took leave of their friends in the capital and set out with their retainers for Salonika, where they arrived at the end of September.

It is very unlikely that Boniface and Mary-Margaret would have carried the Shroud and the Grail around with them during these negotiations and travels. Between the end of May and the end of September they travelled at least eight hundred miles, which at the rate of progress then usual, would have taken them more than four weeks. It is unlikely that they would have removed the relics during this last visit to Constantinople, so the more probable course of events would seem to have been that they left them at Demotika until such time as it was considered safe to take them to Salonika or elsewhere. The man they entrusted them to was Otto de la Roche.

Our next clue to the Shroud's whereabouts comes from a letter written to Pope Innocent III by Theodore Ducas Angelos on 1 August 1205 in the names of himself and his brother Michael, Lord of Epirus. Among Mary-Margaret's Greek supporters was Michael Ducas Angelos Comnenus, a cousin of her first husband Isaac, and of the late Emperor Alexius III. He ruled southern Epirus from his capital at

Arta. Theodore was his illegitimate half-brother. The letter reads as follows:

> In April last year a crusading army, having falsely set out to liberate the Holy Land, instead laid waste the city of Constantine. During the sack, troops of Venice and France looted even the holy sanctuaries. The Venetians partitioned the treasures of gold, silver and ivory, while the French did the same with the relics of the saints and, most sacred of all the linen in which our Lord Jesus Christ was wrapped after his death and before the resurrection. We know that the sacred objects are preserved by their predators in Venice, in France and in other places, the sacred linen in Athens. So many spoils and sacred objects should not be taken contrary to all human and divine laws, nevertheless in your name and in the name of Jesus Christ our Lord, albeit against your will, the barbarians of our age have done just that.
>
> The teaching of Jesus Christ our Saviour does not allow Christians to despoil other Christians of their sacred belongings. Let the thieves have the gold and silver, but let what is sacred be returned to us; and toward this end my brother and lord has placed his greatest trust in the intervention of your authority. With your co-operation, restitution is certain. The faithful await your action and your co-operation. My brother and lord, Michael, awaits the justice of Peter.
>
> Rome: Kalends of August 1205 [1 August][11]

How does this fit in with what we have postulated so far? Almost immediately after he gained possession of his new capital Boniface set out to conquer the rest of Greece. At about the same time Geoffrey de Villehardouin the Younger, the chronicler's nephew, left Syria and landed by chance in southern Greece after a violent storm at sea. Here he met and joined forces with Guillaume de Champlitte and together they carved out for themselves a principality in the Peloponnese. By the spring of 1205 Innocent III was addressing Guillaume de Champlitte as Prince of Achaea and the Morea. The writer of the letter I have just quoted joined his brother Michael in Greece in 1205, and was put in charge of the few remaining Greek strongholds in the Morea, which he managed to hold until 1212.

Meanwhile Otto de la Roche had become Lord (and later Duke) of Athens in late October or early November 1204. Thebes, of which he was also lord, was being ruled after 1211 by Otto's nephew, Guy de la Roche. So, if Theodore was correct in telling Pope Innocent III that the Shroud was in Athens by 1 August, the date on which he wrote to the pope, it must have reached there a considerable time before; first, because the news of its arrival there would have taken some time to reach Theodore and Michael in Epirus, and second, it would have taken yet more time for Theodore to travel from Epirus to Rome, from where he wrote his letter. It looks, therefore, as if Boniface and Mary-Margaret had entrusted the Shroud to Otto de la Roche during the summer or autumn of 1204, and that he was taking care of it on their behalf during the period following their departure from Demotika for Constantinople and until they finally settled in Salonika. If Otto did take the Shroud to Athens, there is some evidence for thinking that he lodged it in the still-standing monastery of Daphni, about six miles from the Acropolis on the road to Eleusis. In 1205 Otto expelled the Greek monks and gave the basilica and monastery buildings to the Cistercians.

So was Monsignor Barnes right after all? Did Otto de la Roche send the Shroud to Besançon soon after he obtained it? On the face of it this might seem so, but my investigations led me to think otherwise. If this were the only evidence we had, we would be justified in believing that Barnes' account was correct. But other evidence does exist and made me hesitate to accept his version of what happened. Theodore's evidence certainly rules out the theory that the Shroud came into the possession of the Templars in 1204 after the sack of Constantinople, for the order never had a house in Athens, and if the order had taken it, Theodore would have known and said so in his letter to the pope.

As one of Boniface's vassals, Otto de la Roche would have been gravely at fault if he had sent such a valuable relic as the Shroud to his father on his own initiative. If, indeed, he did send it, which I very much doubt, he did so with Boniface's knowledge and approval. If that were so, then it was sent before Boniface's death in 1207. After that date, his overlord would in name have been Boniface's infant son Demetrios, but was in fact Mary-Margaret, who was regent for the infant King of Salonika.

But we know that the Besançon shroud was a copy, and that it was destroyed in the French Revolution. If the authentic Shroud was sent from Athens to Besançon it must at some stage have been exchanged for that copy. When? Why? How? Then there is the matter of the Templars' 'idol': if it were *not* the authentic Shroud, it must have been a copy. When, and by whom, and where was that copy made? And if it was made and the Templars *knew* that it was a copy, why did they go to such lengths to prevent it falling into the king's hands in 1307? At that date there were two shrouds in Burgundy: the authentic one we know today and a copy. One of these was at Besançon, the other at Voulaine for reasons I have already explained. There can be no argument about it. Since the de Charny family came into possession of the authentic Shroud, and since we can be sure that Geoffrey de Charny

never obtained it from the Archbishop, Dean and Chapter of Besançon (why on earth would they have given it to him, anyway?) it
follows that the previous owners, the Templars, must have owned it
too. But all this gives rise to even more questions. Since the authentic
Shroud was in Athens in 1205, how did it come into the possession of
the Templars less than seventy years later? Since the Besançon shroud
was a copy, where and when was it made, and were other copies made
during this so far unaccounted-for period? I have shown that the de
Charnys and the Savoys who owned the authentic Shroud in the
fourteenth and fifteenth centuries were not only related to each other,
but shared common ancestors in three, if not four of the principle men
and women who had the handling of it in 1204. One is bound to ask,
therefore, if there were a long-standing Mafia-like conspiracy to
obtain it by fair means or foul. If there were, the next question to ask is
whether these families had any intrinsic right to own it. If the answer
to this question is No, then they must have been blasphemous bandits.
If, on the other hand, they could claim some right to its ownership,
then the matter becomes one of realpolitik rather than banditry.
Indeed, had they been bandits, and not entitled in any way to own it,
then surely Baldwin would have created a tremendous fuss when
Boniface and Mary-Margaret removed it from the Bucoleon. It would
certainly seem that he, at least, felt no qualms about their having taken
it.

But none of this explains how it came into the possession of the
Templars so soon after its apparently legitimate owners had taken
possession of it. Were Boniface and Mary-Margaret acting on their
own behalf, or were they intent on making sure that it came into the
ownership of the Hohenstaufen emperors rather than into that of the
pope or the King of France?

I must now try to answer these questions, and will begin by inviting
you to return to Salonika and to the year 1207. In the course of 1205 the
Emperor Baldwin had been taken prisoner by the Bulgarians and was
presumed dead, his brother Henry assuming the regency and later the
crown (August 1206). During the following autumn Otto de la Roche
arrived to see the new emperor to negotiate a marriage between the
marquis's daughter and the emperor himself. She was then at Salonika
and the marriage was arranged to take place there, but circumstances
prevented this. It did not take place until Candlemas Day 1207 (February) at Constantinople. Throughout most of 1207 Boniface was taken
up with campaigns in Thrace, and it was not until August that he met
his new son-in-law, who told him that the empress was expecting a
baby. The marquis did homage to the emperor and became his man,

to hold his lands from him, as he had held them from his brother, the late emperor. The marquis and the emperor spent two happy days together at Ipsala, a small town one hundred and twenty miles west of Constantinople, and agreed to meet again in October outside Adrianople to make war on the King of Wallachia. So they parted from each other, both in the best of spirits. The marquis went back to Mosynopolis and the emperor to his capital. Five days after his return home Boniface was fatally wounded in a skirmish with some Bulgarians, who cut off his head and sent it in triumph to the King of Wallachia.

The kingdom of Salonika now passed to Boniface's infant son Demetrios, under the regency of his widow Mary-Margaret, and the child was crowned on 6 January 1208 by his brother-in-law the Emperor Henry.

The traces of Mary-Margaret's reign as Queen-Regent of Salonika are few, but what there are throw a little light on the history of the Shroud. There is in the city a very ancient church dating from the ninth or tenth century which was then known as the Basilica of Theotokos (i.e. the church of the Mother of God). Only one royal personage is known to have had anything to do with it, and that was 'Marie de Montferrat'. Somewhere between 1205 and 1222 the name of the church was changed, and it became known as the church of Hagia Paraskevi (Good Friday) or the church of the Akheiropoietos (not-made-by-human-hand). The latter term is the one invariably used and applied to images of the Sindon and Soudarion, so it is not unreasonable to believe that the relic was installed there during this period.

At about the same time the infant King Demetrios was being crowned in Salonika, Guillaume de Champlitte learnt of the death in Burgundy of his elder brother Louis, who had left him an inheritance which he now returned to claim. According to the great French genealogist, Père Anselme, Guillaume de Champlitte had one son by Elisabeth de Mont-Saint-Jean, Eudes, of whom very little is known. He was named after Guillaume's brother, who had come on the Fourth Crusade with him, but who had died in 1204 and who was buried in the Church of the Apostles in Constantinople. Guillaume himself, who died on his journey home, was a cousin of Frederick Barbarossa, and it was his sister Ode who in 1228 sold for 7000 livres half the town of Champlitte to Guillaume de Vergy I, Seigneur de Mirebeau, Seneschal of Burgundy, grandfather of the Jean de Vergy who was the Seneschal of Burgundy at the time the Templars were dissolved. Guillaume de Champlitte left his conquests in Greece in charge of a nephew, presumably intending to return in due course. The precise identity of this nephew is uncertain, for his brother Eudes does not appear to have left issue, and Père Anselme mentions no other brothers who might have done so. It is possible that the nephew was one of the sons of Elisabeth de Mont-Saint-Jean's five brothers. As two of them died without issue, the choice is narrowed to one of the sons of Elisabeth's elder brother, Guillaume de Mont-Saint-Jean, Sire d'Ancy-le-Franc, Salmaise et partie de Vergy; of Jean de Charny; or of Pons de Mont-Saint-Jean, sire de Charny. On the other hand another genealogical source, de Courcelles, says that Guillaume de Champlitte divorced Elisabeth de Mont-Saint-Jean on grounds of consanguinity and married Eustachie de Courtenay, a daughter of the Emperor Peter de Courtenay. But whatever the truth of this, it is certain that Geoffrey de Villehardouin the Younger had become ruler of Achaea and Morea by May 1209.[12]

When Otto de la Roche was invested with the lordship of Athens in the autumn of 1204 it was the beginning of more than a century of Burgundian rule in Boeotia and Attica. After 1210 Otto shared the lordship of Thebes with his nephew, Guy de la Roche. Some time later Guy's sister Bonne received the other half of Thebes which she brought by marriage in the 1230s into the powerful Flemish family of Saint-Omer. Otto returned with his wife and two sons to Burgundy in 1225, leaving all his Greek lands to his nephew Guy, who ruled there till 1263.[13]

It was to Nicholas de Saint-Omer that Mary-Margaret became married in 1207, shortly after the death of Boniface de Montferrat. Her new husband was the son of the titular Prince of Galilee, and a collateral descendant of Godfrey de Saint-Omer, one of the two principle founders of the Military Order of Knights Templar. This marriage lasted little longer than her last, for Nicholas died in 1212, but not before she had borne him two sons, Bela in 1208 and William in 1209 or 1210. Left once more a widow, Mary-Margaret continued to reign as regent for her son, King Demetrios, until he came of age in 1220.

The Emperor Henry of Constantinople died in June 1216 and Pope Innocent III a month later. About the same time Michael Ducas died and was succeeded by Theodore Ducas Angelos (the writer of the letter of 1205 to Innocent III) as Despot of Epirus. He planned to regain Salonika, and perhaps the Shroud, and Mary-Margaret was forced to defend her son's kingdom with Guy de la Roche until help could reach her from France or Constantinople. At the same time Mary-Margaret's brother, King Andrew II of Hungary, having put off for more than twenty years the fulfilment of a vow originally taken by his father, and renewed by himself, to lead a crusade, decided that he had best join the Fifth – an undertaking which, like almost everything else he attempted, ended in complete failure. Andrew had succeeded his nephew Ladislas II as King of Hungary in 1205. Like his English contemporary, King John, he was an incompetent spendthrift, who conducted fourteen unsuccessful wars of aggression in the first fifteen years of his reign and antagonized his nobles thereby, with disastrous consequences for his country and its finances. In 1213 his first wife, Gertrud von Andechs, had been assassinated and two years later he married Yolande de Courtenay, another daughter of Peter de Courtenay, so he was very briefly a brother-in-law of Guillaume de Champlitte. The following year Peter de Courtenay succeeded Henry of Flanders as Emperor of Constantinople.

King Andrew's crusading enterprise brought Hungary to the very brink of bankruptcy, and nothing was achieved by it beyond the acquisition of two exceedingly doubtful relics. One of them was supposed to be the water jug used by Jesus to turn water into wine at the marriage of Cana, and the other was a skull purporting to be St Stephen's. King Andrew was quite delighted with them, for he had bought them within a week of his arrival in the Holy Land for an exorbitant price, which to his way of thinking guaranteed their authenticity. Enchanted with the success of his shopping expedition, he decided that crusading as such was not much fun, so he returned home immediately, bearing in triumph his jug and his skull, content to have fulfilled his vow with such splendid success. This time he decided to travel by land, no doubt fearful for his precious relics' safety, and called in to visit his father-in-law, the emperor, en route. He returned to his capital, Esztergom, by the end of 1218.

All this time, while King Andrew was shopping for relics in Palestine, his sister was trying to beat off attacks from Theodore of Epirus. She held him at bay for three years, but by the end of 1221 Theodore was at the gates of Salonika itself, and early in 1222 he captured it. Mary-Margaret escaped with her eldest son, Kalojan Angelos, whom she had borne to Isaac, and her two youngest sons, Bela and Guillaume de Saint-Omer. King Demetrios of Montferrat, her second son, now aged seventeen, fled to Italy to summon help from his Italian relations and to persuade Pope Honorius to preach a crusade for the defence of his kingdom. He failed in both enterprises.

Mary-Margaret was now forty-seven, three times widowed, the mother of four sons and no longer beautiful or marriageable. There was little she could do beyond return to her native land. King Andrew gave the province of Srem (Sirmium), which had been her dowry when she married the Emperor Isaac in 1195, to her son Kalojan to rule as a semi-independent Hungarian fief. So it was to Srem that she and her sons almost certainly went. Did she take the Shroud with her? She certainly did not leave it in Salonika, and it is unlikely that she sent it to the Holy Land at that particular time. Things were not going well for the crusaders just then. Damietta had fallen in 1221, and the Grand Masters of the Temple and of the Teutonic Order had had to sue for peace. In any case, what reason had she for parting with it?

We can only guess how Mary-Margaret regarded her precious relic. Did she think of herself as its legal owner, or only as a trustee? If so, was she a trustee for her first husband's son, Kalojan or for her second's, Demetrios? Was Demetrios, in turn, its owner or merely its guardian in succession to his father Boniface, for the Hohenstaufen Emperor, Frederick II? Or did it properly belong to Boniface's niece, the Marquise Maria of Montferrat, Queen of Jerusalem in her own right? In the circumstances of her departure from Salonika, there was no alternative but to take the Grail and the Shroud with her to Srem. Though there is no written evidence for this, there are two pieces of circumstantial evidence to support this view. The first, and least convincing, is a circular seal granted by King Bela IV, Mary-Margaret's nephew and Andrew II's successor and son, to the city of Trnava near Bratislava, then in Hungary, now in Czechoslovakia. It consists of two concentric circles of writing surrounding a head of Christ which bears an astonishingly close resemblance to the head on the Shroud. The second is the Sainte Face de Laon, which I have described at some length. But before I consider it in this context, we must turn back to 1204 and enquire what happened to the other cloth, the Mandylion/Soudarion.

The Mandylion too disappeared, even more completely than the Shroud. It could of course have been destroyed: that is the generally accepted view, but I do not agree with it. It was kept in the Blachernae Palace, and a careful reading of the accounts of the sack of Constantinople suggests that whereas there can be no doubt that the relics in the Bucoleon Palace escaped the looters, there is a strong possibility that those in the Blachernae did too. I have pointed out that these two palaces were four miles apart, and that the fires and looting immediately after the crusaders captured the city took place in the area between. The Blachernae like the Bucoleon was a self-contained enclave, and the troops of Count Henry of Flanders who took it were under strict control. Those who ran amok belonged to the five other divisions which had attacked the city. They were far harder to control by their officers, and given the city's enormous size, it is understandable how things could have got out of hand. After all there were hundreds of churches and monasteries there, all of which had their own relics, and it was these and works of art which were destroyed. The treasures of Hagia Sofia were extremely vulnerable to attack, since this building lay outside the palace compounds, and we know that it was ransacked by the soldiers. Let us take a closer look at what Geoffrey de Villehardouin says. After describing how Boniface went straight to the Bucoleon he goes on:

> In the same way that the palace of Bucoleon was surrendered to the Marquis of Montferrat, so the palace of Blachernae was yielded to the Comte de Flandre's brother Henri, *and on the same conditions*. There too was found a great store of treasure, not less than there had been in the palace of Bucoleon. The Marquis of Montferrat and Henri de Flandre each garrisoned the castle surrendered to him, and *set guard over the treasure* [my italics].
>
> The rest of the army, scattered throughout the city, also gained much booty; so much indeed, that no one could estimate its amount or its value. It included gold and silver, table-services and precious stones, satin and silk, mantles of squirrel fur, ermine and miniver, and every choicest thing to be found on this earth. . . .
>
> Everyone took quarters where he pleased, and there was no lack of fine dwellings in that city. So the troops of the Crusaders and the Venetians were duly housed. . . .

I think we can trust Villehardouin's account of what took place, simply because there can be no motive for him to lie about it. We can assume, therefore, that the Mandylion in the Blachernae was *not* destroyed. But the nub of the matter seems to be Bishop Garnier de Trainel's failure to mention either cloth in the list of treasures he was required to draw up after the sack. I submit that the reason he did not include the Sindon and the Mandylion is because he knew that both were safe. Let me remind you of the circumstances: there had been an agreement in March before the city was attacked, as to how the booty was to be divided, and Bishop Trainel had been deputed to make a list of all the relics so that they could be shared out accordingly. The response was patchy, as Villehardouin admits – 'Each man began to bring in such booty as he had taken. Some performed this duty conscientiously, others, prompted by covetousness, that never-failing source of all evil, proved less honest.' This can only refer to the less important relics, not, I am confident, to the Mandylion and Sindon. These must have been among the treasures guarded by Boniface and Henry of Flanders in their respective palaces. As I said earlier, the ceremony described by Robert de Clari in which the *Sydoine* stood up straight every Good Friday at the church of St Mary in the Blachernae must have taken place on Good Friday 23 April 1204. Moreover, Robert de Clari was a member of the Flanders contingent – he came from Picardy – and this Good Friday was the only one on which he was in Constantinople. If I am correct in thinking that Boniface and Mary-Margaret took the Shroud with the agreement of the Emperor Baldwin either for themselves, or more likely for the ultimate benefit of the Emperor Frederick II, it is only reasonable to believe that Baldwin made no objection because his brother had possession of the Mandylion. What happened afterwards is anyone's guess, and mine is that it found its way to Rome. The Doge of Venice and the King of France both obtained much treasure (and many relics) from the sack; the pope alone got nothing.

Now it might be argued that the cloth in Rome, variously described as the Sudarium Christi or the Veronica, had been there since Pope Sergius IV dedicated an altar to it in St Peter's in 1011. But this, and later references to it which I quoted earlier, do not *prove* that the *authentic* cloth was in Rome. Indeed, it could have been a copy. If the Jerusalem hierarchy were convinced that their eight-foot shroud was authentic as late as 1140, it is equally plausible to think that the popes thought that their Sudarium was too. Only after 1171 would they have become aware that the authentic cloths were in Constantinople, and that what they had thought was genuine was only a copy. If news of the existence of the Grail and the Shroud made such an enormous impact in Champagne, Burgundy and Outremer, to the extent that the Fourth Crusade became in part an attempt to wrest them for the Western Church, why not in Rome?

If on the other hand the Mandylion was not sent from Constantinople to Rome in, or soon after, the summer of 1204, it might have been taken by Boniface and Mary-Margaret, and Theodore's letter to Innocent III could be taken to indicate that both cloths were then in Athens. If this were the case, then both cloths probably remained in Salonika until 1222. When the time came to decide where the two should go – let us say about 1229 soon after Mary-Margaret's death or retirement, it could be argued that since the Mandylion had come from Edessa in 944, its rightful owner was Beatrix de Courtenay-Edessa and her husband, Otto von Henneberg. The Mandylion was then sent to Germany, while the Shroud was given to the Templars for the pope and taken by them to their headquarters in Acre. The grand master at this time was Pierre de Montaigu, and I shall return to this possible course of events later.

But there is another scenario we ought to consider. If Mary-Margaret never had the Mandylion, but only the Sindon, a decision concerning its disposal had to be taken at her death. It might be argued that its owner was the Queen of Jerusalem and her husband, Jean de Brienne, for that is where the Shroud came from in the first place. So we now have five possible claimants – Kalojan Angelos, Demetrios of Montferrat, Maria of Montferrat and Jean de Brienne, and the Emperor Frederick II, with the possible addition of Otto and Beatrix von Henneberg. All these claimants were members of what I have called the Shroud Mafia (see Tables 4, 5, 6, 7 and 9). Before I consider this further I want to return to the circumstantial evidence I mentioned earlier, which convinces me that the Shroud was taken to Srem. It hinges upon the origin of the Sainte Face de Laon.

Jacques Pantaléon, later Pope Urban IV, but earlier a canon of Laon, sent the icon to his sister, an abbess in Picardy, in 1249 from Apulia. It bears a Slavonic inscription stating that 'This is the Lord's face on the Cloth', and all experts agree that it is of Balkan origin and dates from the first half of the thirteenth century. A similar icon, lacking the trelliswork background and inscription but almost certainly painted by the same artist, is in the Tretyakov Museum in Moscow. Independent experts have dated this icon to between 1200 and 1217. A third icon, also in the Tretyakov, of the Rostov–Suzdal school, and dating from the late thirteenth century, shows Christ's head strikingly similar to the others, but with a squared background and fringe with the two roundels containing Christ's monograms similar to those on the Laon icon. The origin of all three is clearly the same: the first two may even have been painted at the same time.

The Hungarian authority on icons, Dr Eugen Csocsan de Varallja, is convinced that the Laon icon, and probably the first Tretyakov icon, must have been painted in the Benedictine monastery of Szavaszent-demeter (St Demetrius-on-the-Sava). This abbey was situated in Srem, in what is now northern Yugoslavia, but was then part of Hungary. The monastery was founded by King Andrew I and his brother Bela I of Hungary in about 1057. At that time Srem belonged to the Eastern Empire, although the suzerainty of Constantinople was more theoretical than real. King Bela II found sanctuary there in 1132, when he was threatened with an uprising of his nobility. In 1247 Innocent IV gave it to the Benedictines and placed it under the direct authority of the Bishop of Srem after it had been looted during the Tartar invasion of 1240–41. The monastery was originally under the authority of the Orthodox Church, and as such Slavonic was the language of its monks. It only came under Rome during the pontificate of Honorius III in 1216. It was consequently a newly acquired religious asset when Mary-Margaret and her sons arrived in Srem in 1222. It is the Slavonic inscription on an Eastern-style icon, which has always belonged to the Roman Church, that makes the Sainte Face de Laon so important in the context of the Shroud's history. If one takes the inscription literally, it means that the icon was painted directly from the image on the cloth.

The site of Szavaszentdemeter has been lost. As late as the seventeenth century its name appeared on maps of the region at a location not far from the modern Croat town of Nova Gradiska. Other maps place it further east in or near the city of Sremska Mitrovica, some forty miles west of Belgrade. Throughout its history the abbey was closely associated with the Arpad dynasty, and was the largest monastery in that part of Hungary during the twelfth and thirteenth centuries. If Mary-Margaret took the Shroud with her from Salonika, then it was to Szavaszentdemeter that she most likely carried it. Not only was this a Uniate community within the Roman communion, but it was the chief religious establishment in her son's dukedom.

In 1241 the Tartars invaded Hungary, forcing Bela IV and the royal family to seek refuge in the Templar fortress of Klis, a few miles from Split in Dalmatia. Bela had managed to save the Crown of St Stephen and other crown jewels, and to send them with his queen and children to safety there. Warnings of this impending catastrophe had been sounded as early as 1238, but when the Tartars eventually broke through the Carpathian passes into the broad Hungarian plain, Bela found himself deserted by most of his barons, who resented his attempts to recover the lands his father had so profligately distributed among them. The king was forced to retreat to Croatia, and then down the Dalmatian coast. He reached Zagreb in 1242 from where he sent his family to the coast. Hotly pursued by the Tartars, the king retreated as slowly as he could, eventually reaching Split, where he hoped to cross over to one of the many offshore islands. There were no boats to carry him and his army, so he retreated further down the coast to Trogir, which is built on an islet linked to the mainland by a bridge, which the Hungarians managed to destroy. The Tartars laid siege to the island fortress, but within a few days news reached them of the death of the Great Khan, and as rapidly as they had come, they withdrew eastward through Bulgaria and back to the southern steppes of Russia. By the middle of 1242 the evacuation of Hungary was complete, but the devastation they left behind them was appalling.

Mary-Margaret probably died a decade before the Tartar invasion, and it is unlikely that it was her intention to leave the Shroud in a backwater like Srem. She left no will, or if she did it has not survived, so we are driven once more to speculate. I had traced the Shroud's history to 1222 with some degree of certainty, and to 1230 with rather less. I knew that the Templars owned it by 1293 and probably by 1274, so I was now faced with a gap of between forty and seventy years. It proved to be a harder task and took longer than I had anticipated.[14]

CHAPTER 6

GERMANY AND THE HIDDEN YEARS: 1230–1274

———•———

In the spring of 1201, when Geoffrey de Villehardouin was crossing the Mont Cenis Pass on his way back to Champagne from Venice after concluding the treaty with the doge for the transport of the crusaders to the Holy Land, he encountered his kinsman, Gauthier de Brienne, who was accompanied by Gauthier de Montbéliard, Robert de Join-ville and a large number of other crusaders from Franche-Comté and Champagne. They were on their way to Italy where Innocent III had recruited Gauthier de Brienne as an ally in his struggle against the Hohenstaufen party for the control of Sicily and the kingdom of Naples. Gauthier had married the eldest daughter of Tancred, the last Norman King of Sicily and Naples, who was the pope's ally and an enemy of the Hohenstaufen emperors. Innocent consequently approved of the marriage, and promised to support Gauthier's attempt to conquer the county of Lecce in the heel of Italy and the neighbouring principality of Taranto in Apulia on his way to the Holy Land.

Gauthier's chief lieutenants were his cousins, Robert de Joinville and Gauthier de Montbéliard (see Table 4), and at first his campaign went well. But then it ran into stiffer opposition, and dragged on inconclusively for four years. Finally, in 1205, Gauthier de Brienne was surprised in his camp by the enemy, who cut the ropes of his tent, pulled it down upon him and killed him. His brother Jean took part in the conquest of Constantinople, having gone there with the main body of crusaders, where his valour had gained him much glory and esteem.

On the death of King Amalric II of Jerusalem the barons offered Jean the crown of Jerusalem if he married the Marquise Maria of Montferrat, Boniface's niece and King Amalric I's grand-daughter.

160

Jean de Brienne accepted, and after securing the support of Innocent III and King Philip Augustus of France, arrived in the Holy Land in 1209, was married at once and crowned King of Jerusalem the following year. Queen Maria of Montferrat died in 1221, after which Jean de Brienne returned to France, where he married a second wife, Berengaria of Castile. In 1225 his daughter by Maria, Yolande, now Queen of Jerusalem in her own right, was married to the Emperor Frederick II. She was fourteen and he was thirty. There were two weddings: the first by proxy in Jerusalem in August, the second, in person, at Brindisi on 9 November. Frederick, whose sexual appetite was notorious throughout Europe, and which was wont to get the better of him from time to time, disgraced the proceedings by seducing one of the bridesmaids, who happened to be one of the bride's cousins. History does not relate which, but she was either Marguerite de Brienne, one of Gauthier's daughters, or Sibylle de Noyers, a daughter of Gauthier's cousin, Alix de Brienne, the wife of Clérambault de Noyers. Sibylle de Noyers was the wife of Pons de Mont-Saint-Jean (see Table 4), in time to become Jean de Charny's grandmother.

Whichever lady was the unfortunate victim of the imperial seduction, the affair did nothing to endear the emperor to his new in-laws, least of all to his elderly father-in-law, Jean de Brienne. It is not likely to have done much to increase his esteem in the eyes of the Joinville, Noyers and Mont-Saint-Jean families either.

The young Queen-Empress Yolande was packed off to Frederick's harem in Palermo, where on 25 April 1228, at the age of barely sixteen, she gave birth to a son, Conrad. She died six days later. Her family and friends were outraged, and the episode did nothing to improve the already strained relations between the pope and the emperor. Following this unhappy incident, Frederick at last decided the time had come to fulfil his promise to lead a crusade. He had postponed his departure year after year, but finally embarked at Brindisi on 8 September 1227. A few days later one of his most faithful lieutenants, the Landgrave Ludwig of Thuringia, fell ill and died at sea.[1]

Frederick ordered the fleet to put in to Otranto, where he too fell ill. Rather than postpone the expedition, he decided to send it on without him under the military command of Count Henry of Limburg, and under the spiritual guidance of the newly appointed Patriarch of Jerusalem, Gerold of Lausanne. When the pope heard that the emperor had not sailed after all, he reacted sharply in the belief that Frederick's illness was not genuine, and that he was prevaricating once more as he had prevaricated in the past. Gregory IX was a more earnest man than his predecessor (who had died in March 1227) and was, furthermore, a cousin of that unforgiving Hohenstaufen antagonist, Innocent III. Like Innocent, Gregory was a man with a legalistic turn of mind and an uncompromising belief in papal authority. He disliked Frederick as a man, and strongly disapproved of his morals. He was convinced that the emperor's state of health was not the true reason for the delay, so he excommunicated him, repeating the sentence in St Peter's in November.

Frederick retaliated by denouncing the pope, continued his preparations as if nothing had happened, and set out once more in June 1228. In the meantime his child-bride had borne him a son and died as a result, so that he was no longer the husband of the Queen of Jerusalem, but at best the regent for its infant king, Conrad. This altered his status in the eyes of the local barons, the patriarch and, not least, the pope. The emperor arrived in Cyprus on 21 July where he remained till the beginning of September. He then sailed for Acre, reaching there on the 5th. Meanwhile the news that Gregory had excommunicated the emperor had reached the patriarch, and that the pope had repeated it because Frederick had set out before obtaining absolution. Frederick, needless to say, cared not a fig for all this.

Frederick's position in regard to the throne of Jerusalem was uncertain following Yolande's death. Quite apart from this most of the local notables, both lay and clerical, felt it their duty to have nothing to do with an excommunicate. This particularly applied to the Military Orders of the Temple and Hospital, though the Teutonic knights remained loyal to him, thanks mainly to their leaders, Conrad von Hohenlohe-Brauneck and Hermann von Salza.

Confronted with these spiritual and political difficulties, Frederick had no alternative but to resort to diplomacy. He made a treaty with the Saracens by which he obtained Jerusalem, Bethlehem, Nazareth and western Galilee under certain reasonable conditions together with a ten-year truce. Thus the excommunicate had won back the Holy Places without a blow. The pious and bigoted among both Christians and Moslems were furious. And none were more furious than the patriarch and the Templars; the former because Frederick had flouted ecclesiastical authority, the latter because the Temple area was to remain in Moslem hands.

None of this made much impression on Frederick. He made a ceremonial entry into Jerusalem on 17 March 1229, and next day crowned himself king, in right of his late wife, in the Church of the Holy Sepulchre, assisted only by the Teutonic knights. Patriarch Gerold placed Jerusalem under an interdict, which so enraged

Frederick that he set out there and then for Acre, where the patriarch was living, threw a cordon of soldiers round his palace and the Templars' quarter, threatened to kidnap him and Grand Master Pierre de Montaigu, and to pack them off to Italy. The outcome of all this was the total alienation of the Templars, who in any case owed their allegiance to the pope alone. It was as a result of this quarrel that the first accusations of Templar malpractices were made. We should regard them, therefore, with some degree of suspicion.

But this situation could not last: a way out had to be found for the pope and the emperor to live together in harmony. In the end Frederick did make his peace with the pope, but not until July 1230, a year after he had returned to Italy to defend his lands against his father-in-law, Jean de Brienne, who had invaded them at the head of a papal army. Frederick, having successfully repulsed these attacks, was now ready to come to terms with the pontiff, and to be absolved from his excommunications.

Following the Peace of San Germano, Frederick neglected his duties in Germany during the ensuing years, for the struggle with the papacy was not really ended. Aided by the Lombard cities and many German nobles, the papacy eventually won the day, and Frederick died in 1250, still at odds with the Church.

What, you may ask, has all this to do with the Shroud and the Grail? Before I answer, I must make a further digression to consider the theories advanced by Dr W. K. Müller. Willi Müller is a doctor of medicine whose professional interest lies in the study of diseases of the central nervous system in man and animals. Part of this study has embraced the inherited disease known as Huntingdon's Chorea. It attacks its victims usually in middle age, and occurs in fairly restricted communities – in Britain it is commonest in East Anglia, in America among families descended from seventeenth-century New England immigrants, and in Germany in the district round Würzburg in Franconia. In the course of his investigations, Müller had cause to visit villages in Franconia to examine their parish records, which, due to the good fortune of having escaped destruction during the Thirty Years' War, are more complete than in other parts of the country. He was also interested in the Shroud and its history, and was struck by a number of things which seemed to suggest a connection with the relic in some of the churches he visited. For example, in the churches of Weikersheim and Frauenroth he noticed frescoes and paintings which included coats of arms identical to those of Geoffrey de Charny, the Porte Oriflamme. These arms related to a family called Weinsberg, and in the church of Weinsberg, near Heilbronn, he was struck by sculptural features which included the fleur-de-lys of France. Then there were some strange pictorial carvings over the main portal of the little country church of Oberwittighausen, and certain architectural features which suggested to him that they might have been connected with the public exposition of the relic. All this led him to discover that the churches in question were either founded by or connected with the Hohenlohe-Brauneck and Henneberg families, and more particularly with Conrad von Hohenlohe and Otto von Henneberg-Bodenlauben. Dr Müller and I began to correspond, and in the Easter holidays of 1985 I paid him a visit and had the pleasure of being taken to see these churches. I came away convinced that he was correct in believing that the Shroud spent some time in Germany during the thirteenth century, but I did not agree with him about the way in which it came there. At that time I could not advance a convincing alternative theory, but I returned to Britain determined to reconcile, if possible, his views with my own, and to discover, if I could, new evidence which might throw some light on the matter. Having explained this, we must now return to 1222, when Mary-Margaret fled from Salonika to her native Hungary.

Nothing is known about the former empress after 1229, and it is assumed that she died then or soon after. Her brother King Andrew died in 1235, and the question we must answer is: What happened to the Shroud? How and why did it pass into the hands of the Templars? We know that it did not remain in Hungary; Müller and I believe it went to Germany, and yet it was in France by 1274 if Brother Jean-Denis de Tavernay's evidence is to be believed, for it was not in the Holy Land at that date. The clue which provided the answer to these questions was to be found in the financial state of Hungary after the death of King Andrew.

King Andrew was not on good terms with the Templars. He had invited the Teutonic knights to settle in Burzenland, the area of eastern Hungary and western Rumania north of the Danube and immediately to the east of Srem. His aim was to create a bulwark against penetration from the east by Asiatic nomads. The knights tried to carve out a state for themselves, an activity which caused great resentment in Hungary and led to their expulsion in 1225. Like every other enterprise undertaken by King Andrew, this one ended in failure, and his relations with the Templars had been soured by his flirtation with the Teutonic knights in an area which they hoped to establish themselves. Andrew's relations with the Hospitallers, on the other hand, were somewhat more cordial.

Due to King Andrew's profligacy most of the Crown lands had

been given to the barons or mortgaged to Jewish moneylenders for loans which had to be repaid by his son and heir, Bela IV. There was only one way Bela could extricate himself from his financial embarrassments without antagonizing the barons by demanding that they hand back to the Crown those lands Andrew had so thoughtlessly given them, and that was to appeal for help to his French and German kinsmen, or to the Templars.

The order had become the banker of Europe, as I have already described in Chapter 3. Their activities were confined to four fields: loans, advances and bonds; payments over long distances and the transmission of funds generally; debt-recovery; and payments on current account. Those who wanted to borrow money did not pay interest, as this was forbidden by canon law. Instead the borrower would give the order real estate or personal valuables as security in exchange for a gift of the amount of money required. So long as the 'loan' was outstanding and unpaid, the order kept the income from the estate or the personal valuables. When the borrower died the security was not handed back to the heirs but kept by the order for ever as a counter-gift.

There is no evidence that Bela IV sold or mortgaged the Shroud and the Grail to the Templars or to anyone else. To have done so would have been tantamount to blasphemy. On the other hand there is ample evidence to show that he was able to restore the finances of Hungary in a remarkably short time after his father's death in spite of the havoc wrought by the Tartar invasion five years after he had come to the throne. That the Shroud and the Templars played some part in this recovery seems at least possible.

When, two hundred years later, Marguerite de Charny gave the Shroud to Duke Louis of Savoy, he gave her certain estates in return for so-called 'valuable services'. By this euphemism the sordid business of sale and purchase was tactfully avoided. But if we look at this transaction a little more closely, it is clear that it was not a business deal between strangers but the transfer of an heirloom from one branch of the family to another. The earlier transaction was of precisely the same nature, but in this case the *quid pro quo* was the payment of Bela's debts, and the Templars' role was not so much that of a banker lending money to a client on security as that of a trustee administering the estate for the benefit of the family. Like any trustee the Templars had to be paid for their services. In this case the 'payment' was the possession of the relic. There is, of course, no surviving written evidence for this, but I offer what follows as one possible explanation of events, for it does at least fit such meagre evidence as we do possess.

165

At the end of Chapter 5 I touched upon the question of the Shroud's ownership. It did not belong to the Roman Church or to the pope. It had formerly belonged to the emperors of Constantinople in succession in much the same way that the British crown jewels belong to the kings and queens of Britain in succession. It was not the emperors' personal property, nor did it belong to the state. Like the British crown jewels it belonged to a legal fiction approximately equivalent to the Crown, which is different and separate from the incumbent of the throne. In 1247 (close enough to be significant to the period we are now considering) the Emperor Baldwin II, in exchange for financial support, decreed that all the relics in Constantinople were to belong to the King of France, at that time Louis IX, or St Louis. But the Shroud was different. Throughout its recorded history from the time it was at Lirey down to the death of the late King Umberto in 1984, it has been the private property of a family or group of families, of which the House of Savoy was the ultimate heir. Only since King Umberto's death has it belonged to the Roman Catholic Church. It had, of course, been cared for by the Church, because of its sacred nature, and had most of the time been housed in consecrated buildings, but the Church never owned it as it did the Veronica.

After Mary-Margaret's death, and perhaps for some time before, the question of ownership must have become a highly controversial issue. I have already explained that there were five possible claimants, but in order to help us to conclude which of them was the rightful one, we must take into account what we know of the Shroud's subsequent history.

I hope I have convinced you that it belonged to the Templars from at least 1274, and to the de Charny family from 1307. What we have to decide now is how it passed from Mary-Margaret to the Templars, bearing in mind the strong probability that it spent some years in Germany.

After examining what little evidence I can find, I am left with two possible scenarios. In the first, the Shroud passed directly into the hand of the Templars between 1222 and 1230 in trust for Frederick II. The grand master at the time was Pierre de Montaigu, who was elected in 1219. He had formerly been Preceptor of Provence and Spain, and was succeeded at his death by Armand de Périgord, the former Preceptor of Sicily and Calabria. His term of office lasted until 1244. Both grand masters spent their terms of office in the East. In these circumstances it is more than probable that the Shroud and Grail would have been sent to Acre, the Templars' headquarters in the Holy Land. This is what Müller believes. The notorious hostility which existed between Pierre de Montaigu and Frederick II was attributable, he thinks, in part at any rate, to the grand master's refusal to hand over the relic to the emperor. But with the help of the Teutonic knights, under Conrad von Hohenlohe, the Shroud was seized from the Templars by main force when the emperor attacked them in Acre in March 1229, and was taken back to Europe when he left the following May. Conrad von Hohenlohe was charged with its care, and it was he who brought it to Germany. The trouble with this is that it takes no account of the fact that it returned to the Templars forty years later. Why?

The second scenario takes into account other factors which cannot be ignored, but which are no more than suggestive, and certainly not conclusive. If we assume that Boniface and Mary-Margaret took the relics on behalf of Frederick II, it is hard to understand why she and her executors – presumably her sons Kalojan and Demetrios – would have allowed them to go back to the Holy Land when they were already more than halfway to Germany. Kalojan could not possibly justify any claim to them, even though he was the son of the Emperor Isaac. Demetrios was an exile in Italy, to whom no one paid any attention. This left Mary-Margaret's German relations, Otto von Henneberg, her sister-in-law's brother Berthold von Andechs, Patriarch of Aquilea, and Berthold's sister Hedwig, Duchess of Silesia, better known to history as St Hedwig (see Tables 9 and 13). Otto von Henneberg was a first cousin of the patriarch and of the saint, and was born about 1177.[2] At the age of twenty he took part in the Third Crusade, returning to Germany in 1206, where he remained for two years. On his return to the East he married Beatrix de Courtenay. In 1220 he and his wife sold their property in the Holy Land to the Teutonic knights and returned home to Franconia in 1221. Beatrix and Otto had two sons: Heinrich, who became a monk, and Otto, who married a wife from the Hillenberg family, from whom he separated in 1230 in order to join the Teutonic Order, while she took the veil. The only child of this marriage was given to the Church to bring up. In 1230 Otto and Beatrix sold extensive estates in Germany in order to found a nunnery at Frauenroth. Otto died in 1244 and Beatrix a few years later.

As a German nobleman and part of the Shroud Mafia, Otto was the obvious person with whom to entrust the Shroud on Mary-Margaret's death. The foundation of the abbey of Frauenroth at this particular juncture, and the concurrent wave of piety which swept the Franconian nobility must surely signify some deep religious event to have influenced so many members of the local aristocracy to devote their lives to religion. In addition to the Arpad saints, Elisabeth of Thuringia, Margaret of Hungary, Kunigunde of Cracow and Yolande (Helena) of Poland, there were Berta von Andechs, a sister of Duke Berthold VI, who was abbess of Gerbstadt, her niece, St Hedwig of Silesia, and her nephew, the Patriarch's brother, Ekbert von Andechs, who was bishop of Bamberg. There was also their sister, Mechtild von Andechs, who was abbess of Kissingen near Frauenroth. The Hohenlohe-Brauneck family produced two brothers, Heinrich and Friedrich who were the joint founders of the Abbey of Mergentheim, and no fewer than six grandchildren of Conrad von Hohenlohe were either nuns or monks, not to mention several other members of this family who were Teutonic knights (see Table 11). I suggest that this event was the arrival of the Shroud and the Grail in their midst. But if this is no more than coincidental, there is one other small piece of evidence worth mentioning. Above the handsome tomb in which Otto and Beatrix lie in the chancel of Frauenroth there are the remains of frescoes which include not, as one might expect, their coats of arms, but those of Charny/Weinsberg–Gules, three escutcheons argent. It was Kunigunde von Hohenlohe, the sister of this same Conrad, and of the two founding brothers of Mergentheim, who married Hans von Weinsberg, alias Jean de Charny, somewhere around 1225 to 1230.

The appointment of Jean de Milly in 1228 to succeed Brother Aimard as Treasurer of the Templars, an office he held until 1234 or 1235, takes on some significance in this context. The treasurer was always the Commander of the 'Terre de Jerusalem' and after 1202 Commander of France, and ranked fourth in the hierarchy after the grand master, seneschal and marshal. The treasurer was, of course, the knight responsible for financial affairs as important as the one I envisage taking place at this time. Jean de Milly's precise position in his family's pedigree is uncertain, but that he was a close kinsman of Beatrix von Henneberg's mother, Agnes de Milly, cannot be doubted. It follows that on Mary-Margaret's death her nephew, Bela IV, in whose country it was, would have been in a strong position if he had wished, to use the Shroud as a bargaining counter for the settlement of the debts he had inherited from his father. It seems highly probable, therefore, that he came to some agreement with the Templars to give the Shroud to Otto and Beatrix in return for the payment of these debts. This was the sort of arrangement that Jean de Milly is bound to have viewed with favour, especially in view of the hostility then existing between the order and Frederick II, and more especially since his uncle Philip de Milly had been one of those privileged few

Table 11   HOHENLOHE–BRAUNECK/WEINSBERG (CHARNY)

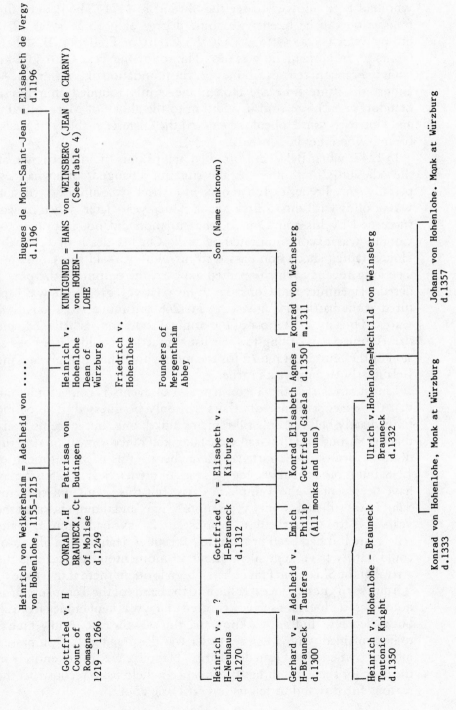

who had been allowed to see the Shroud in 1171. The date of this transaction can be fixed with some degree of probability as 1230, during which year Otto was at the Court of Frederick II, where Conrad von Hohenlohe was too. The following year Otto sold his lands in Franconia to raise money for the foundation of Frauenroth. At almost the same time the Hohenlohe family founded churches at Standorf and Burgerroth in addition to the abbey of Mergentheim, and Gottfried von Hohenlohe entered the Cistercian abbey of Heils-bronn, where he died in 1312.

In 1247, when Baldwin II granted Saint Louis the right to own all the relics in Constantinople, the situation changed somewhat, especially since Frederick II had once more been excommunicated, and was at odds with the Church again. Three years later, when he was succeeded by his son Conrad, the situation did not improve, for Conrad was excommunicated as well. On his death in 1253, the Hohenstaufen succession passed to his two-year-old son Conradin. The long regency which resulted exposed the empire to the pope's hereditary enmity and Conradin to his relatives' greed. He was captured at the battle of Tagliacozzo in 1268 and murdered soon afterwards. Thus by 1254 most of the original protagonists had died, and the Templars, according to their usual practice, could claim possession of the Shroud in return for the money that they had given King Bela nearly twenty years earlier.

I must stress that this reconstruction of events is conjectural, and that the exact sequence of affairs can only be guessed. The period immediately before 1274 still remains a dark one, but it seems likely that the Shroud and the Grail were taken to France some time after the death of Beatrix de Courtenay-Henneberg – this is some time after 1248, but more probably after the death of Frederick II in 1250. It may have been sent to the Temple in Paris, but this seems unlikely, for Saint Louis still had twenty years more to live, and though he spent the years 1248 to 1254 in the East, he must surely have had some say in the relic's fate if it had been brought to his capital. Jean de Joinville, too, could hardly have kept silent about so momentous an event as the arrival of the Shroud in France had it been brought there at that time. It is fruitless to guess. Once it came into the hands of the Templars, their notorious fondness for secrecy ensured that it was kept hidden from all but a select few. Indeed, we know that this was the case. And yet it has to be explained why, when the order was dissolved in 1307, it passed into the ownership of Jean de Charny. Happily, we are not entirely in the dark for there are shreds of evidence to help us to reconstruct the reasons for this and to tell us how it came about.

Some time between 1230 and 1240 a wedding took place in the church of Weinsberg, a small town about five miles from Heilbronn, between Hans von Weinsberg and Kunigunde von Hohenlohe-Brauneck, the sister of the Conrad von Hohenlohe who accompanied Frederick II to the Holy Land in 1228. Hans von Weinsberg's arms are identical to those of Geoffrey de Charny, the Porte Oriflamme – on a field gules, three escutcheons argent. Who was he? The two principle authorities on the pedigrees of the French nobility are Père Anselme and de Courcelles, the former an eighteenth-century and the latter an early nineteenth-century genealogist. They do not always agree, as is to be expected, but neither of them has anything to say about this matter. I have therefore had to speculate once more.

Kunigunde von Hohenlohe is recorded in German records as being of age in 1219. Girls came of age at different periods and in different countries at between twelve and fifteen in the Middle Ages, and boys at between fifteen and twenty-one. It very much depended on whether you were an heiress or not. Princess Margaret of Hungary married the Emperor Isaac when she was ten, and Queen Yolande de Brienne was fourteen when she married the Emperor Frederick II. In Kunigunde's case the chances are that she came of age later than she would have done had she been a royal princess, so we can estimate her year of birth as somewhere around 1204, give or take three years either way. This date accords by and large with the known dates of birth of her siblings.

Turning now to the de Charny family, there are only two called Jean: one was the husband of Marguerite de Joinville and he died in 1323, so he cannot have been the husband of a girl who was of age more than a century earlier. In any case, we know the names of his three wives – Marguerite was his first, followed by Jeanne de Grancey, Dame de Frolois, whom he married in about 1307, and Isabelle de Sancerre of the House of Blois-Champagne, who died in 1320. This Jean de Charny was born about 1270. The other was his great-uncle, and a brother of Elisabeth de Mont-Saint-Jean, the wife of Guillaume de Champlitte, Prince of Achaea. Both French pedigrees say that this Jean died without issue, and it is certainly true that he disappears from Burgundian records after 1224. Statements of this kind often mask a genealogist's ignorance. To give you one excellent example, Geoffrey de Briquenay, Jean de Joinville's second son, is said by Père Anselme to have died without issue, when in fact he went to Naples and became the ancestor of an Italian family of Counts of Sant-Angelo. Consequently it is by no means impossible to believe that Jean de Charny went to Germany, where he became Hans von Weinsberg and married

Kunigunde von Hohenlohe. I must stress, however, that this is pure guesswork.

If, however, my guess is correct, a number of interesting possibilities follow from it. The first, and most important, places a member of the de Charny family squarely in the centre of that group of men who had most to do with the removal of the Shroud and Grail from Constantinople in 1204, and it establishes a link between that family and Otto von Henneberg through Kunigunde's brother, Conrad von Hohenlohe. This Jean de Charny was the right age to have become Hans von Weinsberg, and although he was too young to have taken part in the Fourth Crusade, he grew up in its aftermath and was the brother-in-law of one of its leaders, Guillaume de Champlitte. He disappears from French records a little before the time I reckon the Shroud came to Germany from Hungary.

Hans and Kunigunde had at least one son, and possibly other children as well. What part, if any, they played in the transfer of the Shroud to Germany and then to the Templars is so far impossible to tell, but if the second transfer took place in the 1250s or 1260s, then it would have been Hugues de Mont-Saint-Jean, Seigneur de Charny, Hans' nephew who would have had to do with it. Hugues' son Geoffrey, the martyred Templar, was born about 1251, and was received into the order in 1269 or 1270 by Amaury de la Roche, a close kinsman of Otto de la Roche, and his descendants the Dukes of Athens. Whether Geoffrey's decision to become a Templar rather than a member of another order or to become a priest had anything to do with the Shroud is yet again something we can only surmise. That he was in a good position to keep a watching brief over it on behalf of his kinsmen during the years it was in the order's care, and especially during the critical summer and autumn of 1307, cannot be gainsaid.

I want now to turn our attention to the other family who must have been closely associated with the Shroud's fate during the last thirty or forty years of the thirteenth century, the de Joinvilles. There is no doubt in my mind that Jean de Joinville, the biographer of St Louis, must have played a part in its rescue from the rapacity of Philip the Handsome.

The origins of the House of Joinville are closely linked with those of the House of Brienne.[3] Two brothers, Engelbert and Gozbert, built a castle called Brienne about 950, from which they carried on a campaign of brigandage in the area of Chaumont, Troyes and Saint-Dizier. The King of France, Louis IV, besieged and took it, then destroyed it and banished the brothers. In spite of this setback the brothers quickly recovered. Engelbert married the rich widow of the

Table 12   JOINVILLE/BRIENNE 1140 – 1300

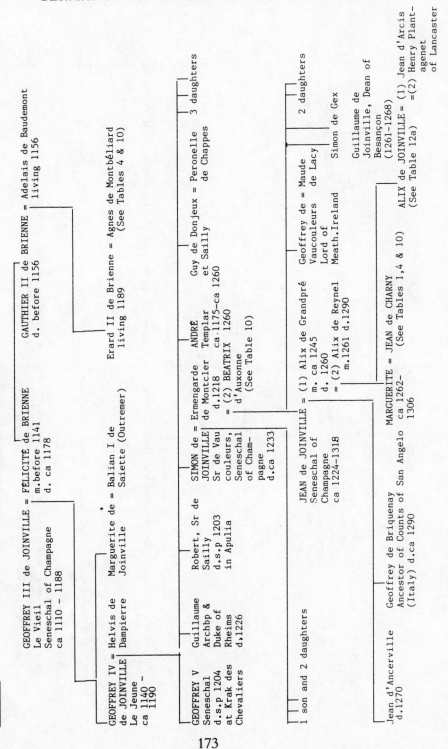

173

Table 12a   JOINVILLE/VERGY/SAVOISY/DE LA FAUCHE/MONTBÉLIARD/ARCIS

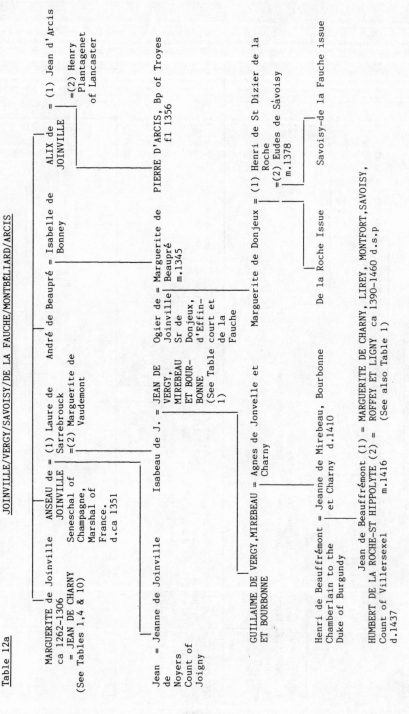

Count of Joigny and, astutely one may think for a brigand, made himself rich by offering to protect religious houses – for a fee – a custom that is still popular with racketeers to this day.

At the beginning of the eleventh century one of Engelbert's cronies, a knight named Stephen, followed his leader's example by extorting protection money from the abbey of Saint-Urbain, near the town of Vaux-sur-Saint-Urbain where he had been born. With the support of the Briennes he began to build a castle not far from his birthplace on a bluff overlooking the Marne at Joinville. Emulating his brigandish patron, Stephen married an heiress and acquired a dowry of more than half a dozen villages and seigneuries at the expense of the monks he was supposed to be protecting. This roisterer's origins and the date of his death are unknown, but it was from him that Marguerite de Joinville, Dame de Charny, was descended.

Details of the earliest generations of the family are meagre and gappy, and it is not until 1127, when Geoffrey III de Joinville succeeded his father in the by now extensive family estates, that we are on firmer ground. Arising from Geoffrey's prowess in the Holy Land in 1147, Count Henry I nominated him Seneschal of Champagne, an office which soon became hereditary in the family. Geoffrey III was a liberal supporter of the Church, and the founder of five abbeys and priories between 1132 and 1146, as well as a generous patron of five more. His brother Guy de Joinville was Archdeacon of Langres and later Bishop of Châlons. Geoffrey married between 1133 and 1140 Felicité de Brienne, the daughter of Erard I de Brienne. With this marriage began a much more brilliant period than the one that had preceded it. Having little by little reached the first rank of the nobility, the descendants of Stephen of Vaux had attained the highest position in the County of Champagne when they received the seneschalship, a position they never lost. The true founder of the family fortunes is without doubt Geoffrey III.

Geoffrey IV succeeded his father in 1188. Before his departure in 1189 on the Third Crusade Geoffrey IV made several donations to a number of abbeys and priories in his own name and the names of his sons, Geoffrey (V) and Robert. He was present at the siege of Acre in October 1189 and died of wounds the following August. Helvis de Dampierre, the wife to whom he had entrusted the care of his estates during his absence, survived him for several years. They had six sons: Geoffrey V, the eldest, succeeded to his father's estates and to the seneschalship; Robert, the second, I mentioned in connection with Gauthier de Brienne and the Fourth Crusade. He accompanied Gauthier to Apulia in 1201, where he probably died, possibly without issue, since his brother Simon inherited his Seigneurie of Sailly in 1203. Guillaume was a churchman, and began his career as archdeacon of his uncle's cathedral of Châlons, to become in turn Bishop of Langres in 1208 and Archbishop of Reims in 1219. He died in 1226.

Simon, Sieur de Sailly after the death of his brother Robert, became Sieur de Joinville on Geoffrey's death. He is not mentioned before 1195, but I will have more to say of him by and by. The fifth brother, Guy, inherited Sailly when Simon inherited Joinville, and the youngest brother, André, joined the Templars and in time became Preceptor of Payns, the order's oldest but not its most important house, dating from the days of its founder, Hugues de Payns. Very little is known about him, though it is assumed that he served in the Holy Land, but when and where is uncertain. Müller believes that he may have been partly responsible for the Shroud's removal to Franconia, and that he may have been buried at Oberwittighausen, but I can find little to support this view, though I cannot disprove it convincingly.

Geoffrey V had accompanied his father to the Holy Land but returned to France on his death. Count Henry of Champagne had become, in the meantime, King of Jerusalem, and had left the conduct of affairs in France to his mother, the Countess Marie. It was for her that Geoffrey V de Joinville now exercised his duties as seneschal. In the quarrel between Richard Coeur de Lion and Philip Augustus, Count Henry of Champagne had sided with Richard. The difference between the two kings, who were both Henry's uncles, arose from the question of the succession to the throne of Jerusalem. Philip favoured Conrad of Montferrat, Isabelle de Lusignan's second husband; Richard, followed by Henry, favoured the rights of Guy de Lusignan. But when Conrad was assassinated and Henry married his widow eight days later, Richard gave him his full support. Guy de Lusignan was consoled with the gift of Cyprus and of all Richard's conquests in Syria. The close friendship between Richard and Henry accounts for the bond which secured the loyalty of the Joinville family to the English king, which was sealed by Richard's permission for Geoffrey to quarter the English arms with his own.

Between 1199 and 1201 Geoffrey de Joinville played a leading part in the preparations for the Fourth Crusade, and especially after the death of Count Thibaut during the search for a successor to lead it. Faithful to his vow, Geoffrey was among the knights of Champagne who reached the Holy Land under the command of Renaud de Dampierre. They went by way of Apulia without taking any part in the conquest of Constantinople. During his absence he left the care of his estates to his brothers, Guillaume and Simon. Like his father before him Geoffrey died in Palestine and was buried in the graveyard of the great crusader fortress of Krak des Chevaliers. He was said by Guyot de Provins to be one of the most valiant knights of his day.

Geoffrey V was succeeded by his fourth brother, Simon. It is not known when Simon was born, but as he did not marry before 1206 it is probable that the year of his birth was between 1180 and 1190. His first wife Ermengard de Montclair came from Merzig, between Saar-brucken and Trier. Simon was old enough to take part in the Albigensian Crusade in 1209, and in 1216 he received a letter from Pope Honorius III, along with other noblemen and bishops in France, urging them to embark on a new crusade and to encourage others to follow their example. Like his fellow barons he disregarded this plea.

During the conflict which arose over the succession to the throne of Champagne following the deaths of Henry and Thibaut, Simon's loyalty to the regent, the Countess Blanche, was somewhat doubtful, which led her to withhold recognition of his claim to the seneschalship of Champagne. In 1219 Simon left France to join his kinsman Jean de Brienne before Damietta, and he was present when the city fell during the summer of that year. He was back in Joinville by September 1221.

Delaborde tells us nothing about the youngest of Geoffrey IV's sons, André de Joinville. It is not even certain whether he was in fact the fifth or the sixth son, but we know he was younger than Simon. This means that he must have been born between 1185 and 1190. If he followed the custom of young noblemen who opted to join one of the military orders, he would have been received into the Templars at about the age of eighteen – between 1203 and 1208. This would indicate that he might have accompanied his elder brothers Geoffrey V and Robert to the Holy Land or to Apulia, but it makes it unlikely that he took part in the diversion to Constantinople. It seems equally unlikely that a youth of this age would have had anything to do with the removal of the Shroud. By 1219, however, André would have been between twenty-nine and thirty-four years of age. The Templars played an important part in the campaign that ended in the capture of Damietta in November 1219, and it is more than likely that he would have taken part in it. The Fifth Crusade ended the following year with the withdrawal of all the Christian forces from Damietta, after which all operations were concentrated in Palestine and Syria, and it was here that André de Joinville is likely to have spent the next few years of his life.

By 1224 Simon de Joinville had lost one wife and married another. His new wife was Beatrix, the daughter of Stephen, Count of

177

Table 13   BURGUNDY-IVREA/ANDECHS-MERAN/JOINVILLE/BRIENNE/COURTENAY

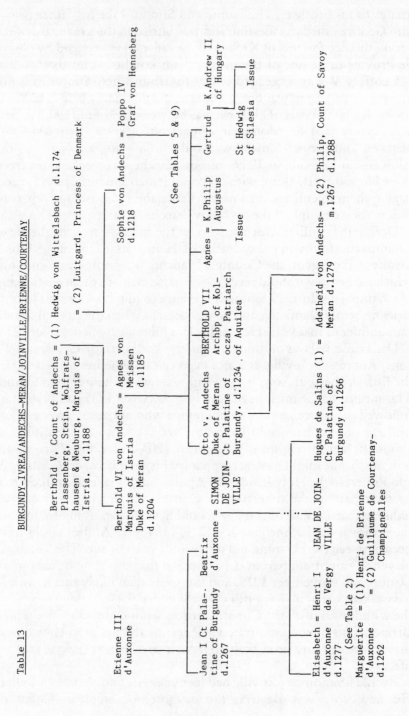

Burgundy and Auxonne and his wife Beatrix, Countess of Châlon-sur-Saône. The new Dame de Joinville was a distant cousin of the Emperor Frederick II, for they shared a common great-great-grandfather in Stephen, Count of Macon, who was killed at Askalon in 1102. His new marriage also linked Simon with both the Montferrat and Champlitte families.[4]

Important as this marriage was, it did not lack its curious aspects. Beatrix's first marriage had been dissolved, something that was less uncommon than one might expect at that time, and she married Simon de Joinville during the lifetime of her first husband, Aimon de Faucigny. We do not know why this marriage, by which there were two daughters, was dissolved, but it seems that the singularity of the situation gave no rise to any embarrassments between the issue of these two marriages. Not only did Jean de Joinville, Simon's son by Beatrix, treat as nephews the grandsons of Aimon de Faucigny, but three other of Simon's sons – Geoffrey, Sire de Vaucouleurs, Simon, Sire de Marnay, and Guillaume – owed their fortune to the relations that the marriage of one of their half-sisters, Agnes de Faucigny, which Peter of Savoy gave them. Peter became known as 'le Petit Charlemagne', though no one guessed when Agnes married him that one day he would become the head of his family. At this period of his career he was a soldier of fortune at the court of King Henry III of England.

In July 1226 Simon was finally granted the hereditary right to the seneschalship of Champagne, which had been withheld from him due to the part he had played after the deaths of Henry and Thibaut. His loyalty was thereby confirmed, and from then on neither he nor any of his descendants deviated from it. It is worth mentioning that Simon and his descendants were the vassals of five important magnates at one and the same time. Simon's supreme overlord was the King of France, but for Joinville and Vaucouleurs and his other domains in that part of France he owed allegiance to the Counts of Champagne. For the lands he had had with his first wife, and for those he had had with his second, he owed allegiance to the Duke of Lorraine and to the Duke of Burgundy. He was also a vassal of the Holy Roman Emperor for lands which came to him through his second marriage in the County Palatine of Burgundy, alias Franche-Comté. This gave him a peculiarly strong position to act as a mediator in any disputes that might arise between these powerful princes.

Not only had Simon done well for himself, he had arranged some prestigious marriages for his sons.

He followed his ancestors' example by supporting the Templars.

Not only was his younger brother André the Preceptor of Payns, but ever since its foundation in 1137 the Joinville family had made generous grants of land and money to the preceptory of Ruetz, about ten miles from Joinville near the village of Bayard. I can find nothing to suggest that the Shroud was ever at Ruetz, which was not a very important house, though it did come under the ultimate control of the Commandery of Champagne at Voulaine.

When Simon died in 1233 he was survived by his second wife, by two daughters of his first marriage and by four sons and two daughters of his second.

This is not the place for a detailed history of the Joinville family, so I must omit a great deal about most of Simon's sons, apart from saying that the second son of the second marriage, Geoffrey de Vaucouleurs, married Maude de Lacy, who brought him vast estates in Herefordshire and Ireland; and that Guillaume, the fourth son of this marriage, was Archdeacon of Salins in 1258, and later Dean of Besançon, a post he held till his death in 1268. Dean Guillaume must have known something about the two Shrouds, and which of them was authentic and which a copy. Moreover, this must also have been known to his brother, Jean de Joinville. The arrival of the relic in France must surely have been known to André de Joinville, who was Preceptor of Payns in 1260, by which time he was an old man approaching seventy, if not older.[5]

Because of his famous *Life of Saint Louis* a great deal is known about Jean de Joinville's early life, and I do not propose to repeat it here. Those who wish to know more should read the late Margaret Shaw's admirable translation, which is published along with her translation of Geoffrey de Villehardouin's account of the Fourth Crusade in Penguin Classics. After Jean's return to France in 1254, by which time he was about thirty, most of the rest of his long life was spent in his native country. He spent the next three years attending to his affairs and seeing to the repair of the damage to his property which had occurred while he was abroad. His mother died in 1260 and his wife soon afterwards, but he had remarried – to Alix de Reynel – by December 1261. His second marriage was much more advantageous than his first, for it brought him the rich Seigneurie of Reynel, a few miles north of Chaumont, of which his new wife had been the sole heiress.

In 1270 Jean's lifelong friend and sovereign, Louis IX, died. During the same year his second son by his first wife, Geoffrey, Sire de Briquenay, came into his inheritance, and three years later married Mabile de Villehardouin, the great-granddaughter of the historian of the Fourth Crusade. On 6 October 1285 Philip the Bold died, and was succeeded by his son Philip the Handsome. By the younger Philip's marriage to the heiress of Champagne and Navarre, the Princess Jeanne, these two provinces were at last united to the Crown of France. This was not, of course, the reason for the antipathy which reigned between Jean de Joinville and the new king – it had deeper roots than that. But Jean de Joinville is conspicuous for his absence from the annual meetings of notables, known as the Grands Jours de Troyes, in 1287, 1288 and 1289. When he reappeared in 1291 he was given an inferior place at Court.

In 1299 there took place at Jean de Joinville's castle of Vaucouleurs a meeting between Philip the Handsome and the Emperor Albert, from which resulted the marriage of Princess Blanche of France, the French king's sister, with Duke Rudolf of Austria. Before the official meeting the two monarchs stayed at Jean's castle of Reynel, and when the negotiations were complete he was charged with the task of escorting the princess to meet her future husband at Hagenau, near Strasbourg. A few months earlier Jean de Joinville had married his youngest daughter Alix to Jean d'Arcis, Sire de Chacenay, later to become the father of that Pierre d'Arcis, Bishop of Troyes, who so strongly disapproved of Geoffrey de Charny's exposition of the Shroud at Lirey fifty years or so later.[6]

Jean de Joinville's disapproval of Philip the Handsome continued to grow. During 1302 the king began to levy illegal taxes to pay for his unsuccessful war against Flanders, and disturbances broke out as a consequence. When the States General were summoned in April 1302 Jean de Joinville was again conspicuous by his absence. The king's quarrel with Pope Boniface VIII was regarded with the strongest disapproval by the erstwhile friend of Saint Louis. The king demanded that Joinville send half his silver to the treasury, and the same demand was made of his two sons, of his nephew de Vaucouleurs and of his cousin de Sailly.

Jean de Joinville was by this time an old man, and Queen Jeanne had been pressing him to write the memoir of Saint Louis by which he is now so well known. The work is a tacit criticism of the saintly king's grandson to be put before the young heir to the throne, Louis le Hutin, the son of Philip the Handsome and Queen Jeanne. By making the young Dauphin acquainted with the life of his great-grandfather, Jean de Joinville thought to inspire him with an ambition to emulate him. To prepare for France a king worthy of his saintly ancestor, and to remind Philip the Handsome of the model he ought to follow, was the inspiration behind the memoir. But we have to remember that it was written over a period of five years beginning in 1303, the year when the aged Pope Boniface VIII had been arrested at Anagni by Philip's agents (he died soon afterwards from the shock of his maltreatment), and that it was finished soon after the king's attack on the Templars.

There are practically no records of Jean de Joinville's life during this – for the Shroud – critical period. It is not known whether he attended the States General called in 1308 in the aftermath of the Templars' arrests. But we can be quite sure that Jean de Joinville strongly disapproved of the king's attack on the order. The very idea that Philip the Handsome might take possession of the precious relic would have been odious to him, and there can be little doubt that he would have done whatever he could to prevent it happening. Although Geoffrey de Charny, his daughter's brother-in-law, did not escape arrest and died a martyr's death, it seems more than probable that he had a hand in the plot to save the Shroud, and that de Joinville would have approved. Receiving the king's secret orders for the arrests, as he must have done as Seneschal of Champagne, during the first two weeks of October, he must have warned his son-in-law, Jean de Charny. Whether Jean de Joinville's sons – Anseau, the future Marshal of France, and André de Beaupré – were in the plot is impossible to say. Neither of them had estates near Voulaine, so it is unlikely they could have done much to further it. The old man's age and experience, coupled with the reflected glory of his long friendship with Saint Louis, ensured that he enjoyed the greatest respect among his younger contemporaries. Whatever the facts, we can be sure that the plan to save the Shroud met with the old seneschal's approval. Jean de Joinville's qualities have been compared with those of Joan of Arc – sincere piety, moral purity, loyalty, courage, love of his king, pity for the poor of the Lord. They were inscribed on his tomb when, at last, the old man died on Christmas Eve 1317.[7]

When Marguerite de Charny realized in the 1450s that she was not going to have any direct heirs of her own, she began to weigh up in her mind to which of her many kinsmen she should entrust the Shroud when she died. She was descended from Otto de la Roche through her grandmother, Jeanne de Vergy, and from Joscelin I de Courtenay, Count of Edessa, through her great-grandmother, Marguerite de Joinville. She shared a common ancestry with the Brienne Kings of Jerusalem, and was a close kinswoman of the ruling Houses of France, England, Hungary, Savoy and the Counts of Hohenlohe-Brauneck. Through her mother's mother, Simone de Méry, she was descended from Geoffrey de Joinville de Vaucouleurs, Jean de Joinville's younger brother. Her second husband, Humbert de la Roche-Saint-Hippolyte, Count of Villersexel, was, like herself, also a direct descendant of Otto de la Roche. Her Joinville, Vergy, Courtenay, Milly and Brienne kinsfolk were all part of the Shroud Mafia which had known all about these relics ever since they had come to the notice of King Amalric and his entourage in 1171: her kinsman Duke Louis of Savoy, and his wife Anne de Lusignan, included among their titles those of the kingdoms of Cyprus and Jerusalem, the marquisate of Montferrat, the principalities of Achaea and Morea, and Perpetual Vicar of the Empire. Who could have had a better claim to the Shroud than they?

And here I rest my case. To speculate further would only be to advance more ingenious surmises. There is, however, one further matter concerning the Holy Grail which has caused me much puzzlement, and it is this: Why, in an age when even kings and noblemen were nearly all illiterate, does the Grail appear only in medieval literature? Why are there not corresponding pictures and sculptures to illustrate the object and the legends surrounding it? It seemed incredible that such popular legends were not reflected equally widely in the art of the time. But yet, when you go to galleries and museums and ask to see a medieval painting of the Grail, you will find none earlier than the fifteenth century, and these will be of the Grail as a chalice. If the Grail's true form and nature were forgotten by writers in the years between Wolfram's *Parzival* and the middle of the fourteenth century, the same must be true of painters and sculptors. If such paintings and sculptures of the Grail and its ceremonies were made in the thirteenth century, then they must have survived under other titles. It was to show that paintings, frescoes and sculptures of the Grail and the Shroud it contained *do* exist that I embarked in 1985 on the last stage of my quest, which I will now describe.

CHAPTER 7

THE GRAIL AND THE SHROUD IN ART

———●———

To solve the riddle of the Grail in art, I had to go back to the beginning. If, I said to myself, the identity of the Grail could be forgotten, or so completely confused, within a century of the appearance of the first romances, the same must apply to pictorial likenesses of it. If such an iconography existed, it seemed to me that I would find it under some foreign title unrelated to either the Grail or the Shroud. The noblemen and clerics who saw the holy cloths and their reliquaries in Constantinople must have inspired painters and sculptors to depict them just as they inspired troubadours and poets to write about them. So was there such a genre of paintings and sculptures? I found the answer among works of art variously described as the Mass of St Gregory, the Man of Sorrows or the Image of Pity, and, strangest of all, St John the Baptist. In order to form some kind of mental image of what I was looking for I went back to Robert de Clari's description of the interior of the Church of the Mother of God of the Pharos. This is what he tells us:

> The Holy chapel . . . was so rich and noble that there was not a hinge nor a band nor any other part such as is usually made of iron that was not all of silver, and there was no column that was not of jasper or porphyry or some other rich precious stone. . . . Within the chapel were found many rich relics. There were two pieces of the True Cross as large as a man's leg and as long as half a *toise* [about 3½ feet]; there was also the iron of the lance with which our Lord's side was pierced, and two of the nails which were driven through his hands and feet. There was a crystal phial with some of his blood; there was the tunic he wore, which was taken from him when they led him to Mount Calvary; there was the blessed Crown with which he was crowned, and which was made of reed with thorns as sharp as the points of daggers. . . . There was still another relic in this chapel, which I

had forgotten to tell you about; for there were two rich vessels of gold hanging in the midst of the chapel by two heavy silver chains. In one of these vessels there was a tile and in the other a cloth. . . .

In an earlier passage describing the church of St Mary in the Blachernae Palace, Robert de Clari writes: 'Here was kept the sydoine in which our Lord had been wrapped, which stood up straight every Good Friday, so that the features of our Lord could be plainly seen there.'

And let me remind you of what Pope Stephen III is reported to have said in the eighth century: 'At the first hour of the day [Christ appeared] as a child, at the third as a boy, at the sixth as an adolescent and at the ninth hour visible in his full manhood, in which the Son of God went to his Passion when he bore for our sins the suffering of the Cross.'

Before considering these descriptions of the holy cloths, the sanctuaries in which they were kept and ceremonies in which they were used, we must have a look at the whole subject of Christian iconography from the time of Constantinople up to the time when these relics became known in the West, for it helps us to understand the different attitudes held by the Eastern and Western Churches. Edward Gibbon covers this in the *Decline and Fall of the Roman Empire*, and I think you will find it helpful if I quote him at some length.

The primitive Christians, he tells us, were 'possessed with an unconquerable repugnance to the use and abuse of images'. Under the successors of Constantine the more prudent bishops 'condescended to indulge a visible superstition for the benefit of the multitude; and after the ruin of Paganism they were no longer restrained by the apprehension of an odious parallel. The first introduction of a symbolic worship was in the veneration of the cross and of relics. . . .' Gibbon goes on to tell us that

a memorial more interesting than the skull or sandals of a departed worthy is the faithful copy of his person and features, delineated by the arts of painting and sculpture. . . . At first the experiment [of creating such images] was made with caution and scruple: and the venerable pictures were discreetly allowed to instruct the ignorant, to awaken the cold, and to gratify the prejudices of the heathen proselytes. By a slow though inevitable progression the honours of the original were transferred to the copy. . . .

Writing about the Mandylion, Gibbon tells us that before the sixth century there were copies distributed far and wide throughout the empire.

Of these pictures the far greater part, the transcripts of a human pencil, could only pretend to a secondary likeness and improper title: but there were some of higher descent, who derived their resemblance from an *immediate* [my italics] contact with the original, endowed for that purpose with a miraculous and prolific virtue . . . such is the Veronica of Rome, or Spain, or Jerusalem, which Christ in his agony and bloody sweat applied to his face, and delivered to a holy matron.

This passage must surely apply to the Soudarion/Mandylion, for had Gibbon been referring to the Sindon, he would have mentioned that more than Christ's face was delineated on the cloth. His use of the phrase 'immediate contact' must mean that certain of these copies were made from the actual cloths themselves, of which the Sainte Face de Laon is almost certainly one. Presumably the eight-foot copies mentioned by Bishop Arculf and those of Compiègne and Besançon which were also eight foot long must have been made as direct copies. That only the frontal image was copied is natural enough in the circumstances, for it is unlikely that artists would have wanted to copy the dorsal image as well. To have copied the whole shroud image head to head would only have added to the complexity of the design without adding to its immediate appeal to the faithful, to whom it would be revealed from a distance and in circumstances of great solemnity. As Gibbon says, 'The worship of images had stolen into the church by insensible degrees, and each petty step was pleasing to the superstitious mind, as productive of comfort and innocent of sin.'

The iconoclastic movement of the eighth and ninth centuries did away with all images of Christ except in the Eucharist, and decreed that image-worship was corrupt and pagan, and that all such idolatrous monuments should be destroyed. But in time images of Christ and the saints crept back, though in a more restricted manner in the East than in the West. It was in that tradition that the artists who painted the Laon and similar icons were working, so there seemed little chance of finding any depictions of the Grail before the twelfth century, when it first became known in the West. Indeed, I did not expect to find any before the middle of the thirteenth century.

May I now remind you of how the Grail is described in the romances so that we can have some kind of general picture of it in the back of our minds? This will help us to look for paintings and sculptures which may bear titles far removed from the subject they were designed to portray. By the fifteenth century the Grail was thought of as a chalice, and from that time pictures of it as a communion cup, often with an elaborate spired or dome-shaped cover, can be seen in pictures or as illustrations of manuscript copies of the romances. I have one in mind which shows it borne by angels appearing in the middle of a circular table with a hollow centre round which King Arthur and his knights are seated.

Let us start with Walter Map and his *Quest of the Holy Grail*.

A man seems to come down from heaven garbed in a bishop's robes with a crozier in his hand and a mitre on his head; four angels bear him on a throne, which they set down next to the altar on which the Holy Grail is lying. He approaches the silver altar and prostrates himself before it. After an interval the door of the chapel opens and angels bring two candles, a cloth of red samite and a bleeding lance to the altar. They place the candles on it, one lays the cloth beside the Holy Vessel and the fourth holds the lance upright over it so that the blood running down the shaft is caught in it. As soon as this has been done the bishop rises and lifts the lance a little higher above the Holy Vessel, which he then covers with the cloth.

Next he acts as if he were going to consecrate the Host, but after pausing a moment, he takes the Host 'in the likeness of bread' from the Vessel, and raises it aloft; the figure of a child descends, whose face glows and blazes as brightly as fire. The heavenly child enters the bread, which now takes on human form. When the bishop has stood for some time holding this up to view, he replaces it in the Holy Vessel. This is the point in the Mass where the priest pronounces the words '*Hoc est enim corpus meum*'. Having discharged his function as a priest, the bishop goes up to Galahad and kisses him, and then after saying a few more words, vanishes. The knights then see the figure of a man appear out of the Holy Vessel, unclothed and bleeding from his hands, feet and side. He then takes the Holy Vessel and going to Galahad, who is kneeling before the altar and gives him the Host, which he places on Galahad's tongue. Here is Christ in person giving Communion to the purest and most valiant of the Knights of the Round Table.

Walter Map must surely be recalling what William of Tyre had told him about the Masses of the Shroud he had witnessed in Constantinople during the course of his visits there. The similarities are close enough to justify this assumption, and different enough to show that they are not written from personal experience. William of Tyre had made two visits to Constantinople and was well received on both occasions by the emperor. He must certainly have taken part in the ceremonies at the church of the Mother of God in Bucoleon, and possibly also at the Blachernae Palace. There was ample opportunity during the Lateran Council in 1179 for him to have told Walter Map about them.

But what I have just quoted is not all. Walter Map ends his *Quest of the Holy Grail* with a description of Sir Galahad's coronation as King of Sarras, which reflects what we know about Byzantine ceremonial.

> When the end of the year came round, on the anniversary of the day when he had first won the crown, he and his companions arose early in the morning. And when they came to the temple, they looked at the sacred Vessel, and they saw a handsome man dressed like a bishop and he was on his knees before the table. . . . He rose and began the Mass of the Glorious Mother of God. And when he came to the mystery of the Mass and had removed the platter from the sacred Vessel, he called Galahad and said: 'Come forward, servant of Jesus Christ, and thou shalt behold what thou hast desired to see.' Then Galahad stepped forward and looked within the sacred Vessel. And when he looked in, he began to tremble violently, as soon as mortal flesh began to gaze on the things of the spirit. Then Galahad stretched forth his hand towards Heaven, and said: 'Lord, I adore thee and thank thee that thou hast brought my desire to pass, for now I see clearly what tongue could not tell nor heart conceive. Here I behold the motive of courage and the inspiration of prowess; here I see the marvel of marvels.'

Picture to yourself the Shroud, with its image of the wounded man, the traces of blood on arms, side and forehead. Think of the agony of the nails driven through hands and feet and of the appalling effort of breathing when trying to ease the pain as he hangs from the cross. Even the most hardened sceptic could not fail to be moved by the contemplation of such suffering. How much more must men in the age of faith have been moved? Galahad's reaction, so vividly described here, recalls the fear that some of the Templars said they felt when first seeing the 'idol'. The sequences beginning 'Come forward and behold . . .' and 'Lord, I adore thee . . .' recall the evidence given by Hugues de Pairaud to the Inquisition at his trial, when he said that during the Templar ceremony the brethren were abjured to 'come and adore him who has made us and not left us'. The Templars, the Knights of the Round Table and the artists who painted the 'Mass of St Gregory' are all inspired by the same source – the Mass of the Sindon of Christ as celebrated in Constantinople, in which the body of our Lord is made to appear as in the flesh.

This is even more explicitly described in the *Perlesvaus*. Here Gawain sees the figure of Christ rising from the Holy Vessel with the spear in his side. He is flanked by two other figures, so that we are left with an almost exact literary version of the earliest Masses of St Gregory, where one finds the altar on which the upper part of Christ's body is seen emerging from the casket, witnessed by two figures, usually St Peter and a bishop or pope. In the sequel to the *Conte del*

Graal Gawain's vision of the Requiem Mass and of the spiritual feast that follows it differs from the *Perlesvaus* account in that here we have a bier, perhaps representing the Grail casket with the corpse of Jesus representing the Sindon within it. Here Gawain sees each knight receiving the host from Jesus' own hand, and the spear hangs nearby to remind us of the wounds he suffered for our sins.

Although these descriptions seem to establish a link between the Grail romances, the Mass of St Gregory and the Shroud Masses of Constantinople, there remains the Joseph of Arimathea element, which we must now consider. This legend, as Robert de Boron tells it, is as follows: The vessel in which Christ made his sacrament at the Last Supper was first given by a Jew to Pilate, and then by Pilate to Joseph of Arimathea, who used it at the deposition from the cross to catch a few drops of the Messiah's blood.

Before commenting on this I should explain that, as with other authors of Grail romances, considerable controversy surrounds Robert de Boron, not the least of which concerns his identity. Like Walter Map, Robert de Boron inserts a few words about himself. He writes: 'At the time that I related [the history of the Grail] to my lord Gauthier in peace, who was of Mont Belyal, it had never been related.' Because Robert tells us that one of the twelve sons of Bron and Enygeus betakes himself to the west to the 'vaus d'Avaron' (translated as Vales of Avalon by most Arthurian commentators) which they equate with the marshlands round Glastonbury; and because Robert describes himself in one place as Meistre de Bouron, and in another as Messire de Beron, some authorities translate this as meaning that he was an Anglo-Norman writer from Burun alias Boreham, in Essex, and that he was a remote ancestor of Lord Byron. This completely disregards the fact that he writes in the Burgundian dialect, and that there is a village called Boron about twelve miles from Montbéliard in Franche-Comté. If Mont Belyal and Gauthier, its lord, are equated to Gauthier de Montbéliard, a number of interesting facts flow therefrom. According to Geoffrey de Villehardouin, Count Gauthier de Montbéliard was one of the noblemen who, accompanied by Geoffrey and Robert de Joinville, Otto de la Roche and Guillaume de Champlitte, followed Boniface de Montferrat to the Fourth Crusade. Further enquiries reveal that Gauthier de Montbéliard died in the Holy Land in 1212, and that he had married Burgundia de Lusignan, a daughter of King Amalric II of Jerusalem (Amalric I of Cyprus) and Eschiva d'Ibelin. Burgundia was the stepdaughter of Queen Isabella of Jerusalem, the former wife of Conrad of Montferrat and of Count Henry of Champagne, and mother of Maria de Montferrat, (La Marquise),

Queen of Jerusalem. Gauthier de Montbéliard was also the brother-in-law of Count Berthold von Katzenellenbogen, who had married his sister, Alix de Montbéliard. This couple's daughter-in-law was Eschiva de Saint-Omer, whose nephew Nicholas de Saint-Omer was the former Empress Mary-Margaret's third husband. Gauthier de Montbéliard was also a first cousin of Jean de Brienne, King of Jerusalem, and consequently would have been, had he lived, a first cousin once removed by marriage to the Emperor Frederick II. He was also a not too distant kinsman of Simon de Joinville, Otto de la Roche and Otto von Henneberg-Bodenlauben. In view of all this I think we can say with some degree of assurance that Robert de Boron learnt about the Shroud from Gauthier de Montbéliard. None of this explains the Glastonbury connection, however. (See Table 10.)

The association of Joseph of Arimathea with the conversion of Britain, and more especially with Glastonbury, can be traced to a revision of William of Malmesbury's *De Antiquitate Glastoniensis Ecclesiae* in about 1247. A forged charter of 1220 claimed that disciples sent over by St Philip and St James built the first church at Glastonbury, but St Philip does not appear in the Grail legends. Gradually, however, the monastic authorities seem to have incorporated some of the novel claims made by the French romancers, and to have added that the leader of St Philip's mission was Joseph of Arimathea. This can, perhaps, be best explained when one realizes that the Abbot of Glastonbury in the late 1160s, when news of the Shroud first began to trickle through to the West, was Henri de Blois. Apart from being the grandson of William the Conqueror and a brother of King Stephen of England, he was an uncle of Henri I, Comte de Champagne, Chrétien de Troyes' patron. He was also Bishop of Winchester, so it can hardly be coincidental that we find he was the commissioner of a fresco for the Sepulchre Chapel in his cathedral which shows Christ enveloped in the Shroud.

But it was not until 1367 that the legend was taken seriously enough to warrant the report that Joseph of Arimathea's body had been found at Glastonbury, though King Arthur's was said to have been discovered there in 1191. By the end of the fourteenth century John of Glastonbury had given official sanction to the account of Joseph's history in the *Estoire del Saint Graal*. But John made certain changes, most significant of which were the total omission of the Grail and the substitution of the two cruets containing the Saviour's blood and sweat – relics which Robert de Clari 164 years earlier had said were among those in the church of the Mother of God of the Pharos. So by the middle of the fourteenth century, when Geoffrey de Charny and

Jeanne de Vergy first exhibited the Shroud at Lirey, all memory of its connection with the Grail romances had been forgotten.

When people began to think of the sacred Vessel as a chalice, commentators found the presence of a dish in association with the blood of Christ very difficult to explain. Representations of the Saviour's head set against a circular, dish-like nimbus were then confused with St John the Baptist's, which Salome had asked to be presented to her on a charger. Such a mistake was all the easier to make since the head in question was not crowned with thorns. Unaware of any connection with the Soudarion and Sindon, scholars like A. E. Waite interpreted the '*scutella lata*' – wide platter – of Chrétien and Hélinand, and the vessel in which Robert de Boron says that Christ made his sacrament of the Last Supper, as the paschal dish. In one respect they came near the truth, though the idea that this 'dish' might be a shallow rectangular reliquary containing the burial cloths of Christ never occurred to them. The shallow rectangular box from which Christ seems to be rising in pictures and sculptures of the Mass of St Gregory has been misinterpreted as a coffin, with the result that some of these pictures are entitled 'the Risen Christ', and explained as representations of the Resurrection, which they most certainly are not. In the latter case the tomb is usually painted as it is described in the Gospels as a rock-hewn cave, and not as a coffin. Indeed a moment's reflection will tell us that there is no mention in the Gospels or anywhere else of a coffin in connection with Christ's burial.

By the time these pictures became widespread in European art the Grail as the Shroud's reliquary had been forgotten and replaced by the notion of a chalice for reasons I explained in the first chapter. Nevertheless faint memories of the Shroud and the Soudarion lingered on in a shadowy form. Take, for example, the tradition of the three miraculous hosts of Andechs, which were traditionally associated with St Gregory, once the true connection between the Andechs-Meran family and the Shroud had been forgotten. Yet there was still a memory of a Sudarium Christi at Andechs which persists to the present day. I shall return to this later.

In the Württembergische Landesbibliothek at Stuttgart there is a psalter which belonged to the Landgrave Hermann of Thuringia, Wolfram von Eschenbach's patron. It is one of the most beautiful illuminated, late Romanesque, German manuscripts in existence. Folio 73 shows the Crucifixion of Christ, which is of particular significance in the history of art and to this investigation. In the long series of portrayals of the Crucifixion it had been customary to depict Christ as nailed to the cross with four nails, one in each hand and foot.

The Landgrave psalter, which dates from 1211/1213, is the first to show him nailed by three nails. From this date onwards, it became the accepted custom to depict the crucified Christ in this fashion, to the point where we would now regard a depiction with four nails as odd. This change in the way of portraying this subject coincides with the new way of portraying Christ as described earlier, and can be directly attributed to a knowledge in the West of the Shroud. A close examination of the mysterious image on the cloth shows that only one nail was used to secure the feet to the cross, so the artist who illuminated the Landgrave's psalter must have learnt this from someone who had seen the Shroud. Landgrave Hermann's son Ludwig IV married the Princess Elisabeth of Hungary in 1221. She was the sister of King Bela IV and niece of the ex-Empress Mary-Margaret. She was born in 1207, and after her husband's death devoted herself to good works and was eventually canonized. Her mother was Queen Gertrud of Hungary, Mary-Margaret's sister-in-law. Thus, the most probable informant was one of Queen Gertrud's brothers, either Ekbert von Andechs, Bishop of Bamberg, or Berthold von Andechs, Archbishop of Kalocsa, later Patriarch of Aquileia.

The fact that the oldest three-nail Crucifixions are German and not French is a significant pointer in favour of my thesis that the Shroud reached France by way of Hungary and Germany. That the earliest example of this type of Crucifixion is to be found in an illuminated manuscript in private hands means that the information upon which it was based was known in Germany from as early as 1211 or 1213.

During the Albigensian Crusade (1209–44) those who said that Christ had been nailed to the Cross with three nails were condemned as heretical. Pope Innocent III declared that '*Fuerunt in Passione Domini quattuor clavi quibus manus affixae et pedes affixi*' (There were in the Lord's Passion four nails with which his hand and feet were fixed [to the cross]).

This tradition lasted well into the fourteenth century in Italy, for Giotto's painting of St Francis of Assisi receiving the stigmata shows Christ having been crucified with four nails. Giotto died in 1337, so it is quite clear that the tradition of the three nails, deriving from the Shroud, did not become known in Italy (and probably also in France) until later in the fourteenth century. This can be explained by the fact that from the third quarter of the thirteenth century until Geoffrey de Charny exhibited the Shroud at Lirey in 1353 no one had had a chance to examine it closely, for after it left Germany the Templars took care to hide it from public view.

Having mentioned the Mass at St Gregory several times, it is perhaps time that I said something more about the history of this iconographic theme. There are few such themes to have been so thoroughly studied as this, and both it and its twin subject, Christ, the Man of Sorrows or, as it is sometimes called, the Image of Pity, still remain highly controversial. Just as writers have mistaken the Grail for a chalice after its long sojourn in the Balkans, Hungary and Germany, and its subsequent disappearance during the ninety or so years it belonged to the Templars and the de Charny family, so artists attributed to St Gregory the ceremony which is described in the Grail legends, in which Christ appeared in person from the sacred vessel to serve Mass to Galahad, Perceval, Bors and others worthy to receive it.

In his study of 'The Image of Pity in Santa Croce in Gerusalemme', Carlo Bertelli discusses a small mosaic icon which is preserved in this church in Rome, and which was first brought to the notice of art historians by A. Thomas in his essay 'Das Urbild der Gregoriusmesse' in 1933. It is a mosaic by a thirteenth-century Italian master but in the Byzantine style, which makes it a possibly unique case of this Byzantine technique in Italian art. In 1960 it underwent drastic renovation, so that the confused array of little cubes that A. Thomas saw in the 1930s has now regained a proper unity, with its many fragments in their proper places.

The mosaic is encased in a large wooden reliquary shaped like a triptych, which when closed looks like any plain eighteenth-century aedicula, and which is surmounted with a pediment on which a gilt inscription reads: *Fuit S. Gregorii Magni Papae*. This reliquary is in fact almost certainly of thirteenth-century origin. When it is open it reveals a number of small cases in a grid-iron pattern which entirely surround the icon and completely fill the two wings. These little cases are framed by metallic strips held together by small nails with rosette-shaped heads, and there are 218 of them. Each case is carved into the thickness of the wooden panel and contains (or has at some time contained) a relic wrapped in silk. Apart from the obvious difference that this grid-iron pattern is horizontal and vertical rather than diagonal like the diaper background of the Sainte Face de Laon and the other heads of Christ I have mentioned earlier, the general impression of this icon is much the same, though in this case it is set in a three-dimensional grill rather than against a painted background. By making the reliquary in this way, the grid-iron surround can house a large collection of minor relics in close proximity to the figure of Christ on the icon itself.

The mosaic shows Christ's body down to the waist, the hands crossed, as in the Shroud, but over the abdomen rather than the pelvic area, with the bleeding side wound well in sight. During restoration the Santa Croce mosaic revealed another secret. When it was removed from its grid-iron reliquary, a standing figure of St Catherine was found on the back of the panel to which the mosaic is fixed. This figure is set against a golden diapered or trelliswork background very similar to that of the Sainte Face de Laon. Carlo Bertelli suggests that this was painted by a Western artist unfamiliar with his alien, Byzantine model, and that it raises almost as many questions as it answers. The mosaic itself closely resembles another of the same subject from the monastery of the Birth of the Virgin near Evrytania, in Aetolia, once part of the Duchy of Athens over which Otto de la Roche and his descendants ruled at that time, and which is attributed to a Byzantine workshop of the early fourteenth or late thirteenth century. There is, however, a remarkable difference in the iconography. The Santa Croce mosaic shows Christ's body down to the waist, whereas in the Evrytania one, the Saviour is represented only as far as the chest, and his hands are not shown at all.

The Roman mosaic is enclosed in a silver-gilt frame originally containing ten lozenge-shaped enamels, of which seven still survive. Three of them represent scenes from the Passion, while the four at the corners are decorated with coats of arms, leaving one to suppose that the missing ones were probably also scenes of the Passion. The coats of arms are particularly interesting. They are the arms of Anjou, of the Orsini-Montfort family, the del Balzo family and the shield of the Holy Sepulchre. The association of Anjou with the Holy Sepulchre is a royal connotation, and refers to the Angevin claim to the Kingdoms of Jerusalem and Hungary, and (through the marriage of Philip of Anjou to Isabella de Villehardouin) to the principality of Achaea and the Morea. The red and white fesses surrounding the Angevin shield of lilies refers to the marriage of King Ladislas IV of Hungary to Elizabeth of Sicily of the house of Anjou, and to the marriage of Princess Maria of Hungary, King Ladislas' sister, to King Charles II of Sicily, Naples and Jerusalem. On Ladislas' death the crown of Hungary passed to the descendants of Charles and Maria of Sicily. The other coats of arms and the painting of St Catherine date the icon to around 1370 or 1380 and link it to the church and hospital of St Catherine in Galatina in Apulia, not far from Lecce and Bari, the area of Italy once part of the Byzantine Empire.

The church of Santa Caterina di Galatina has a representation of the Man of Sorrows carved into the pediment of its main portal, which dates from the fourteenth century. In this case the hands are crossed over the chest, the fingers resting against the armpits, the body emerging from a rectangular box. The church and hospital were built by Raimondello Orsini del Balzo who visited Mount Sinai in 1380–81, and it seems possible that the mosaic may have been obtained from there. Bertelli concludes that it is a Byzantine work of the late thirteenth or early fourteenth century; that it was brought to Mount Sinai before 1380, when it came to Italy, and that it was given to Santa Croce in Rome about 1386.

If he is right this modifies current views on the origin of the Mass of St Gregory. To begin with we no longer have to look for a supposed sixth- or seventh-century prototype in Rome. When this icon was taken there, the iconography of the Western Man of Sorrows was so well known in Europe that the mosaic cannot be claimed to be the first image to have introduced these features to the West. The exhibition 'Europäische Kunst um 1400' held in Vienna in 1962 counted no less than seventeen items which were related to the representation of the Man of Sorrows. But before we go further we must make sure whether it is to this mosaic and to the church of Santa Croce that references are made in the early versions of the legend of the Mass of St Gregory.

Nothing had ever been heard of the miraculous Mass of St Gregory in connection with Santa Croce before 1452. Two hosts with the imprint of the cross have been preserved at Andechs since about 1182, and are known as the Sacramentum Gregorii. The hosts are believed to have been found in a case which is painted on the inside with the figures of the Lamb and the Man of Sorrows. A painting attributed to Michael Wohlgemut at Andechs represents the miraculous Mass of a pope, but whether of Gregory the Great or Leo IX is uncertain. It is worth recalling that the reigning Duke of Andechs-Meran in 1182 was Berthold IV. He was the father of Queen Gertrud of Hungary and the uncle of Otto von Henneberg-Bodenlauben. He was also the father-in-law of Beatrix, Duchess of Swabia, who was a daughter of Count Otto of Burgundy. By themselves these genealogical scraps may not mean much, but taken in conjunction with what I have tried to describe before, they assume a deep significance. But I digress: the representation of the Man of Sorrows among the *Arma Christi*, or instruments of the Passion, was an established iconographic scheme as early as the late thirteenth century.

The main difficulty in dealing with the origin of the Mass of St Gregory lies in the fact that it is not connected with any historical event or any dogmatic belief but, according to Bertelli, 'is rooted in the unpredictable vagaries of folk-lore'. This, of course, puts it in precisely the same situation as the Grail itself. The legend concerning this particular Mass emphasizes the vision of Christ in exactly the same way as the Grail romancers envisage it. The Santa Croce mosaic was a carefully executed reproduction of a vision of Christ which the saintly pope was supposed to have experienced during his life. But under the illustrations of the *Arma Christi* in the Royal Manuscripts to which I have just referred, is reproduced the prayer of Pope Innocent III for the Holy Face. Frequently the *Arma Christi* and the Veronica were reproduced together and attracted similar indulgences if looked at intently and devoutly. But there is no firm evidence to account for the origin of this legend: nor does it allow an attribution to St Gregory.

In the vernacular literature of the Middle Ages the name of St Gregory was often misused for any pope just as Constantine's was misused for any emperor. The mosaic's origin was soon forgotten, just as the true nature of the Grail was forgotten, and its long-established connection with the Eucharist, which had struck Western observers as early as the eleventh century, became almost unnoticed. No Greek icons are known to be the reproductions of a historical vision. The Greek fathers thought that an icon should mirror an unchangeable, eternal prototype.

To sum up: the origin of the Mass of St Gregory cannot be firmly linked to any historical event, but the iconography can be said to date from about the fourteenth century. This is not so far removed from 1260, the date said by Professor Grabar to mark the beginning of the vernicle, or hanging cloth representation of the Soudarion. This date more or less coincides with the transfer of the Shroud to the Templars and its disappearance for nearly a century. Such evidence as I have been able to present seems to suggest that it was only between 1222, when the ex-Empress Mary-Margaret took the Shroud and the Grail to Sirmium (Srem) until it passed out of the possession of the heirs of Otto and Beatrix von Henneberg-Bodenlauben some forty or fifty years later, that artists had any chance of making faithful copies of them. The memory of the Soudarion and Sindon Masses faded from memory, dying out with the generation which had witnessed them between 1171 and 1204. A vague tradition persisted in the romances of the Holy Grail in literature and in paintings and sculptures mistitled Mass of St Gregory. The great majority of the surviving Masses of St Gregory date from the fifteenth and sixteenth centuries, by when all association with the Shroud Masses of the Bucoleon and Blachernae churches and with the Grail reliquary had been completely forgotten.

The chronology of the earliest examples of the Man of Sorrows is as artificial as it is hypothetical. The only thing known for certain is that the earliest Eastern form dates from twelfth-century Novgorod. There are murals in Trebizond in Anatolia and at Sopočani and Gradač in Serbia dating from the end of the thirteenth and beginning of the fourteenth centuries. The earliest Western example dates from 1293 and is in a Franciscan prayer-book from Genoa. This has led people to think of the Man of Sorrows as a peculiarly Franciscan creation, but it was also favoured by the Dominicans from almost as early a period. Its function is to be seen in the emotional participation in the sufferings of Jesus.

But the link between the so-called Mass of St Gregory and the sacred cloths – particularly the Veronica – was not forgotten in Germany. There are more than thirty examples of the Mass of St Gregory in the Warburg Institute's collection of photographs on this subject, the great majority of which are from the fifteenth or sixteenth centuries. About half of these, all of them of German or Flemish provenance, include the Veronica; all, without exception, show the body of Christ from the waist upward, but with the hands in varying positions. The majority, however, show the hands crossed on the chest or the lower abdomen as in the Shroud. The casket from which the body emerges differs from one version to another, with a tendency for it to become more elaborate in the later ones. Not all artists have included the casket, though most do. The majority also include the instruments of the Passion. In one Spanish example the Shroud is shown draped over the edge of the casket from which Christ's body is emerging, and in another of the Spanish-Flemish school of the fifteenth century, which comes from an altarpiece of the school of Memling, Christ is shown kneeling on the edge of the Grail casket supported by angels, whereas another of the Memling school shows the whole body of Christ standing on the altar. As might be expected, the later the version the more elaborate the composition and the more fanciful the attitude of Christ.

I want now to consider another aspect of this problem. The Templars were accused of worshipping an idol, and the answers they gave under torture seem to suggest that some versions of it were three-dimensional, whereas others seem to have been pictures. Since nothing pagan was found when Philip the Handsome's men took over the Templars' establishments, we can conclude that these were perfectly orthodox paintings and sculptures. Nevertheless some of the 'idols' were said to have had two or three heads, or to have represented a single head on a dish. Could these have been three-dimensional representations of the Mass of St Gregory and Man of Sorrows theme? It seems at least very likely that some of them were. In order to throw light on this subject we must go back to the Grail legends themselves and consider them in connection with a genre of medieval alabaster or stone carvings which are now listed as heads of St John the Baptist. It is not easy to understand how some of the more elaborate of these carvings came by this nomenclature, and as I read the Grail romances and the evidence of the Templars it seemed clear that they were in reality representations of Christ's head surrounded by a nimbus, and that they derive from the same source as such icons as the Sainte Face de Laon.

In the *Peredur* version of the Grail romance two maidens bring in a man's head on a platter, and there is blood in profusion round it. Since John the Baptist does not figure in these stories it has been necessary to find some other explanation for this particular description of the sacred vessel. Mary Williams suggests that the tradition of the severed head in a dish was developed from the legend of the feasting of Brân's retinue in the presence of his head in a royal hall as described in the Welsh legend *Brânwen*. R. S. Loomis, another distinguished Arthurian scholar, and Helaine Newstead have also argued in favour of this Celtic origin. Loomis is quite sure that the Grail was not a chalice or a ciborium, but as Chrétien and Hélinand say, a '*scutella lata et aliquantulum profunda*', 'a wide and somewhat deep platter'. This corresponds to the Welsh description of it as a *dysgl*, translated into Latin as '*scutella lata et ampla*' – 'a wide and capacious platter'. Thus the function and form of the Grail corresponded exactly with the *dysgl* of Rhydderch, or the magic vessel of the legendary god Brân, son of Llyr. The similarity between the shallow dish-like reliquary in which the Shroud was kept and this legendary *dysgl* was so close that it was easy to combine the two in the later Christian stories – hence the subsequent confusion. During the century and a half when the Shroud and the Grail went missing, it is understandable how this confusion arose. Though this Celtic explanation cannot be entirely rejected, since the Grail legends have an indubitable Celtic ancestry, there is another explanation which we must now consider.

In 1824 there was a lively correspondence in *The Gentlemen's Magazine* initiated by a Dr Meyrick and carried on at considerable length in an article by W. A. St John-Hope. Dr Meyrick had advanced the theory that certain alabaster carvings originating in Nottingham in the fifteenth century or end of the fourteenth represented the legend of the miraculous image of Christ's face as described in the story of Abgar of Edessa – in other words they related to the Mandylion/Soudarion. Dr Meyrick makes it clear that this was the general view held by savants in the eighteenth century, and he linked these carvings with the

Veronica – or vernicle as he calls it. In the sixteenth century, however, he had noticed that references in inventories to these alabasters called them representations of John the Baptist. St John-Hope then countered with a defence of the latter view, and put forward five alternatives for consideration.

1 That they represented the head of St John the Baptist on a charger with the figures of saints and angels.
2 That the central subject was the image of Christ's face given to Abgar.
3 That the three persons of the Trinity were represented.
4 That the central head and disc represented the vernicle.
5 That the sculptures represented a variation on the theme of the Mass of St Gregory.

In most of these panels, of which two excellent examples are to be seen in the Burrell Collection in Glasgow, the main feature consists of a bearded head, closely resembling the head on the Shroud, set against a large circular disc beneath which is a much smaller figure of Christ from the waist upwards, the body emerging from a rectangular box or casket. In the more elaborate versions a third and smaller figure set against an oval dish emerges from above the head, the whole composition crowned with an elaborately carved gothic canopy. In the simpler versions the central figures are flanked by St Peter on the left and a bishop carrying a processional cross on the right. In the other, more elaborate carving, which forms the central section of a triptych, the triple group is flanked on the left by statuettes of St James and St Catherine above St Peter, and on the right by St Antony and St Margaret above the bishop. The smallest, praying figure, above the head, is supported by two angels.

There are two further variants: one in which the head appears with the small figure in base, and one in which four saints appear, but without the accessory figure added at the top. The smallest tablets mostly belong to the first and third class and the largest to the second. In practically every case the left-hand saint (as you view the carving) is St Peter with key and book; the right-hand figure is invariably a bishop or archbishop in cope and mitre holding a cross or a book.

The accessory at the base of all four variants is either a half-length figure of Christ standing in a square or polygonal box, or the Lamb of God. A solitary example has instead of either of these a seated figure of the Virgin with the infant Christ.

The small figure of Christ at the base of the composition is invariably naked, usually wearing the Crown of Thorns. The position of the arms, however, varies, scarcely any two examples being alike. The hands are either bound at the wrists or so disposed as to show the marks of the nails. Sometimes one of them points to the wound in the side. In no instance is the right hand raised in blessing. This corresponds exactly to the upper half of the frontal image of the Shroud as folded in the manner I described in Chapter 2. There can be no doubt that herein lies the underlying inspiration for both these alabaster and stone carvings on the one hand, and of the Mass of St Gregory and Man of Sorrows paintings on the other. Both symbolize Christ's death and Passion, not his Resurrection, and all derive from the Byzantine Masses of the Shroud and Grail. The upper, larger head common to all the panels represents the Soudarion/Veronica image, while the smaller, lower figure represents the Sindon. In a much earlier, though similar composition, carved in the timpanum of the south transept door of the former Cistercian abbey of Heilsbronn in Franconia, the relative positions of the two images are reversed. In this case the body of Christ is seen emerging from the Grail, his left hand raised in blessing and his right pointing to the side wound. The Grail itself is draped with a cloth on which is sculpted the Veronica head, while angels hold a much larger cloth – the Sindon – above the figure of Christ. The central figures are flanked in this case by a monk and a pope on one side and by a monk and a bishop on the other.

In carvings where a third accessory occurs, this generally consists of two angels holding up, in a cloth or a painted oval, a small naked figure. This might represent the soul of Christ or the Holy Ghost. In such cases the central, largest head could represent God the Father, with God the Son in base and God the Holy Ghost emanating from the Father's head. In four of the six most elaborate carvings, the upper pair of saints includes St Catherine while two have figures of St James the Greater. Only seven of the first type, eight of the second, five of the third and five or six of the fourth type are known to exist in England. Earlier, and simpler versions are to be found on the continent, such as those at Santa Caterina in Galatina and at Heilsbronn, where they have been included in the decoration of church portals. That carvings such as these Nottingham alabaster examples could have been made for the Templars, and that they could have been made to appear as idols by a hostile Inquisition, cannot be doubted. That all derive from the same source is equally clear.

Because some of the Nottingham examples show a gash on the forehead of the principal figure, St John-Hope explained this in terms of John the Baptist who was struck on the head by Herodias' knife. But can this really be so? The traces of blood on the forehead of the man of the Shroud emanate from wounds caused by the Crown of Thorns, but if tradition dictated that the head be depicted *not* wearing a Crown of Thorns, the only way an artist could indicate the wounds it had made would be in this fashion. The tradition of a bearded head on a large disc similar to a platter was well known to both poets and artists in the thirteenth and fourteenth centuries. Later generations have confused them with the head of John the Baptist, but it is more reasonable to suppose that they derive from the portrayal of Christ's face seen through the circular opening in the Grail casket as illustrated by the monk who painted the Sainte Face de Laon.

The same goes for the bearded, bleeding head the Templars were accused of worshipping. Those who created such heads, whether in paintings or as sculptures, like the Grail romancers, interpreted in their own individual fashion the imagery transmitted to them by those who had actually seen the relics in Constantinople. In the case of the stories, Welsh and French elements were inextricably blended, thus causing scholars much difficulty and perplexity in sorting out the various sources. One of the greatest causes for confusion in the literature as well as in art arises from the ambiguity of the word 'cors', which has at least five meanings in modern and medieval French. It can be translated as horn, corner, court, course and body. Since corner, court and course make no sense in the context, and because horn can only be taken to refer to a drinking horn or a Horn of Plenty, we are left with the remaining meaning of body. The Grail castle, Corbenic, must be taken to mean the castle which contained the blessed (*benic, benoit* or *benit*) body of Christ, or *Corpus* Christi. The sacramental wafer is likewise the body of Christ, which explains the symbolism which underlies not only the Mass of St Gregory pictures but also the Grail ceremonies in the romances. What else can the *Graal* and the *Oiste* which sustain the lives of the Fisher King's father and Joseph of Arimathea be? Due to these ambiguities the Welsh vessels of plenty, the platter and the drinking horn have been converted into the Grail and the Body of Christ. The true nature of the Grail, its shape and its size, as well as its connection with the burial linen of Christ, was certainly known to Chrétien de Troyes, Robert de Boron and Walter Map and probably to Wolfram von Eschenbach too. Since the patrons they wrote for also knew, they had no need to be more explicit than they were. With their deaths, subsequent poets and authors, who were not in the secret, gradually came to understand these things, until the Grail had taken on an entirely new form as the Chalice and even the Sang Real or Holy Blood, now interpreted as a kind of sacred Y-chromosome.

While the Shroud was in Germany the latticework casket in which it had been kept in Constantinople was replaced by a new reliquary either by those who were in charge of it during the lifetime of Otto and Beatrix von Henneberg-Bodenlauben or, more probably, after it came into the hands of the de Charny family. I would be merely guessing if I were to speculate about this further. All I can say is that the casket in which it was kept at Lirey and subsequently in Chambéry and Turin is definitely not the Grail casket of former centuries. The Grail casket, however, was far too holy to be cast lightly on one side, and a faint clue to its fate is to be found in a painting of the Man of Sorrows in the abbey of Heilsbronn, near Ansbach in Franconia. Towards the end of the thirteenth century Gottfried von Hohenlohe-Braunek, the nephew of Kunigunde von Hohenlohe, who married Hans von Weinsberg (Jean de Charny), and the son of the Emperor Frederick II's faithful vassal, Conrad von Hohenlohe-Braunek, entered the Cistercian Order, and passed most of his life at Heilsbronn, where he died in 1312. As a young man he almost certainly saw the Shroud when it was in Franconia, and of course he was well aware of his aunt's connection with its French owners, the de Charnys, who were his close cousins. In 1350 Abbot Friedrich von Hirzlach commissioned a painting of Christ, the Man of Sorrows, which is generally regarded as possibly the first of its kind in Germany. It hangs in the north aisle of Heilsbronn minster, now the town's parish church.

The painting is life-size, and shows our Lord standing with his hands folded across the upper part of the abdomen, left over right, in such a way as to show the wounds in the hands and the side. The latter is just below the right breast. The body is draped in a long blue sheet or cloth – it can hardly be described as a robe – which hangs over the left shoulder and right elbow and loosely across the middle of the body in such a way as to leave the legs visible below the knees. The feet are apart and bear the wounds of the nail. On Christ's left side can be seen the Lance, and behind his head the Cross's beam on which a coil of rope is hanging. On the right side, on a level with the head, which is encircled by a golden nimbus, are the three nails and the flagrum. The whole composition is set against a raised, trelliswork background, which Professor Heinrich Pfeiffer, SJ, believes to be a cast of the Grail. He suggests that a negative image of it was made in beeswax and then a positive one of stucco, and that this was then attached to the wooden planks on which the picture is painted. The lowest layer of this stucco cast appears to have been a large piece of purple cloth embroidered with gold thread in a foliate pattern. This was overlaid with a criss-cross of gold strips fixed by plate-like nails with rosette heads (possibly originally set with precious stones) at the points of intersection. The general effect closely resembles that of the diaper background of the Sainte Face de Laon, except that this one is three-dimensional and stands proud of the figure of Christ itself. A border or framework about three inches wide, of gold leaf, with a running pattern of vine leaves, forms the topmost layer. Professor Pfeiffer and Dr Müller suggest that what we see is a cast of the banner part of the Labarum Constantini, which originally covered the Shroud's casket. If they are right, then we can see exactly what the Holy Grail looked like.

The modern notion that an artist must be 'original' was by no means shared by most people in the past. An Egyptian, a Byzantine or a medieval artist of Western Europe would have been greatly puzzled by such a demand. He would not have understood why he should invent new ways of planning a church, of representing the sacred story, or of decorating a reliquary when the old ones had served their purpose so well, and, moreover, for so long. The pious donor who wanted to create a new casket for a holy relic not only tried to procure the most precious materials, but he would seek an old and venerable example of how it should be decorated. In nearby Nuremburg there are two very similar reliquaries dating from the fourteenth century. One of them – in silver and with criss-cross strips of gold – contains the relics of St Sebald and stands in a shrine in the nave of the church dedicated to him. The other is in the German National Museum, and once contained the relics of the Passion belonging to the Holy Roman Emperors. These caskets were decorated with the sacred grill pattern because the most precious relic of all, the Shroud, had been kept in a casket decorated in this manner. The very notion of the trellis was equated in the minds of medieval artists with the idea of sanctity of a very exceptional kind.

The same argument applies to the paintings called the Mass of St Gregory. The tradition of Christ's appearance above an altar at Mass had been handed down by those who had witnessed the Shroud Masses in Constantinople (and while the only written account we have is Robert de Clari's this does not, of course, mean that he was the only Westerner to be present at such a Mass or the only one to have written or spoken about it on his return home). Artists interpreted this story as best they could, ignorant no doubt that the body of Christ was identical to the mysterious image of the upper part of a crucified man on a piece of cloth. Naturally they envisaged the body of Christ in the round, not as an image of one. And as time passed, and the original eye-witness descriptions were forgotten, artists began to depict the whole body of Christ upon the altar, not just the upper part of what was in reality the partially unfolded Shroud. Artists were not out to create a convincing likeness of nature, so much as to convey the content and the message of the sacred object and the story surrounding its appearance at Mass.

It is perhaps significant that it was St Gregory himself who said that painting can do for the illiterate what writing does for those who can read. He reminded those who were against all paintings that many members of the Church could neither read nor write, and that for the purpose of teaching them, images and paintings were as useful as the pictures in a picture-book are for children. In the case of the Gospel stories and the stories of the lives of the saints there remained the sacred and sanctified texts to which the literate could refer. But the stories of the Shroud Masses do not occur in the Bible or in the lives of the saints, and furthermore they had been disseminated by word of mouth and only appeared in a garbled form in the stories of the Holy Grail. The cloth itself had been hidden for nearly a century, so that all artists had to go on was the memory of a tradition, something entirely vague and amorphous. We must also remember that from the twelfth century until after the collapse of the Latin Empire of Constantinople in 1261 there was more contact than formerly or since with the art of Byzantium, and that many Western artists tried to emulate the sacred images and icons of the Eastern Church. Artists were not concerned with the imitation of natural forms, but rather with the arrangement of a traditional sacred story.

If this explanation is correct it follows that the Grail, after being copied by German artists, may have remained in Germany after the Shroud passed into the hands of the Templars, and there is likewise the possibility that it might have survived unrecognized in some church or castle. Fantastic though this may at first sight appear, it is no more fantastic than the survival of the Dead Sea Scrolls or Tutankhamen's treasure. Since Grail seekers have been looking for a chalice or the record of Jesus' supposed descendants all these years, it is not surprising that they should have ignored a shallow, rectangular box had they happened to stumble upon one in the course of their investigations. Beside the clues offered by the reliquaries in Nuremberg I have just mentioned, the grail tradition lived on elsewhere in Bavaria. At Denkendorf, near Stuttgart, there is a crypt on whose walls can be seen diaper frescoes almost identical in pattern with that of the Sainte Face de Laon, even to the tassels along the bottom. This crypt contains an empty tomb and a head of Christ on a circular dish-like nimbus, closely resembling those seen on the Nottingham alabasters. If, as I have suggested, the criss-cross motif can be traced to the repetition of Christ's initial, X, then much is explained.

There remains one more grain of evidence to support my theories, which commentators on the legends seem to have overlooked. It concerns the part played by the family in the legends. Take Wolfram's version by way of example, for it applies more or less equally to the other three early versions. Parzival, the hero, is Trevrizent's nephew; the Fisher King, Anfortas, the son of Frimutel and grandson of Titurel, is Trevrizent's brother. Anfortas is the brother not only of Trevrizent, but also of Herzeloide and Repanse de Schoie, the Grail Bearer. The Red Knight, Ither von Gaheviez, is Parzival's cousin; so is Sigune. Parzival himself is the son of Gahmuret and Lohengrin's father. Much is made of the supposed descent of these characters from Joseph of Arimathea, and complex genealogical trees can be drawn to illustrate the relationships between the various protagonists.

If I have done nothing else in this book, I think I can claim to have shown how closely related to one another were the men and women who had most to do with the Shroud between 1171, when it was first seen by King Amalric I and his entourage, right down to 1453, when Marguerite de Charny gave it to her kinsfolk, Duke Louis and Duchess Anne of Savoy. Is it merely coincidental that this historical family network is reflected in the romances? Can it be that the Shroud Mafia was the Grail Family? I leave you to answer that question.

INCENDIUM AMORIS, OR THE HEAT PHENOMENON OF MYSTICS AND HEALERS

———•———

American scientists involved in STURP – the Shroud of Turin Research Project – have put forward two suggestions to explain the image on the cloth. One of them suggests some very brief but intense burst of 'photographic' radiation involving heat sufficient to scorch but not burn the cloth. The other proposes a thermo-nuclear 'flash in a milli-second of time', which strikes me as being much the same. Father Herbert Thurston, SJ, wrote a treatise in 1952 on the *Physical Phenomena of Mysticism* (Burns Oates) in which the following account of the life of St Philip Neri appears:

> Philip felt such a heat in the region of the heart that it sometimes extended over his whole body, and for all his age, thinness and spare diet, in the coldest days of winter it was necessary, even in the middle of the night, to open the windows, to cool the bed, to fan him while in bed and in various ways to moderate the great heat. . . . Cardinal Crescenzi, one of his spiritual children, when he touched his hand, it burned as if the saint was suffering from a raging fever. . . . Sometimes in saying office, or after Mass, or in any other spiritual action, sparks, as it were of fire, were seen to dart from his eyes and from his face.

When surgeons performed an autopsy on him after his death they opened the body to find a swelling under his left breast which proved to be due to the fact that two of his ribs were broken and thrust outward. . . . There can be no dispute that the injury was there, and had been for many years. Fr Thurston goes on to say, quite rightly, that such physical phenomena can hardly be regarded as witnessing to any abnormal increase in the temperature of the body. None the less the claim is made that phenomena do occasionally occur for which no parallel can be found in the pathological records known to medical science. In the case of Padre Pio, who during World War II lived in a

206

village in the Gargano peninsula of eastern Italy, and who was marked with the stigmata, the clinical thermometer used by his doctor in visiting him professionally was unable on more than one occasion to register the patient's high temperature, and was broken by the unprecedented expansion of the mercury in it.

There is considerable evidence to suggest that some energy flows from the faith healer to the patient, and that this either initiates or augments the patient's 'self-repair' system. Experiments at the University of Illinois and at the Medical Research Foundation on Long Island on the reaction of enzymes to the laying on of hands by a faith healer reveal that the net effect of the healer's treatment was identical to that caused by exposure to high magnetic fields. This cannot be said to prove that healing energy is identical to magnetism in nature, of course, for no trace of any magnetic field has ever been picked up in the vicinity of a healer. But that the healer did something remarkable to the enzymes in solution was undeniable. Photographs of healers taken by a lensless, electrical process before, during and after healing sessions, known as the Kirlian process of photography, suggest that psychic healing involves a dynamic, detectable interchange of energy between the healer and his patient. When Jesus healed the woman with an issue of blood (Mark 5:30) he 'immediately knowing in himself that virtue had gone out of him, turned . . . and said, "Who touched my clothes?"' In 1970 Dr Thelma Moss and Kendall Johnson built a Kirlian device using a 12-volt, high frequency (3,000 hertz) spark to form a corona image on ordinary 4×5 Kodak film. They observed a definite and sizeable increase in the width of the corona surrounding the fingertips of the patient and a corresponding decrease in the same parameters of the healer's halo. Unfortunately, this is not conclusive evidence of the transfer of energy from healer to patient, for alcoholic consumption can produce marked corona differences. Nevertheless, Dr William Tiller, chairman of the Department of Material Sciences at Stratford University in America, has reported that it takes several days after death has been officially pronounced by a physician before the fingertips lose their glow. Moss and Johnson found that the corona surrounding the fingertips of five hundred normal people varied in width from a sixteenth to a quarter of an inch. In the case of one healer, even in a non-healing situation, the blotches of vivid blue surrounding her fingertips stretched far beyond the normal limit of one quarter inch. When she was asked to think she was in the process of healing and in the full healing state, the resulting corona resembled a solar flare emanating from the sun.

The haloes believed to crown the heads not only of Jesus and

Christian saints, but also of Hindu and Buddhist gods and mystics, may be exceptionally intense fields which Kirlian equipment can record in weaker form. Needless to say, experimental evidence cannot confirm this theory – maybe it never will. No one is able to explain the phenomenon, though there can be little doubt of its reality.

Corona discharge is an electrical discharge, a movement of electrons, that may run over a short physical range when a high-intensity electric field exists in a gaseous atmosphere. This discharge will cause a glow without necessarily producing sparks. Examples of such naturally occurring discharges that produce glowing coronas or haloes are St Elmo's Fire, the glow that sometimes appears round high-tension power lines, and the sparking or crackle that can occur when taking off one's clothes on a cold winter's night. That the images of the Sindon and Soudarion may have been made in some such fashion is a subject for further investigation, but not by me.

TEMPLAR ESTABLISHMENTS UNDER THE JURISDICTION OF THE GRAND PRIORY OF CHAMPAGNE

———●———

ESTABLISHMENTS	DEPARTMENTS	DATES OF CHARTERS
VOULAINE – Grand Priory of Champagne	Côte d'Or	1175
1 Bure – Commandery	,,	1120/1224
Bissey-la–Côte	,,	1209
Beneuvre	,,	1307
Châtillon-sur-Seine	,,	1144
Lucenay-le-Duc	,,	1224
Avôsne	,,	1147
Uncey	,,	1147
Thoisy-le-Désert	,,	1202
Dijon	,,	1165
Curtil	,,	1295
St Philibert or Velle-sous-Gevrey	,,	1204
2 Mormant – Commandery	Hte-Marne	1120
Marac	,,	1159
Richebourg	,,	1199
3 Epailly – Commandery	Côte d'Or	1215
Courban	,,	1230
Louesme	,,	1209
Thoire-sur-Ource	,,	1209
4 Montmorot – Commandery	,,	1197
Busserotte	,,	1299
Montenaille	,,	1197
5 La Romagne – Commandery	,,	1144
Courchamp	,,	1144
St Maurice-sur-Vingeanne	,,	1225
Montigny-sur-Vingeanne	,,	1225
Charmoy	Hte-Marne	
Rougeux, Arbigny, Genrupt	,,	

ESTABLISHMENTS	DEPARTMENTS	DATES OF CHARTERS
Broncourt, La Chassagne	,,	
Valeroy, Montormentier	,,	
Broye-les-Loups	Hte-Saône	
Barge, Neuvelle	,,	
Autrey	,,	1191
Champlitte	,,	1191
Fouvent	,,	1191
6 Avalleurs – Commandery	Aube	1172
Buxières	,,	1307
Polisot, Levigny, Avanthieres	,,	
7 Fontenotte – Commandery	Côte d'Or	1307
8 Dijon (Fauverney) – Commandery	,,	1281
9 Beaune (St Jacques) – Commandery	,,	1207
Vandenesse-sous-Châteauneuf	,,	1237
Sombernon	,,	1234
10 Demigny-près-Chagny – Chapel	Saône-et-Loire	1225
11 Châlon-sur-Saône – Commandery	,,	1150
Sevrey	,,	1234
Montbellet-près-Macon	,,	1307
Givry	,,	1230
Buxy-le-Royal	,,	1234
12 Le Saulce d'Iland-Pontaubert – House	Yonne	1209
Domécy-sur-le-Vaux	,,	
13 St Marc-près-Tonnerre – Commandery	,,	1186
Fontenay	,,	1214
14 Auxerre – Commandery	,,	1199
Mesry/Montigny, Le Saulce d'Ecolives	,,	1216
Valan, St-Bris, Moneteau	,,	1260
Villemoson – Former commandery	Nièvre	1189
Molay	,,	1250

NOTE: The Auxerre Commandery came under the Grand Priory of France whose headquarters were at the Temple in Paris.

15 Macon – Commandery	Saône-et-Loire	?
Belleville-sur-Saône	Rhône	1223
Peyzieu	Ain	1298
16 Beugnay-en-Charollais – Commandery	Saône-et-Loire	?

NOTE: Macon and Beugnay came under the Grand Priory of Auvergne whose headquarters were at Lyon.

ESTABLISHMENTS	DEPARTMENTS	DATES OF CHARTERS
FRANCHE-COMTÉ		
1 Dole – Commandery (Senior)	Jura	1181
Baverans – Sub-Commandery	,,	?
Salins – Sub-Commandery	,,	1279
Arbois – Sub-Commandery	,,	1249
Besançon	Doubs	?
Sales – Sub-Commandery	Hte-Saône	?
Villedieu-en-Fontenette – Sub-Commandery	,,	?
Valentigney	,,	?
Dammartin – Sub-Commandery	Doubs	
2 Bresse et Bugey – Commandery de la Musse	Ain	1200
Espesses	situation unknown	?
Tessonges	situation unknown	?
3 Feuillées – Commandery	Ain	?
4 Arroyer-en-Bugey – Commandery	,,	?
CHAMPAGNE		
1 St Amand-près-Vitry – Commandery	Marne	?
2 La Neuville – Commandery	,,	?
3 Braux – Commandery	Hte-Marne	?
4 Ruetz – Commandery	,,	?
5 Thors – Commandery	,,	?
6 Esnouveaux – Commandery	,,	?
7 Bonnevaux – Commandery	,,	?

1156   Spas–Mirozski frescoes (circa).

1157   Richard Coeur de Lion born.

1161   Walter Map returns to England, joins royal household. Philip de Milly marries and becomes Sr. d'Outrejourdain.

1162   Amalric I succeeds to throne of Jerusalem; divorces Agnes de Courtenay.

1165   Philip de Milly joins Templars.

1167   Amalric I m. Maria Comnena.

1168   William of Tyre, ambassador to Constantinople.

1170   Philip de Milly elected Grand Master of Templars.

1171   Apr.–June: Visit of Amalric I and entourage to Constantinople. Death of Philip de Milly.
Boniface of Montferrat m. Elena di Busca (of Savoy). Death of Henry of Blois, Abbot of Glastonbury and Bishop of Winchester.

1174   Death of Amalric I; Baldwin the Leper succeeds as K. of Jerusalem.
Joscelin III, Ct of Edessa and Reynald de Châtillon released from prison. Reynald de Châtillon m. Stephanie de Milly.

1175   Voulaine presented to Templars by Duke Hugh III of Burgundy.
Earliest date for Chrétien de Troyes' *Conte del Graal*,

1177   Philip, Count of Flanders visits Constantinople. Death of William of Montferrat.

1178   Philip of Flanders in Antioch.

1179   Philip of Flanders returns to France. Lateran Council opens; attended by Walter Map and William of Tyre.

1180   Median date for *Conte del Graal*. Death of Emperor Manuel Comnenus.

1181   William of Tyre returns to Holy Land. Death of Henri I de Champagne.

1182   William of Tyre returns to Rome. Walter Map begins *De Nugis Curialium*.

1185   Death of William of Tyre. Margaret of Hungary m. Emperor Isaac Angelos.

1186   Birth of Prince Arthur of Brittany.

1188   Latest date for *Conte del Graal*.

1189   Accession of Richard Coeur de Lion. Geoffrey IV de Joinville joins Third Crusade; present at siege of Acre. Walter Map leaves royal household and returns to England.

1190   Death of Geoffrey IV de Joinville of wounds; Geoffrey V succeeds to Seneschalship of Champagne. Birth of Jacques Pantaléon (future Pope Urban IV).

1191   Death of Philip of Flanders in Holy Land. King Arthur's tomb allegedly discovered at Glastonbury. Pope Celestine III shows the Veronica to Philip Augustus.

1195   Emperor Isaac Angelos deposed; Alexius III succeeds.

1196   K. Philip Augustus m. Agnes von Andechs–Meran.

1197   Frederick II born. Walter Map appointed Archdeacon of Oxford.
Innocent III elected pope. Geoffrey IV de Joinville dies. Otto von Henneberg-Bodenlauben goes to Holy Land.

1199   Spas-Nereditsa frescoes. Death of Richard Coeur de Lion.
        28 Nov: Tournament of Écri-sur-Aisne – genesis of 4th Crusade –
        attended by Geoffrey V de Joinville.
1200   Earliest date for the composition of *Peredur*. Latest date for sequel to
        Conte del Graal. Earliest date for *Parzival*. Ash Wednesday: Conference
        of Compiègne; Baldwin of Flanders and Theobald of Champagne take
        the cross.
1201   Mar: Geoffrey de Villehardouin and Frankish ambassadors in Venice.
        24 May: Death of Theobald of Champagne.
        Aug/Sept. Boniface of Montferrat goes to France and is elected leader of
        the Crusade.
        Autumn: Prince Alexius Angelos flees from Constantinople to Philip of
        Swabia.
        Christmas: Boniface, Philip and Alexius discuss attack on
        Constantinople.
        Gauthier de Brienne in southern Italy fighting for the pope against
        Hohenstaufens.
1202   19 Dec: Death of Hugues de Vergy. Gauthier de Montbéliard joins 4th
        Crusade.
1203   June: Crusaders reach Constantinople.
        5–17 July: Siege of Constantinople.
        19 July: Crusaders enter Constantinople.
        1 Aug: Coronation of Alexius IV, co-emperor with Isaac.
        Murder of Prince Arthur of Brittany. K. Andrew II m. Gertrud of
        Andechs-Meran.
1204   4 Feb: Alexius IV deposed by Murzuphlus; murdered 10 Feb.
        6 Apr: first Crusader attack on Constantinople repulsed.
        12 Apr: second Crusader attack succeeds, followed by sack.
        23 Apr: Robert de Clari sees Good Friday mass of the Soudarion.
        15 May: Boniface of Montferrat m. Empress Mary-Margaret.
        16 May: Coronation of Baldwin as emperor.
        End of May: Boniface and Mary-Margaret leave Constantinople with
        the Shroud; arrive at Mosynopolis; go to Demotika. Boniface quarrels
        with Baldwin.
        End of Aug: Baldwin returns to Constantinople; attempts to patch up
        quarrel with Boniface.
        Sept: Boniface and Mary-Margaret return to Constantinople from
        Demotika.
        End of Sept: Boniface and Mary-Margaret reach Salonika.
        Oct. (circa): Otto de la Roche appointed Duke of Athens; guarding
        Shroud there.
1205   Spring: Guillaume de Champlitte appointed Prince of Achaea.
        1 Aug: Theodore Ducas Comnenus Angelos writes to Innocent III
        telling him that the Shroud is in Athens.
        Emperor Baldwin taken prisoner. Andrew II succeeds as K. of Hungary.
        Death of Gauthier de Brienne. Demetrios of Montferrat born.
1206   Aug: Henry crowned Emperor of Constantinople.
        Earliest date for *Perlesvaus*. Otto von Henneberg-Bodenlauben returns to

Germany from Holy Land. Berthold von Andechs appointed Archbishop of Kalocsa.

1207   Spring: Boniface campaigning in Thrace.
Aug: Boniface meets Emperor Henry.
Sept: Boniface of Montferrat killed.
Oct/Nov: Mary Margaret m. Nicholas de Saint-Omer.
Innocent III initiates procession of the Veronica. Wolfram incorporates Lohengrin into *Parzival*.

1208   6 Jan: Demetrios of Montferrat crowned K. of Salonika. Mary-Margaret regent.
Guillaume de Champlitte leaves Greece for Burgundy and dies.
Otto von Henneberg-Bodenlauben returns to the Holy Land. Guillaume de Joinville appointed Bp. of Langres.

1209   Jean de Brienne lands in Palestine.

1210   1 Apr: Walter Map dead by this date. Latest date for *Parzival*. Guy de la Roche co-duke of Athens.

1212   Latest date for *Perlesvaus* and Robert de Boron's *Joseph of Arimathea*.
Death of Etienne de Mont-Saint-Jean and Gauthier de Montbéliard.
Frederick II Holy Roman Emperor.

1213   Queen Gertrüd of Hungary assassinated. Landgrafenpsalter Crucifixion.

1215   Fourth Lateran Council. K. Andrew II m. Yolande de Courtenay.
Earliest date for *Vulgate Cycle* (? uncertain). Hélinand of Froidmont mentions the Grail in his *Estoire del Graal*.

1216   Emperor Henry dies; Peter de Courtenay succeeds. Death of Innocent III, Honorius III succeeds. Michael Ducas Comnenus dies, Theodore Ducas Comnenus Angelos succeeds as Despot of Epirus. Andrew II goes on crusade. Szavaszentdemeter comes under Roman jurisdiction.

1218   Andrew II returns to Hungary from Holy Land. Theodore Ducas attacks Salonika. Berthold von Andechs appointed Patriarch of Aquilea.

1219   Guillaume de Joinville appointed Archbp of Reims. Pierre de Montaigu appointed Grand Master of Templars. Simon de Joinville leaves France for Holy Land; joins Jean de Brienne at Damietta. Guillaume I de Vergy appointed Seneschal of Burgundy.

1220   Otto and Beatrix von Henneberg sell their Syrian lands to Teutonic Knights. Forged charter claims evangelical foundation for Glastonbury.

1221   Sept: Fall of Damietta (5th Crusade) Simon de Joinville returns to France. Autumn: Salonika besieged by Theodore Ducas. Otto and Beatrix v Henneberg return to Franconia. Death of Queen Maria of Montferrat–Jerusalem.

1222   Theodore Ducas captures Salonika; Mary-Margaret goes to Hungary. Kalojan Angelos, Duke of Srem. Philip Augustus appoints Templar treasurer his executor. Theobald IV of Champagne m. Agnes de Beaujeu.

1223   July: Death of Philip Augustus. Aug: Coronation of Louis VIII. Jean de Brienne at Court. Earliest date for painting of Sainte Face de Laon.

1224   Jean de Brienne returns to Italy. Last mention of Jean de Mont-Saint-Jean in French records; moves to Franconia to become Hans von Weinsberg?

1225   Aug/9 Nov: Weddings of Frederick II and Yolande de Brienne-

Jerusalem. Jean de Brienne in Rome to protest against Frederick's
seduction of his niece.
1226 Accession of Louis IX. Gerold of Lausanne appointed patriarch of
Jerusalem. Death of Archbp Guillaume de Joinville.
1227 Death of Br Aimard, Templar Treasurer; succeeded by Jean de Milly.
Mar: Death of Honorius III; election of Gregory IX.
Sept: Frederick II embarks for Holy Land; death of Ludwig of Thuringia;
Frederick postpones his departure. Pope excommunicates Emperor
Frederick II.
1228 Apr: Queen-Empress Yolande gives birth to Conrad von Hohenstaufen
and dies. Jean de Brienne appointed regent of Constantinople, *de facto*
emperor.
June: Frederick II sails for Holy Land; arrives Sept. Quarrels with
Patriarch Gerold and Templars.
1229 18 Mar: Frederick crowned K. of Jerusalem. Besieges Acre; accuses
Templars of malpractices. Death or retirement of Mary-Margaret.
1230 Otto v. Henneberg meets Conrad v. Hohenlohe at imperial court in
Italy; they return to Germany by autumn.
July: Treaty of San Germano; excommunication of Frederick lifted.
Sainte Face de Laon in Bari (?); Blessed Juliana of Liège promotes idea of
feast of Corpus Christi, supported by Jacques Pantaléon.
1231 Otto and Beatrix v. Henneberg sell property for the Church. Death of St
Elisabeth of Hungary (widow of Ludwig of Thuringia).
1232 Death of Pierre de Montaigu; election of Armand de Périgord as
Templar Grand Master.
1234 Death of Jean de Milly, Templar Treasurer.
1235 Death of Andrew II of Hungary. Latest date for *Vulgate Cycle*
(uncertain). Jean de Joinville appointed Seneschal of Champagne.
1236 Br. Gilles appointed Templar Treasurer.
1238 Emperor Baldwin II gives Crown of Thorns to St Louis.
1240 Jacques Pantaléon appointed Canon of Laon. Baldwin II offers True
Cross as guarantee for Templar loan. Tartar invasion of Hungary. Death
of Guillaume I de Vergy; Henri de Vergy succeeds as Seneschal of
Burgundy.
1241 Tartars reach Dalmatia; flight of Hungarian royal family to Klis.
1244 Death of Otto v. Henneberg. Jacques de Molay born. Death of Armand
de Périgord; Guillaume de Sonnac succeeds as Templar Grand Master.
1247 Innocent IV gives Szavaszentdemeter to Benedictines. Emperor Baldwin
II cedes all Constantinople relics to St Louis. Geoffrey de Joinville de
Briquenay born. William of Malmesbury's *De Antiquitate Glastoniensis
Ecclesiae* revised.
1248 Death of Beatrix von Henneberg. St Louis and Jean de Joinville leave
France for the Holy Land.
1249 Jacques Pantaléon sends Sainte Face to Laon.
1250 July: Death of Guillaume de Sonnac; succeeded by Renaud de Vichier as
Templar Grand Master. Death of Frederick II; succeeded by Conrad.
1251 Conradin of Hohenstaufen born. Geoffrey de Charny (Templar) born.
1254 Jean de Joinville returns to France with St Louis.

1260   Guillaume de Joinville appointed Dean of Besançon; André de Joinville
       preceptor of Payns by this time; death of Jean de Joinville's first wife,
       Adelaide de Grandpré; death of his mother, Beatrix d'Auxonne.
       Professor Grabar's date for change in Veronica image representation.
1261   Jacques Pantaléon elected pope (Urban IV). Pierre de Charny appointed
       papal chamberlain.
1265   Hugues de Pairaud received into Templars (approx.). Pierre Allemandi
       preceptor of Montpellier-St Gilles.
1268   Dean Guillaume de Joinville of Besançon dies.
1269–70   Geoffrey de Charny received into Templars.
1273   May: Guillaume de Beaujeu elected Templar Grand Master.
1274   Guillaume de Beaujeu attends the Council of Lyon.
1278   Jean de la Tour appointed Templar Treasurer.
1285   6 Oct: Death of Philip the Bold; accession of Philip the Handsome.
1291   Fall of Acre; death of Guillaume de Beaujeu. Hugues de Pairaud
       appointed Templar Seneschal. Thibaud Gaudin elected Grand Master.
1292   16 Apr: Death of Thibaud Gaudin; succeeded by Jacques de Molay.
1293   Templar General Chapter at Montpellier, Shroud exhibited. Franciscan
       Man of Sorrows in Genoese MS.
1294   Dec: Boniface VIII elected pope.
1295/6   Winter: Templar General Chapter at Paris. Jacques de Molay in
       England for inauguration of Guy de Foresta as Visitor of England.
1296   Autumn: Templar General Chapter at Arles.
1297   Jacques de Molay in Cyprus.
1300   Geoffrey de Charny the elder born (approx.). Jacques de Molay takes up
       residence in Paris Temple. Commandery of Mormant founded.
1302   Apr: Estates General meeting; Jean de Joinville absent. Jean de Joinville
       begins to write his memoirs.
1306   Autumn: Jacques de Molay returns to France from Cyprus visit.
1307   May: Jacques de Molay meets Clement V at Poitiers.
       July: Templar General Chapter in Paris; steps taken to safeguard the
       Shroud.
       14 Sept (or 27): Philip the Handsome signs order for the arrest of the
       Templars.
       12 Oct: Jacques de Molay attends funeral of Catherine de Valois.
       13 Oct: All Templars in France arrested. Shroud removed from Voulaine
       to Charny stronghold by this date.
       18 Oct: Blanche of Burgundy m. Edward of Savoy.
       27 Oct: Clement V protests to Philip the Handsome.
       Henri de Vergy, Canon of Langres, later Cantor of Besançon, dies.
1310   Death of Jean de Vergy, Seneschal of Burgundy.
1318   Death of Jean de Joinville, Seneschal of Champagne.
1323   Death of Jean de Charny.
1345   Geoffrey de Charny leaves for Smyrna. He remains there for a year.
1349   Battle of Crécy. Geoffrey de Charny captured by the English. Besançon
       cathedral burnt down; Shroud copy goes missing.
1352   Geoffrey de Charny released by English and returns to France.
1353   Geoffrey de Charny founds church at Lirey; Shroud exhibited.

1356   Battle of Poitiers; Geoffrey de Charny killed.

1360   Death of Guillaume de Vergy.

1362   Geoffrey de Charny the younger is knighted.

1367   Joseph of Arimathea's 'body' found at Glastonbury.

1375   Geoffrey de Charny II appointed Bailli of Caen.

1380/81   Raimondello Orsini del Balzo visits Sinai; brings icon to Galatina.

1386   Raimondello presents icon of Sinai (Man of Sorrows) to Sta Croce in Gerusalemme, Rome.

1389   Second public exhibition of Shroud at Lirey. Bishop d'Arcis complains about it.

1398   Geoffrey de Charny II dies; Marguerite inherits his lands.

1418   Shroud moved from Lirey to Montfort.

1437   Humbert de Villersexel dies.

1449   Canons of Lirey press for return of the Shroud. Marguerite de Charny takes it to Belgium.

1453   Marguerite de Charny gives Shroud to Duke Louis and Duchess Anne of Savoy.

1460   Death of Marguerite de Charny.

POSTSCRIPT

After I had finished writing this book my attention was drawn to a theory advanced in 1902 by Baron Joseph du Teil, based on a statement by Philibert Pingon, the 16th-century historian of the House of Savoy, in which the Baron suggests that the Shroud was brought directly from Greece to Lirey between 1316 and 1325 by Agnes de Charpigny, Dame de Vostitza (in the Peloponnese), the wife of Dreux de Charny, elder brother of Geoffrey I de Charny. Pingon says that the Shroud was brought to France by Marguerite de Charny because of the unsettled state of affairs in Greece, Asia (Minor) and Syria, but the Baron points out that Pingon mistook Marguerite for her great-aunt, Agnes de Charpigny (see Table 1).

Du Teil's theory cannot, however, be sustained unless we reject all the Templar evidence as described in Chapter 3. On the other hand, if Pingon is correct in stating that the Shroud was removed from Greece because the situation there was so unsettled, and if the Templar evidence is correct, then it follows that the Shroud reached France before 1274 (see page 92). The situation in Greece was particularly unsettled following the battle of Pelagonia in 1259, which led, two years later, to the collapse of the Frankish Empire of Constantinople. At the same time it must be noted that the Templars of Frankish Greece came under the jurisdiction of the Templar Province of Apulia, and that the Commander of that province, prior to his election as Grand Master in 1273, was Guillaume de Beaujeu, who was the first to hold special chapters in honour of the so-called 'idol' (see page 87). Table 3 shows how Guillaume de Beaujeu and his family were related to the family of Mont-Saint-Jean/Charny.

If this is correct, it would appear that the Shroud was kept in Athens (probably in the Parthenon, then the cathedral of the Virgin Mary) from about 1205 to around 1261, and that it was entrusted to the Templars to prevent it falling into the hands of the Greek Orthodox clergy should the restored Greek emperor of Constantinople recapture Frankish Greece, as then seemed possible. This seems a more plausible explanation than the one I gave in Chapter 6, page 165. On the other hand the German and Hungarian evidence has to be explained, and it seems to me more likely that it relates to the Shroud of Besançon rather than to the Shroud of Turin. After all, Otto, Duke of Andechs-Meran became Count Palatine of Burgundy, whose capital is Besançon, in 1231, and his daughter, Adelheid, married as her first husband Hugh, Count of Châlon-Salins, first-cousin of Jean de Joinville. Otto, his successors and the Chapter of Besançon would be reluctant to admit that their Shroud was a copy and not the genuine article, which goes some way to explain why there should have been accusations of fraud against Geoffrey de Charny and his Shroud when it was exhibited at Lirey. Whichever way you look at it, the Shroud Mafia was determined to keep both the original and the copy very firmly in the family. The final answer to these questions has yet to be given.

May 1987

BIBLIOGRAPHY

Allgemeine Deutsche Biographie

Alphandéry, P.,   *La Chrétienté et l'idée de croisade* (Paris, 1954).

Angelow, D.,   *L'influence du Bogomilisme ou les Cathares* (Sofia, 1968).

Anselme, Père,   *Histoire de la maison royale de France* (Paris, 1726–33).

Arnold, B.,   *German Knighthood, 1050–1300* (Oxford, 1985).

Baigent, M., Leigh, R., and Lincoln, H.,   *The Holy Blood and the Holy Grail* (London, 1982).

Barber, M.,   *The Trial of the Templars* (Cambridge, 1978).

Barta, Beend, Nagy *et al,   History of Hungary* (London, 1975).

Baunel, J., *Histoire d'une seigneurie du midi de la France* (Montpellier, 1971).

Belperron, P.,   *La croisade contre les Albigeois* (Paris, 1961).

Bernadac, C.,   *Le mystère d'Otto Rahn* (Paris, 1978).

Bertelli, C.,   *The Image of Pity in Santa Croce in Gerusalemme* (London, 1967).

Bishop, Morris,   *The Pelican Book of the Middle Ages* (London, 1971).

Boccacci, Giovanni,   *De Casibus Virorum Illustrium* (Strasburg, 1475?)

Bonnet, Emile,   *Les maisons de l'Ordre du Temple dans le Languedoc* (Nimes, 1933).

Boron, Robert de,   *Roman de l'Estoire dou Saint Graal* (English trans: London, 1861).

Bradford, Ernle,   *The Great Betrayal* (London, 1967).

Brown, E. A. R.,   *The Cistercians in the Latin Empire of Constantinople* (New York, 1958).

Brown, Peter,   *The World of Late Antiquity* (London, 1971).

Butler, Samuel,   *Lives of the Saints* (London, 1981).

Cabrol, Fernand,   *Dictionnaire d'Archéologie Chrétienne*, Tome VIII (Paris, 1903–53).

Chenaye-Dubois, de la and Badier,   *Dictionnaire de la noblesse* (Paris, 1844).

Chevalier, U.,   *Etude artistique sur l'origine du saint suaire* (Paris, 1900).

Chifflet, J. J.,   *De linteis sepulchribus Christi* (Paris, 1767).

Churchill, W. S.,   *History of the English-speaking People* (London, 1956).

Clari, Robert de,   *Conquest of Constantinople* (Trans. E. H. Neal: New York, 1936).

Cognasso, D.,   *Un imperatore bizantino della decadenza:* Bessarione XXXI.

Colledge, M. A. R.,   *The Parthians* (London, 1977).

Comureaux, C.,   *Histoire de Bourgogne* (Paris, 1977).

Courcelles, *Histoire généalogique et héraldique des pairs de France* (Paris, 1824).

Courtepée, Claude, *Description du duché de Bourgogne* (Dijon, 1847–8).

Crubellier, M. and Juillard, C., *Histoire de la Champagne* (Paris, 1969).

Dailliez, L., *Les Templiers – ces inconnus* (Paris, 1972); *Les Templiers – Gouvernement et Institutions*, Tome I (Alpes Meditérannée Editions, 1980).

Daniel-Rops, H., *Cathedral and Crusade* (Trans. J. Warrington: London, 1957).

Delaborde, H., *Jean de Joinville et les sieurs de Joinville* (Paris, 1894).

Devic and Vaissette, *Histoire générale de Languedoc* (Toulouse, 1885).

Dictionnaire étymologique de français (Paris, 1979).

Dictionnaire étymologique de la langue latine

Dosset, J., 'Un évêque cathare', *Bulletin philologique et historique* (1965).

Drews, R., *In Search of the Shroud of Turin* (New Jersey, 1984).

Du Cange, *Les familles d'Outremer* (Ed. E. G. Rey: Paris, 1869).

Dumoulin, G., *Conquêtes et trophées des Normands français* (Rouen, 1658).

Duvernoy, J., *La catharisme* (Toulouse, 1929).

'L'Eglise dite bulgare du Catharisme occidental', *Byzantinobulgarica*, VI (1980).

Eschenbach, W. von, *Parzival* (Trans. A. T. Hatto: London, 1980).

Eusebius, Pamphili, *Life of Constantine the Great* (London, 1636).

Every, G., *The Mass* (Dublin, 1970).

Fine, J. V. A., *The Bosnian Church* (New York, 1975).

Finke, H., *Papstum und Untergang des Templerorden* (Münster, 1907).

Finlay, G., *A History of Greece* (Oxford, 1877).

Fleckenstein, J. and Hellmann, M., *Die Seigneurie de Joscelin und der Deutschen Orden* (Stuttgart, 1974).

Frolow, A., 'Recherches sur la déviation de la IVe Croisade vers Constantinople', *Revue de l'Histoire des Religions*, CXLV–VI (1954); *La Peinture du moyen âge en Yougoslavie* (Paris, 1954).

Gantz, J. (Trans.), *Mabinogion* (London, 1967).

Gauthier, Jules, *Notes iconographiques sur le saint suaire de Besançon* (Besançon, 1883).

Gibbon, Edward, *Decline and Fall of the Roman Empire* (London, 1910).

Glossarium mediae et infimae Latinitatis (Niort, 1884).

Godfrey, John, *The Unholy Crusade* (Oxford, 1980).

Gospel of Nicodemus (Trans. from *The English Recusant Litterature*, Ilkley, 1975).

Gospel of St Peter (Trans. J. A. Robinson and M. R. James: London, 1892).

Gospel of Thomas (Trans. L. Johnston: London, 1960).

Grabar, A., 'On the Sainte Face of Novgorod in the Tretyakov

Museum', *Cahiers Archéologique*, Tome XII (Paris, 1976); 'La Sainte Face de Laon', *Seminarium Kondakovianum* (Prague, 1935).

Green, Maurus, *Enshrouded in Silence, Ampleforth Journal* (1969).

Grousset, R., *Histoires des Croisades et du royaume franc de Jerusalem* (Paris, 1934–6).

Hamilton, Bernard, *Monastic Reform, Catharism and the Crusades 900–1300* (Variorum Reprints, 1979).

Harvey, J., *The Plantagenets* (London, 1967).

Haskins, C., 'A Canterbury Monk at Constantinople', *Eng. Hist. Revue* XXV (1910).

Heller, John, *Report on the Shroud of Turin* (Boston, 1983).

Homan, B., *Geschichte des ungarischen Mittelalters* (Berlin, 1943).

Hope, W. A. St J., 'On the Sculptured Alabaster Tablets called St John's Head', *Archaelogica* 52 (1890).

Hopf, Karl, 'Geschichte Griechenlands', *Allgemeine Enzyclopädie des Wissenschaft und Kunsten*, LXXXV–VI.

Howarth, S., *The Knights Templar* (London, 1982).

Inglis, Brian, *Natural and Supernatural* (London, 1977).

Jackson, T. G., *Dalmatia* (London, 1887).

Janin, Raymond *Les églises et monastères des grands centres byzantines* (Paris, 1975).

Joinville, J. de, *Histoire de Saint Louis* (Paris, 1952).

Kelley, T. E., *Structural Study of the Perlesvaus* (Geneva, 1974).

Kitchin, G. W., *History of France* (Oxford, 1881).

Krekic, Barisa, *Dubrovnik, Italy and the Balkans in the Middle Ages* (Paris, 1961).

La Monte, J., 'The Lords of Sidon in the XII and XIII centuries', *Byzantion* XVII (1944/5); 'Lords of Caesarea', *Speculum* XXII (1947); 'The Viscounts of Naplouse', *Syria* XIX (1938).

Larousse, *Dictionnaire d'ancien Français: moyen âge et rennaissance* (Paris, 1947).

Laurent, J. and Claudon, F., *Les Templiers et les Hospitaliers en Bourgogne et Champagne méridinale XIIe–XIIIe siécles* (Variorum Reprints).

Lavirotte, C., *Memoire statistique des Templiers en Bourgogne* (Dijon n.d.).

Lea, H. C., *History of the Inquisition* (London, 1888).

Lewis, Charlton T. and Short, Charles, *Oxford Latin–English Dictionary*.

Lexicon Mediae et infimae Latinitatis (Paris, 1866).

Lizerand, Georges, *Le dossier de l'affaire des Templiers* (Paris, 1923).

Loge, Abbé, *Histoire du Comte de la Roche et de St Hippolyte* (Besançon n.d.).

Lognon, J., *'The Frankish States in Greece 1204–1311'* (see K. M. Setton, *A History of the Crusades*, Philadelphia, 1962).

Loomis, R. S., *The Grail: From Celtic Myth to Christian Symbol* (Cardiff, 1963).

Loos, M., *Dualist Heresy in the Middle Ages* (London, 1974).

Macartney, C. A., *A Short History of Hungary* (Oxford, 1962).

Male, E., *L'art religieuse de la fin du moyen âge en France* (Paris, 1931).

Map, Walter, *Quest of the Holy Grail* (Trans. P. Matarasso, London, 1969); *Death of King Arthur* (Trans. J. Cable, London, 1971); *De Nugis Curialium* (Trans. T. Wright, London, 1850).

Mas Latrie, L. de, *Histoire de l'Ile de Chypre* (Paris, 1855).

Matthews, J., *At the Table of the Grail* (London, 1984).

Melville, M., *La vie des Templiers* (Paris, 1951).

Michel, F., *Le Roman du Saint Graal* (Paris, 1841).

Mignard, M., *Statistiques des possessions de la milice du Temple en Bourgogne* (Paris, 1853); *Le coffret du duc de Blacas* (Dijon, 1856).

Monmouth, Geoffrey of, *History of the Kings of Britain* (Trans. Lewis Thorpe, London, 1966).

Neal, E. H. and Wolff, R. L., *The Fourth Crusade* (Philadelphia, 1912).

New Catholic Encyclopedia (New York, 1967).

Nicol, D. M., *The Fourth Crusade*, Cambridge Modern History IV (Cambridge, 1966).

Oldenbourg, Z., *Le bûcher de Montségur* (Paris, 1959).

Onasch, K., *Icons* (London, 1963).

Paris, Matthew, *Chronica Majora*, 7 Vols., (Pub. 1872–80).

Passati, C., *Supersense* (London, 1975).

Pauphilet, A., *Robert de Clari et Villehardouin* (Paris, 1953).

Payen, J. C., *Motif du retenir dans la littérature française mediévale des origines a 1230* (Geneva, 1968).

Petit, R., *Histoire des ducs de Bourgogne de la race capétienne* (Paris, 1885).

Piaget, A., *Le Livre de Messire Geoffroi de Charni* (Romania, 1897).

Piquet, Jules, *Les Templiers* (Paris, 1939).

Pirie-Gordon, M., 'The Reigning Princes of Galilee', *Eng. Hist. Rev.* XXVII (1912).

Puech, H. C. and Vaillant, A., *Le Traité contre les Bogomiles* (Paris, 1945).

Queller, D., *Mediaeval Diplomacy and the Fourth Crusade* (Variorum, 1980).

Rahn, Otto, *Le Croisade contre le Graal* (Paris, 1934).

Raymond, G., *Gestes des chyprois* (Geneva, 1887).

Reinach, S., 'Le Tête magique des Templiers', *Rev. de l'Hist. des Religions* (1911).

Rey, E. G., 'Les Seigneurs de Montréal', *Rev. de L'Orient Latin*, IV (1896).

Riant, Paul, *Dépouilles Religieux: Innocent III, Philippe de Souabe et*

BIBLIOGRAPHY

Boniface de Montferrat Exuviae Sacrae Constantinopolitani (Geneva, 1877–1904).

Rietstap, J. B., *Armorial générale:* Gouda 1884 (London, 1969–71).

Röhricht, R., *Regesta Regni Hierosolymitani* (Innsbrück, 1893).

Rossiter, S., *Blue Guide to Greece* (London, 1971).

Rudt de Collenberg, W. H., 'The Rupenides, Hethumides and Lusignans', *Familles de l'Orient Latin XIIe–XIVe siecles* (Variorum, 1983).

Runciman, S., *Families of Outremer* (London, 1960); *A History of the Crusades* (Cambridge, 1952); *The Fall of Constantinople* (Cambridge, 1965).

Schwennicke, D., *Europäische Stammtafeln* (Stuttgart, 1975–).

Setton, K. M., *A History of the Crusades* (Philadelphia, 1962).

Seward, Desmond, *Monks of War* (London, 1972).

Shaw, M. R. B., *Joinville & Villehardouin* (London, 1967).

Sinor, D., *History of Hungary* (London, 1959).

Skrobucha, H. and Neubert, L., *Icons in Czechoslovakia* (London, 1971).

Smith, Donald M., *The Letter* (DMS Publishers, 1953).

Sox, David, *Relics and Shrines* (London, 1979).

Spectrum International (1982–84).

Squillante and Pagani, *Vita della Ven. Serafina di Dio* (Rome, 1748).

Stevenson, K. E. and Habermas, G. R., *Verdict on the Shroud* (London, 1981).

Studi, V. and Testi, *Miscellanea Giovanni Mercati* (Rome, 1946).

Szalay, L. V., *Geschichte Ungarns* (Pest, 1866).

Talbot Rice, D., *The Icons of Cyprus* (London, 1937); *Birth of Western Painting* (London, 1930); *Yugoslavian Medieval Frescoes* (Greenwich, Conn. 1955).

Theiner, A., *Vetera Monumenta Historica Hungariam Sacram* (Rome, 1895).

Thurston, H., *The Physical Phenomena of Mysticism* (London, 1952).

Tilbury, Gervase of, *Otia Imperialia III* (Hanover, 1787).

Topping, Peter, *Studies in Latin Greece 1205–1715* (London, 1956).

Tyre, William of, *Receuil des histoires des croisades* (Paris, 1844–95).

Usseglio, L., *I marchesi di Monferrato in Italia ed in Oriente durante i secoli XII e XIII* (Turin, 1926).

Van Os, H. W., 'Discovery of an early Man of Sorrows in a Dominican Triptych', *Journal of Warburg and Courtauld Institutes*, XLI.

Vasiliev, A. A., *History of the Byzantine Empire* (London, 1952).

Voinovitche, L., *Histoire de Dalmatie* (Paris, 1934).

Wailly, M. N. de, *Villehardouin et la Conquête de Constantinople* (Paris, 1874).

Waite, A. E., *The Holy Grail* (London, 1953).

Wakefield, W. L. and Evans, A. P., *Heresies of the High Middle Ages* (New York, 1969).

Wakefield, W. L., *Heresy, Crusade and Inquisition in Southern France* (London, 1974).

Wentzel, Hans, *Das Turiner Leichentuch Christi und das Kreuzigungsbild der Landgrafenpsalter* (Stuttgart, 1952).

Werther, M., *Die Allianzen des Arpaden* (Vienna, 1887).

Wilson, Ian, *The Turin Shroud* (London, 1978).

Wolff, R. L., *Studies in the Latin Empire of Constantinople* (London, 1976).

Zarek, Otto, *History of Hungary* (London, 1935).

NOTES

---•---

Chapter 1   The Grail Identified

1   T. S. Kelley, *A Structural Study of the Perlesvaus*, Droz. Geneva 1974.
2   Pauline Matarasso (trans.), *The Quest of the Holy Grail*, Penguin Classics 1969.
3   James Cable (trans.), *The Death of King Arthur*, Penguin Classics 1971.
4   S. Runciman, *A History of the Crusades*, Vol. 2, Peregrine 1965.
5   Minnesinger is the German equivalent of troubadour, and means a lyric poet and reciter of ballads.
6   R. S. Loomis, *The Grail from Celtic Myth to Christian Symbol*, Cardiff 1963.
7   A. T. Hatto (trans.), *Parzival*, Penguin Classics 1980.
8   A. E. Waite, *The Holy Grail – Its Legends and Symbolism*, London 1953.

Chapter 2   The Shroud of Turin: 1353–1985

1   Ian Wilson, *The Shroud of Turin*, Gollancz 1978.
2   Fulk of Anjou was the grandfather of Henry II Plantagenet, King of England, by his first wife. Through the marriage of Fulk's granddaughter, Princess Sibylla of Jerusalem, to Guy de Lusignan (see Table 5) the Dukes of Savoy, by the marriage of Duke Louis to the Lusignan heiress Anne (see Table 7) became heirs to the crusader kingdoms of Jerusalem and Cyprus.
3   Herbert Thurston, SJ (trans.), 'Memorandum of P. d'Arcis', *The Month*, Vol. CI, 1903, pp. 17–29.
4   Aymon was a member of the House of Savoy.
5   She was Jeanne de Vergy, and Geoffrey himself was the great-great-grandson of Elisabeth de Vergy. The de Charny family claimed direct descent from Manassé de Vergy, who lived in the ninth century.
6   Meister von Hallein, 1453. German National Museum, Nuremberg. Ref GM 1120/21.
7   This will be discussed at greater length in Chapter 7.
8   Private correspondence and conversations with the author.
9   The word *pharos*, besides its better-known meaning of 'lighthouse' is used by Homer and other Greek writers for 'cloak', 'winding-sheet' and 'shroud'.

10 Translated from the Greek by Bernard Slater and boys of Bradford Grammar School, assisted by the Rev. John Jackson.

11 M. and J. O. Wardrop and F. C. Conybeare, *Studia Biblica et Ecclesiastica*, Oxford 1900.

12 Riant, *Exuviae Sacrae Constant*, ii:211.

13 N. Mesarites in A. Heissenberg (ed.), *Die Palastrevolution des Johànnes Komnenos*, Würzburg 1907.

14 The 'Chi' or 'X' motif was used heraldically to commemorate Christ, and the diagonal crosses of St Andrew and St Patrick on the Union Jack perpetuate this idea.

15 Bishop John Robinson in a paper entitled 'The Shroud of Turin and the grave-clothes of the Gospels', written in 1977, makes the point that the *soudarion*, according to St John, was 'over the head' (*epi tes kephales*), and that the same word was used concerning Lazarus' burial, where his face was bound round (*pereidedeto*) with a napkin (*soudarion*). *Soudarion* is a loan word from the Latin and defines the object not by its material but by its function, namely to wipe away sweat. The confusion arises when it comes to decide what function such a cloth played in the burial of Jesus: it was round Lazarus' face and over Jesus' head. Bishop Robinson says: 'The only position . . . which fits both these descriptions . . . is of something tied crossways over the head, round the face and under the chin. In other words it describes a jaw-band.' This description does not seem to be correct when there were *othonia*, which were thin strips of cloth, available to do the job more efficiently. To lay a thin cloth or veil over the features with reverence would seem far more likely.

Father Albert R. Dreisbach, of the Atlanta International Center for Continuing Study and Exhibit of the Shroud of Turin, does not believe that a cloth or veil placed over the face would have been marked in the same way as the Shroud itself. He supports the view by saying that there are no markings in the genital region because Jesus was wearing a loin-cloth. But this argument does not hold water, because the hands are folded over the genitalia and come between them and the Shroud.

Chapter 3   The Idol of the Templars: 1274–1307

1 The Kings of Jerusalem occupied what is now known as the el-Aqsa Mosque at the southern end of the Temple complex, of which the Dome of the Rock is the central feature, standing over the Rock of Zion.

2 Jules Piquet, *Les Templiers*, Hachette 1939.

3 Malcolm Barber, *The Trial of the Templars*, Cambridge University Press, 1978.

4 *Dixit quod dictum caput habebat quattor pedes duos ante ex parte faciei et duos retro.*

5 Stephen Howarth, *Knights Templar*, Collins 1982.

6 This Templar's name appears in the Latin proceedings as Charniaco, which some commentators have translated as Charnay. Since the same Latin word is found in references to the family of Lirey, it is reasonable to assume that they are the same.

Chapter 4   The Plot to Save the Shroud: 1307

1   Geoffrey of Monmouth, trans. Lewis Thorpe, *The History of the Kings of Britain*, Penguin 1966.
2   Maud was the widow of Guy de la Roche, Duke of Athens (see Table 2a) and the daughter of Florent de Hainault by Isabelle de Villehardouin, Princess of Achaea and the Morea.
3   See Appendix B for a diagram and list of the Templar hierarchy in Burgundy and Champagne.

Chapter 5   The Real Quest of the Holy Grail: 1171–1222

1   Robert de Joinville was the third son of Roger de Joigny, Lord of Joinville, whose mother, Hodierne de Courtenay, was Agnes de Courtenay's great-aunt. They were consequently first cousins once removed (see Table 12).
2   Bernard Hamilton, 'The Elephant of Christ: Reynald of Châtillon', *Studies in Church History*, Vol. 15, London 1978.
3   A. Frolow, 'Recherches sur la déviation de la IVe Croisade vers Constantinople', *Revue de l'Histoire des Religions*, Vols. CXLV and CXLVI.
4   Paul Alphandéry, 'La Chrétienté et l'idée de Croisade'; D. M. Nicol, 'The Fourth Crusade', *Cambridge Medieval History*, Vol. IV, 1966. H. Daniel-Rops, trans. John Warrington, *Cathedral and Crusade*, London 1957.
5   In accordance with a custom which endured up to the fall of the Romanoff dynasty in 1917, the consorts of emperors always took a new name on their marriage. In this case Princess Margaret took the name of Mary, and is so called in Greek sources. In this work, however, I shall refer to her by both names: Mary-Margaret.
6   Victor Amadeus II (born 1666) was Duke of Savoy, Chablais, Aosta, Geneva and Montferrat, Prince of Piedmont, Achaea, Morea and Oneglia, Marquis of Saluzzo, Susa and Italy, Count of Geneva, Romant, Nice, Asti and Tende, Lord of Vercelli, Fribourg and Mont-Saint-Jean, Marquis of Ceve, Dolc'aqua e Marro, Prince and Perpetual Vicar of the Empire, King of Cyprus and Jerusalem..
7   Amalric had married Maria Comnena immediately after the death of her first husband, Rainier of Montferrat.
8   List of Byzantine Emperors 1143–1204. See also Table of Ruling Monarchs.

1143–80	Manuel I Comnenus
1180–83	Alexius II Comnenus
1183–85	Andronicus I Comnenus
1185–95	Isaac II Angelos (deposed)
1195–1203	Alexius III Angelos
1203–04	Isaac II with his son, Alexius IV Angelos
1204	Alexius V Murzuphlus

9   Geoffrey de Villehardouin, trans. M. R. B. Shaw, *The Conquest of Constantinople*, Penguin Classics 1963.

10   Berthold von Katzenellenbogen was married to Alix de Montbéliard, daughter of Amadeus de Montbéliard and Gertrude von Habsburg. Amadeus' sister, Agnes de Montbéliard, was the wife of Erard II de Brienne, father of Gauthier and Jean de Brienne.

11   The original is to be found in Chartularum Culisanense folio 126. This translation is by courtesy of Fr Pasquale Rinaldi.

12   Guillaume de Champlitte designated his cousin Robert as his heir of the Morea provided he arrived within a year and a day, but as Robert failed to do so, Geoffrey de Villehardouin was adjudged to be heir. His son Geoffrey II succeeded as Prince of Achaea in 1228. He was succeeded by his brother Guillaume, who died in 1278. Achaea would have then come into the possession of Philip of Anjou, nephew of St Louis, Guillaume de Villehardouin's son-in-law, had Philip not died in 1277. Instead it went to Philip's father, Charles of Anjou, who was King of Jerusalem and Sicily, Duke of Apulia and Prince of Capua. He died in 1285. Guillaume de Villehardouin's daughter Isabella reigned as Princess of Achaea with her second and third husbands, Florent of Hainault (1289–97) and Philip of Savoy (1301–07), a nephew of Amadeus V.

13   Guy de la Roche was succeeded by his son John (1263–80) and by John's younger brother William (1280–87). William was succeeded by his infant son Guy II (Guyot) de la Roche and by his wife, Helena Comnena. In 1291 Helena married Hugh of Brienne, Count of Lecce, whose first wife had been the late Isabella de la Roche, sister of Duke William. Guyot de la Roche died without issue in 1308 and was succeeded by Hugh of Brienne's son Walter, but he was killed in 1311, after which the Duchy of Athens passed into Catalan hands.

14   Srem (Sirmium) and the Fruška Gora were part of the Byzantine Empire in 1165. At that time the Hungarian Church came under the sceptre of the Byzantine emperor so that the royal crown of Hungary remained subject to the emperor's sovereignty. There was no question of the Hungarian Church being subordinated to the Patriarch of Constantinople. In 1172 Henry the Lion, Duke of Saxony, visited Constantinople on pilgrimage. He succeeded in reconciling the two emperors, Manuel and Frederick Barbarossa, who were then at odds with each other. There is a strong possibility that Henry saw the Shroud and Mandylion during his visit and took news of them back to Germany.

Chapter 6   Germany and the Hidden Years: 1230–1274

1   The Langrave's wife was Elisabeth of Hungary, a sister of Bela IV (see Table 9).

2   Otto's father, Count Poppo IV von Henneberg, was the husband of Sophie von Andechs and brother-in-law of Berthold VI, Marquis of Istria and Duke of Meran. Of Duke Berthold's eight children, his eldest daughter Agnes was Queen of France, the wife of King Philip Augustus; his second, Gertrud, was Queen of Hungary.

3   M. Delaborde, *Les Ancêtres de Jean de Joinville*, Paris, 1894.

4. Jean de Joinville, the son of this marriage, was the first cousin of Hugues

228

de Salins (his mother's nephew), whose wife was Adelheid von Andechs-Meran. She was a niece of Queen Gertrud of Hungary, and hence a cousin by marriage of Otto von Henneberg-Bodenlauben. Jean de Joinville was also, through his mother, a first cousin of Henri de Vergy, Seneschal of Burgundy, who had married Elisabeth, another of Jean's mother's nieces. One of this Elisabeth's sisters, Marguerite, married first Henri de Brienne, Seigneur de Venizy, and as her second husband, Guillaume de Courtenay, Seigneur de Champignolles. Another sister, Blanche, was the wife of Guichard de Beaujeu, a cousin of Guillaume de Beaujeu, the Templar Grand Master who instituted the Shroud ceremonies in 1274. See Tables 3, 8, 10 and 13.

5   The strain of longevity in the Joinville family is unusual for the period. Jean de Joinville lived to be ninety-three or ninety-four; his sister Helvis was approaching eighty when she died; their mother lived to about seventy, and although the date of André's death is unknown, he must have been between seventy and eighty.

6   Alix de Joinville later married Henry Plantagenet, Earl of Lancaster, the nephew of King Edward I of England, thus removing the de Joinville connection with that country.

7   Jean de Joinville had at least eight children by his two wives. His eldest son Geoffrey de Briquenay was born about 1247 and went to Italy where he became the ancestor of the Sant-Angelo family of Naples. His daughter Marguerite, who later married Jean de Charny, was the eldest child of his second marriage, born about 1262. Anseau, originally Sire de Rimaucourt, inherited Reynel after his brother's death, succeeded his father as Seneschal of Champagne and was ultimately a Marshal of France. He died in 1340. Anseau's daughter Isabelle was the wife of Guillaume de Vergy, Seigneur de Mirebeau (the son of Jean de Vergy, Seneschal of Burgundy). Her husband's daughter by his second marriage was Jeanne de Vergy, the wife of Geoffrey de Charny, the Porte Oriflamme de France. Finally there was Alix, whose marriage in 1300 to Jean d'Arcis has been mentioned. Her second marriage to Henry Plantagenet took place in 1307. She died in about 1336 or 1337.

INDEX

230

231

INDEX

233

INDEX

239

THE SHROUD AND THE GRAIL

© This edition

Bristol PA, USA

© World rights
Sandviks Bokforlag a.s
Stavanger, Norway

ISBN 1-881445-17-18

Printed in Belgium

THE
TROLL CHILDREN
AND THE
PRINCESS

Story by
Eli Aleksandersen Cantillon

Retold by
Sarah Hewetson

Illustrated by
Francois Ruyer

Designed by
Lene Eintveit

"Hush," Aja said to her little brothers.
They stopped their game and listened.
"I think someone is crying."

Uffe, Olle, and little Klaffe nodded.
They had heard it too.

The four troll children crept toward the
sound, which was coming from the forest.

As they tiptoed closer,
they saw a girl crying as
she sat on a rock.

"Can we help you?”
Aja asked bravely.

The girl looked up at the
little trolls, let out a yell,
and hid behind a tree.

Then Aja spied something
glittering in the grass.
“Is this yours?” she asked.

The girl nodded and came
out from behind the tree.
“I'm Princess Lara,” she said,
“and that is my crown.”

"I was crying because I have lost my horse. We stopped to rest beside a lake and I fell asleep. When I woke up, Lily was gone," the princess told them. "I've been looking for her for hours."

"We'll help you find Lily," Aja said. And off they all went.

They walked for a long time. When they came to a small lake, they decided to rest.

Suddenly, up popped five little heads topped with little red hats. "Have you seen our oats?" one of them asked. "We stopped for a swim at the lake and when we came out of the water, our sack was gone."

"We haven't seen your sack," the princess said. "We are looking for my horse, but we can help you look for your sack, too."

So they all set off together.

One of the gnomes made up a little song,
and they all sang it as they marched along.

"This is no time for songs!" grumbled
the oldest gnome.

But they kept singing so loudly that they couldn't
hear him. So he gave up and started to sing along
with the others.

After a while, they came to a lake. "This is where
Lily and I stopped to rest," the princess said.
"This is where we left our sack of oats,"
the oldest gnome said.

"Thieves must have stolen both of them!" Olle said.
"Let's search for their tracks around the lake,"
Aja said. So they split into two groups and set off in
opposite directions.

But little Klaffe was soon bored. "I'd rather go up
the hill and look for berries," he told his sister.
"All right," Aja said, "but don't wander off."

Klaffe found a patch of berries
and sat down to eat. Suddenly
he saw something in the grass.
It was a curved, silver object
with holes in it. Klaffe put it
in his pocket and went back
to join the others.

As night approached, the two groups met up, but no one had found any trace of the thieves. They sat around a fire trying to figure out what happened to Lily and the oats.

After a while, Klaffe snuggled up against the princess. He couldn't get comfortable with the strange object in his pocket, so he took it out.

"That's Lily's shoe!" Princess Lara exclaimed.
"Klaffe must have found it on the hill," Aja said.
"The thieves must have gone that way, because
Lily and I were never on the hill."

They were so excited it took them a long time to fall asleep. In the morning they were awakened by loud shouts. "The ghosts are after me!" the voice yelled. As the creature came closer, they saw it was a frightened old fox.

"Tell us what happened," the oldest gnome said.

"I was out for a walk and I heard noises coming from a barn. I peeped through a window and saw ghosts!" the fox gasped.

"Are you sure they were ghosts?" Aja asked. "Well, I definitely saw something white moving in there!"

"The thieves!" everyone exclaimed. "Thieves!" the fox shrieked. "They're more dangerous than ghosts!" And he dashed off into the forest.

"Lily and the sack of oats must be with the thieves," Princess Lara said. So they headed quietly over the hill to the barn.

When they reached the barn, the princess bravely marched up to the door and shouted "The king's daughter orders all thieves to come out right now!" Nothing happened.

"Come out or my father will make you peel potatoes in his palace for the rest of your lives!"

The barn door opened slowly and a shaggy head appeared. It was a brand new foal. Behind the foal was a beautiful white horse. "Lily!" Princess Lara shrieked. "You're safe!"

Then the oldest gnome came out of the barn carrying a big sack.

"We've solved the mystery. Lily took the oats knowing she'd need food while she hid to have her foal."

The princess noticed that Lily had eaten most of the oats. "Don't worry," she said. "My father will give you two sacks of oats for helping find Lily."

The gnomes were very happy. "We have enough oats here to have a porridge party," the oldest gnome said. And they all set off singing a happy gnome song.

The party was lots of fun, but Aja knew that she and her brothers should head home. So Princess Lara gave them a ride on Lily and the foal followed.

When they arrived home, Princess Lara said, "Thank you for helping me find Lily. As soon as her foal is big enough, I want you to have him. But you have to promise we can visit often."

Aja, Uffe, and Olle jumped up and down with excitement. But little Klaffe was silent. He had already fallen asleep with a big smile on his face.